Advance Praise for *We Win, They Lose*

"In this high-stakes competition between freedom and authoritarianism, there is nothing static about superpower advantage. It can vanish in an instant—and there is no substitute for American leadership. *We Win, They Lose* serves as a compelling manifesto, presenting authentic policy solutions founded on the principles of peace through strength. Kroenig and Negrea's book is essential reading for all deeply engaged in the intricacies of foreign affairs."

—Keith Krach, Chairman of the Krach Institute of
Tech Diplomacy, Former Undersecretary of State,
and Former Chairman/CEO of Docusign and Ariba

"Kroenig and Negrea have produced their own winner, an audacious fusion of Trump and Reagan for victory in what they see as a new Cold War with China. Their forceful prose and pungent policy prescriptions are sure not merely to shape but to upend the mounting debate over Republican foreign policy."

—Jacob Heilbrunn, Editor of *The National Interest*

"Matt Kroenig and Dan Negrea's book is yet another proof of their superb intellect, strong moral compass, and unique understanding of the complexities of today's world. Their intense belief in the values of freedom and democracy as underpinnings of security and prosperity also represents the Free World's shield against the assaults of authoritarianism."

—Mircea Geoana, Deputy Secretary General of
NATO and Former Foreign Minister of Romania

"*We Win, They Lose: Foreign Policy and the New Cold War* is a must-read not only for policymakers and national and economic security experts, but also for anyone who wants to better understand critical decisions US leaders have made in the past and how the gleaned learnings can foster a brighter American future. Dr. Kroenig and Mr. Negrea have done an impressive job of explaining complex issues, and this book will serve as an invaluable resource for future administrations."

—Kimberly A. Reed, Former Chairman, President, and CEO of the Export-Import Bank of the United States

"Matthew Kroenig and Dan Negrea have written an extremely important book: *We Win, They Lose.* I wholeheartedly agree with their premise that America should strive for a situation where the CCP loses the will or capacity to challenge America's vital interests. This book could easily serve as the first draft of a national security strategy for future Republican presidents."

—Daniel F. Runde, Senior Vice President at CSIS and Author of *The American Imperative: Reclaiming Global Leadership through Soft Power*

"This well-researched book replete with concrete policy recommendations is a valuable contribution to one of the most sober and urgent discussions of our time: how America and the Free World can defend our freedom and prosperity in the face of the malign and aggressive actions of the PRC and the other new axis of evil countries."

—Michelle Giuda, CEO of Krach Institute for Tech Diplomacy at Purdue and Former Assistant Secretary of State for Global Public Affairs

"This book is a must-read for anyone interested in US foreign policy, as well as for students of geopolitical dynamics. The authors lay out clearly and with plentiful evidence the case for a new foreign policy, to the benefit of US citizens and global peace."

—Simeon Djankov, Director for Policy, London
School of Economics and Political Science,
Former Deputy Prime Minister of Bulgaria

"Kroenig and Negrea have utilized past foreign policy successes to create a critical roadmap that we must use going forward. This book is an essential read for anyone who wants to understand and craft solutions to deal boldly with America's current challenges and adversaries."

—Manisha Singh, Former Assistant Secretary of
State for Economic and Business Affairs

"Kroenig and Negrea have written a timely and important explainer that lays out the future of a principled conservative foreign policy vision. Their clearly articulated vision serves as an important field guide for how we can make sure America does win this new twilight struggle."

—Kelley Currie, Former Ambassador-at-
Large for Global Women's Issues

"Many who quote the German military theorist Carl von Clausewitz's maxim about war being 'a continuation of politics by other means' forget the context was an argument that force is not an end unto itself, but one instrument among others in the toolkit of statecraft, to be guided by a grand strategy to achieve the goals of the nation-state. Drawing lessons from the West's victory in the First Cold War, Matthew Kroenig and Dan Negrea offer a compelling and updated conservative strategic vision for defining the objectives and, ultimately, winning America's New Cold War."

—J. Peter Pham, Former U.S. Special Envoy for
the Sahel and Great Lakes Regions of Africa

"America will triumph over tyranny when our leaders heed lessons for a winning foreign policy presented by Matthew Kroenig and Dan Negrea in their guide to conservative foreign policy: *We Win, They Lose: Foreign Policy and the New Cold War*. Office holders, candidates, scholars, journalists, and all who believe America to be the last best hope for the world need to read this book."

—Robert L. "Bob" Livingston, Former
Chairman Appropriations Committee

"Intellectually rigorous and policy relevant, this is the most sophisticated articulation of a conservative internationalist grand strategy for America in the 21st century. Kroenig and Negrea outline how the next Republican administration should deal with the challenges of our new era of great power competition!"

—Ionut Popescu, Adjunct Professor at Texas Tech
University, Recipient of the 2023 Freedom and Opportunity
Academic Prize by The Heritage Foundation

"Matthew Kroenig and Dan Negrea's *We Win, They Lose: Foreign Policy and the New Cold War* is a critical, and timely, contribution to the discussion of US foreign policy in the era of great power rivalry between the United States of America and The People's Republic of China. Their book proposes a refreshing return to realism as the foundation of United States foreign policy when naked aggression by countries hostile to the United States is no longer a relic of history. This book is a must-read for all persons, both Democrats and Republicans, interested in how the United States should navigate the complex world of great power rivalry they refer to as the New Cold War."

—Michael George DeSombre, Former
US Ambassador to Thailand

"European policymakers would be well advised to read *We Win, They Lose*. Not only does the book candidly lay out what a future Republican foreign policy may look like. But it will also help Europeans understand more clearly the rationale, a mixture of realpolitik and values, that underpins Republican foreign policy priorities."

—Markus Jaeger, Adjunct Professor at Columbia University, Member of the German Council on Foreign Relations

ALSO BY MATTHEW KROENIG

Author or Co-Author

*The Return of Great Power Rivalry: Democracy versus
Autocracy from the Ancient World to the U.S. and China*

*The Logic of American Nuclear Strategy:
Why Strategic Superiority Matters*

A Time to Attack: The Looming Iranian Nuclear Threat

*Exporting the Bomb: Technology Transfer
and the Spread of Nuclear Weapons*

The Handbook of National Legislatures: A Global Survey

Co-Editor

*Nonproliferation Policy and Nuclear Posture: Causes and
Consequences for the Spread of Nuclear Weapons*

Causes and Consequences of Nuclear Weapons Proliferation

ALSO BY DAN NEGREA

Lead-Editor

*The Freedom and Prosperity Equation: Exploring the Most Durable
Path to Development for Countries around the World*

WE WIN THEY LOSE

Republican Foreign Policy & the New Cold War

MATTHEW KROENIG & DAN NEGREA

FOREWORD BY MIKE POMPEO

A REPUBLIC BOOK
ISBN: 978-1-64572-092-8
ISBN (eBook): 978-1-64572-093-5

We Win, They Lose:
Republican Foreign Policy and the New Cold War
© 2024 by Matthew Kroenig and Dan Negrea
All Rights Reserved

Cover design by Jim Villaflores

Republic Book Publishers
New York, NY
www.republicbookpublishers.com

Published in the United States of America
1 2 3 4 5 6 7 8 9 10

To our wives and children:
Olivia, Eleanora, and Henry Kroenig
Nikki, Victoria, Peter, and Michael Negrea

Contents

Contents

Foreword

by Mike Pompeo

It was the honor of a lifetime to serve as CIA director and secretary of state in the administration of Donald J. Trump, and I am proud of our many foreign policy accomplishments. We ended a failed, decades-long policy of accommodating communist China and instead ushered in a new era of great power competition. We deterred Putin's aggression in Europe and strengthened the NATO alliance. In the Middle East, we wiped ISIS off the battlefield. We withdrew from Obama's disastrous Iran nuclear deal and replaced it with a "maximum pressure" campaign. The pressure contained the mullahs in Tehran and helped bring about a historic Middle East peace in the form of the Abraham Accords.

It pains me, therefore, to see many of these accomplishments being undone by the Joseph R. Biden administration. Biden's weakness invited Putin to launch the largest war in Europe since World War II, and his lack of a clear strategy for aiding Ukraine is contributing to needless death and destruction. His toothless diplomacy with Iran has permitted the Islamic Republic to become a de facto nuclear weapons power. And his obsession with trying to cooperate with China on climate change and other issues weakens the free world's competitive position against the communist regime in Beijing.

What we need to reverse these losses and once again strengthen American global leadership is a new president armed with a powerful, conservative foreign policy blueprint. Fortunately, such a plan is exactly what Matthew Kroenig and Dan Negrea provide in this gem of a book.

Kroenig and Negrea are among the country's leading foreign policy thinkers, and I benefited from their writings often while I was in office.

In *We Win, They Lose*, Kroenig and Negrea outline a brilliant and compelling "Trump-Reagan Fusion" for uniting the Republican Party on foreign policy and winning the New Cold War with communist China. It starts with the enduring wisdom of Reaganism and updates it for the twenty-first century with Trump's "America First" principles. It then applies this framework to help readers understand the challenges—and the solutions—to every major foreign policy issue facing the United States today, from defeating communist China to enhancing border security. For example, the book envisions a transformed world—a world of American victory—where the CCP and its evil counterparts no longer undermine the United States' vital interests. This state of affairs is envisioned either through the CCP's voluntary capitulation or its incapacitation. Importantly, the book clarifies that while the United States should support champions of democracy within China, the form of governance the Chinese people choose is their own prerogative, not a subject of US preference.

We Win, They Lose is an authoritative guide to conservative foreign policy in the twenty-first century. It is a must-read for anyone who wants to better understand a conservative approach to global affairs. Every GOP presidential candidate and member of Congress can benefit from the wisdom in these pages. I look forward to seeing many copies spread around the White House, the Pentagon, and the State Department come January 20, 2025.

—*Mike Pompeo,* 70th United States Secretary of State

Preface

In the summer of 2021, leading conservative officials and thinkers gathered in Jackson Hole, Wyoming, for a retreat on the future of the Republican Party's foreign policy. Over two days, the participants assessed President Donald J. Trump's foreign policy record, analyzed domestic and international trends, and debated the future direction for the party's policies. It was a big-tent gathering that included: former senior Trump administration officials; former officials from past Republican administrations, including "Never Trumpers"; sitting members of Congress; and conservative academics and think tank experts.

Two things stood out in the discussions. First, there was a lot of agreement. Despite the public perception that the Republican Party is deeply divided, participants at this conference were basically united around the core principles of a conservative foreign policy, their understanding of the state of global affairs, and the strategies and policies necessary to advance US interests. Second, there were a few (but only a few) heated disagreements, but the divides seemed bridgeable. Indeed, the debates were not primarily about divisions over the Trump legacy per se but ran along longstanding ideological and policy cleavages within the party, such as the relative importance of values and interests or whether the United States should reduce its presence in the Middle East to devote more attention to Asia. At one point, a prominent US senator summed up the view of many in the room when he said, "What we really need is a Trump-Reagan fusion."

That statement was the inspiration for this book. We decided to take up that challenge and articulate the foreign policy synthesis around which the Republican Party can coalesce.

MATTHEW KROENIG AND DAN NEGREA

A variety of institutions and individuals made this book possible. We would like to thank the Atlantic Council and its CEO, Fred Kempe. We are fortunate to work at one of the most impactful, nonpartisan foreign policy think tanks in Washington, DC. The ideas in this book were heavily shaped by our daily interactions with the Atlantic Council staff and US and allied government officials and experts too numerous to name, but, in a way, they are the co-authors of this book. The Atlantic Council's talented staff played a key role in conducting background research, preparing footnotes, and other necessary tasks. We could not have finished the book so quickly without the able assistance of Jeffrey Cimmino, Danielle Miller, Sydney Sherry, Soda Lo, and Imran Bayoumi. Of course, the Atlantic Council is a nonpartisan organization that does not stand for any particular party or policy other than its mission statement of "shaping the global future together." The arguments in this book, therefore, represent solely the views of the authors, not of the Atlantic Council as an organization.

Matthew would also like to thank Georgetown University where he concurrently teaches courses on government and foreign service. One of the secret joys of instructing is that teachers often learn as much from their students as their students learn from them.

For constructive feedback on the ideas in this book, we would like to thank: Alex Alden, Peter Berkowitz, Sam Buchan, James Carafano, Todd Chapman, Spencer Chretien, Matthew Continetti, Michael DeSombre, Colin Dueck, David Feith, Jacob Heilbrunn, Brian Hook, Andrew Marshall, Ionut Popescu, Amanda Rothschild, David Wilezol, and John Zadrozny. Any remaining errors or misjudgments are the authors' responsibility.

We would like to thank the Ronald Reagan Presidential Foundation and Institute and its Washington director, Roger Zakheim, for hosting the aforementioned foreign policy retreat.

Finally, we would like to thank our friends and families. We appreciate your patience as we spent many mornings, evenings, weekends, and holidays hunched over our laptops, or on telephone and Zoom calls, working through the ideas in this book. We hope that the end result—helping the United States develop a sound foreign policy to deal with the serious challenges facing the country—was worth the sacrifice. Most importantly, we want to recognize our wives and children: Olivia, Eleanora, and Henry Kroenig and Nikki, Victoria, Peter, and Michael Negrea. This book is dedicated to you.

Introduction

In 1977, Ronald Reagan was discussing foreign policy with his future national security advisor, Richard V. Allen. When the conversation turned to the presidential candidate's plan for managing the Cold War with the Soviet Union, Reagan's blunt statement shocked his longtime confidant.[1]

The prevailing US policy toward the Soviet Union at the time was *détente*. Masterminded by President Richard Nixon and his national security advisor, Henry Kissinger, *détente* was based on the assumption that the United States was a declining power, the Soviet Union was on the rise, and the best Washington could do was lock in parity with its Communist rival through a series of arms control agreements meant to stabilize the relationship. This policy was continued in modified forms by Nixon's successors, Presidents Ford and Carter.[2]

Reagan did not buy it. He saw the Soviet Union as an evil empire. A policy of coexistence presumed an unacceptable moral equivalence between America and the Free World on one hand, and the Soviet Union and its captive nations on the other. Perhaps more importantly, he believed America's free-market, democratic system possessed inherent strengths and that the Soviet Union's Communist system was fundamentally flawed. He bet that if Washington took the gloves off and forced Moscow to compete, the United States could ultimately prevail.

As he explained to Allen, "My idea of American policy toward the Soviet Union is simple, and some would say simplistic. It is this: We win, and they lose."[3]

Three years later, Reagan was elected president and pursued that clear strategic vision. By the time he left office, the United States had won the First Cold War.

Unfortunately, after a quarter-century respite from major power competition, a New Cold War has emerged, this time with the People's Republic of China (PRC). The United States did not choose this confrontation; China is forcing it upon us. While China has challenged the United States for many years, Washington only awoke to this reality in 2017 when President Donald J. Trump declared "great power competition" with China and Russia the greatest security threat facing the nation.[4] This New Cold War may be even more dangerous than the first one because China is wealthier and more powerful than the Soviet Union ever was.[5] Moreover, China is deepening its strategic partnerships with other revisionist and expansionist autocracies, including Russia, Iran, and North Korea.

By calling this confrontation a New Cold War, we are not saying it is exactly like the First Cold War. There are, of course, important differences. Still, there is a key, defining similarity: both cold wars were global confrontations between the United States and an autocratic, great power rival regarding the future of the world. Will we live in a world that reflects US interests and values or one dominated by a hostile dictatorship?

It is early days, and the United States is still grasping to define its strategy. A good strategy begins with clear goals, but Washington has not yet settled on a clear objective for its struggle with China. Some say this confrontation will continue indefinitely, with no end in sight. Others say the goal should simply be to avoid World War III. These answers are unsatisfactory.

Inspired by Ronald Reagan, we suggest a straightforward goal for the New Cold War with China: we win, and they lose. By this, we mean simply that America should strive for a situation where the Chinese Communist Party loses the will and/or the capacity to challenge America's vital interests.

Designing and prosecuting such a strategy will be aided by a conservative worldview. We will explain the fundamental differences between conservative and progressive philosophies and how they result in consistent and predictable foreign policy disagreements. Conservatives tend to believe that the objective of US foreign policy is to advance American interests in a dangerous world. Progressives generally want the US government to cooperate with other nations to solve shared global challenges. Neither is right or wrong per se, and a progressive worldview may have made sense in more benign international environments, such as during the 1990s. But we argue that a conservative worldview is better suited for the coming confrontation with China. It is no accident, after all, that it was Reagan, a Republican president, who won the First Cold War.

Some might argue that, unlike in Reagan's time, the Republican Party today is too divided to pursue a coherent strategy on anything.[6] But this view is incorrect. While there are real divisions within the party, the outline of a new foreign policy consensus exists just beneath the surface. The existential threat posed by the Chinese Communist Party (CCP) is a central, unifying theme.[7] We call this emerging Republican foreign policy doctrine the Trump-Reagan fusion. Reagan set the basis for the modern Republican Party for nearly forty years with his commitment to individual liberty, free markets, and a strong national defense.[8] These traditions are alive and well among conservatives. But Trump updated what it means to be a conservative. His America First policies refocused the GOP on the interests of all Americans and confronting countries, such as China, whose economic policies harm American interests.[9]

Together, Reagan and Trump have been the most influential Republican presidents of the past several decades, and any viable GOP foreign policy must necessarily build on both presidents' legacies. Indeed, we believe the Trump-Reagan fusion we describe in this book could define Republican foreign policy for a generation or more and will help the United States to prevail in its confrontation with China.

Starting from this baseline, the book then provides a coherent and comprehensive understanding for every major foreign policy issue facing the United States. In each subject, we provide the theoretical underpinnings, historical background, and a recommended conservative approach for addressing the issue area. Topics covered include: defense, trade, values, China, Russia, Iran, North Korea, allies and institutions, border security and immigration, energy and the environment, and more.

We hope that the Republican Party can coalesce around a sound foreign policy vision, because the world has entered a dangerous new era. While we are patriots and always wish the American president well, we fear that the administration of President Joseph Biden is not up to the task. Biden's secretary of state, Antony Blinken, for example, has said that US-China relations are a blend of "competition, cooperation, and confrontation."[10] He is only about one-third right. The reality is that relations between Washington and Beijing are increasingly defined by their most confrontational elements.[11]

In short, this book argues that there is an emerging Republican foreign policy doctrine for the twenty-first century that is better suited than progressive alternatives to achieve victory in the New Cold War with China.

We have experienced the evolution of the party's foreign policy firsthand. Indeed, we helped to shape it. Matthew served in the Department of Defense and the intelligence community, and in 2022 he was appointed by the US Congress as a Republican commissioner on a bipartisan commission to review US strategic forces policy. Dan was a successful Wall Street executive for decades before coming to Washington to serve in the Trump administration on Secretary of State Mike Pompeo's policy planning staff and, later, as the State Department's special representative for commercial and business affairs. Currently, we both manage centers at a nonpartisan Washington, DC, foreign policy think tank, the Atlantic Council, where we meet with politicians, policy experts, and US and allied government officials almost daily. Few are better positioned to write a book about Republican foreign policy today.

We wrote this book for many purposes. First, we wanted to provide a handbook for Republican politicians, political candidates, staffers, policy experts, journalists, and voters about where the party stands on the major issues. We hope that this book will become a resource for conservative US leaders for decades to come. If they are preparing for a debate in a national election or at Thanksgiving dinner, this book can help them get up to speed on the major issues. More ambitiously, we aspire for this book to become a first draft of the national security strategy for future Republican presidents.

Second, we wanted to help define the legacy of Trumpism for conservative foreign policy so that others do not misunderstand and misuse it. We worry that some conservatives are learning the wrong lessons from the Trump administration, invoking Trump's name to champion policy positions that border on isolationism. They label themselves Republicans, but their policy prescriptions are often indistinguishable from those on the Far Left. While in office, Trump was skeptical of some preexisting, foreign commitments, but he was no isolationist. We think it would be a mistake to follow a foreign policy of retreat in the name of Trumpism.

Third, we wanted to explain the conservative worldview to fair-minded progressives. As staff at a Washington, DC-based, nonpartisan think tank, we frequently interact with left-leaning colleagues from the United States and abroad, including US and allied government officials, academics, journalists, and other policy experts. They sometimes dismiss conservative viewpoints and what they see as an incoherent Republican foreign policy. We are tiring of defending conservative foreign policy in weekly personal interactions. Now we can simply hand them a copy of our book.

Some readers may think that a Trump-Reagan synthesis is an oxymoron given that these men's personalities and worldviews are so different. In many respects, they are correct. In other ways, however, these men may be more similar than many appreciate.[12] They were both outsiders to Washington politics. They were both Democrats before they became Republicans. They were both entertainers before becoming politicians. They were both belittled as unserious and castigated as reckless. Despite the naysayers, however, they were the most influential Republican presidents of the past seventy-five years, and their ideas significantly transformed the conservative movement. One cannot make sense of mainstream Republican thinking today without understanding both Reagan and Trump.

Of course, the possibility of a Trump-Reagan fusion in foreign policy does not mean that we are blind to the real differences within the Republican Party. Like any healthy party in a flourishing democracy, there is constructive debate on many issues. In an attempt to identify different camps, people apply labels such as realists, neoconservatives, national conservatives, and so on.[13] But, as we argue in this book, there are common principles, worldviews, and policy approaches that bring conservative foreign policy thinkers together under one tent and that distinguish them from their progressive counterparts on the other side of the aisle.

Some readers may be more interested in biographies of Reagan or Trump, chronicles about their administrations, or accounts about the scandals in which they were involved, such as the Iran-Contra Affair or the violence at the US Capitol on January 6, 2021.[14] There are plenty of sources of information for readers interested in these subjects, and we do not intend to reprise that material here. This book instead will focus on understanding Reagan's and Trump's key contributions to conservative foreign policy and apply their insights to the New Cold War with China and the foreign policy challenges facing the country.

In doing so, this book fills an important void. The vast majority of foreign policy books are written by left-leaning authors for a left-leaning audience. Most authors of foreign policy books are journalists and academics, and most journalists and academics are Democrats. Simply look at the record of political campaign donations of the employees of the Council on Foreign Relations, Georgetown University, or *The New York Times*.[15] This means that they do not really understand or sympathize with a conservative worldview. Mainstream accounts of Republican foreign policy, therefore, are written from the outside looking in, as if the author is trying to explain an exotic tribe in a faraway land. We are better positioned to explain authoritatively how Republicans think about foreign policy.

Conservative foreign policy experts have written good books in recent years, but these are almost all on specific issues and do not provide a holistic picture. Elbridge Colby's *Strategy of Denial* proposes a strategy for defending US interests against Chinese military aggression.[16] Aaron Friedberg's *Getting China Wrong* explains how the US foreign policy community underestimated the China threat after the end of the First

Cold War.[17] In *The Kill Chain*, Christian Brose warns that the Pentagon is not well equipped to adopt the newest military technology.[18] These books all make a meaningful contribution, but none provide a comprehensive overview of conservative foreign policy.

Other books do look at conservative foreign policy writ large but were written in, or focus their subject matter on, different eras. Colin Dueck's *Age of Iron* and Henry Nau's *Conservative Internationalism* provide histories of conservative nationalist and conservative internationalist foreign policy thinking, respectively, but they do not offer a comprehensive overview on where the party stands on the major foreign policy issues today and in the future.[19] Paul Miller's *American Power and Liberal Order* lays out a "conservative internationalist grand strategy," but it was written before Trump's rise to political power and does not grapple with what Trumpism means for US foreign policy.[20] In *Only the Strong*, Tom Cotton presents his vision for the future of the United States, including in foreign policy. But this book, and others by leading Republican politicians, serve more as memoirs and high-level statements of principles than as scholarly efforts to study foreign policy problems and their solutions.[21]

In sum, this book is distinctive in that it provides a comprehensive interpretation of conservative foreign policy as the world enters the second quarter of the twenty-first century. Most importantly, it is unique in explaining how the Republican Party fused the traditions of Reaganism with the innovations of Trumpism to arrive at a new synthesis adjusted for the realities of the present era.

The rest of the book will continue in several parts. The first part of the book sets the stage. Chapter One grounds the discussion by explaining the purpose of US foreign policy and the key differences between a progressive and conservative American foreign policy. Chapter Two reviews the Biden administration's foreign policy record. It will argue that Biden was well-intentioned, but on important issues—such as the struggle with China, Russia's war in Ukraine, border security and immigration, the Iranian and North Korean nuclear challenges, energy and climate, and the withdrawal from Afghanistan—Biden's foreign policy failed to deliver for the American people.

Part II is the core of the book. It explains the Trump-Reagan fusion in the principal foreign policy domains of security, economics, and values. Chapter Three makes the case for a defense and security policy centered around the notion of "peace through strength." Chapter Four articulates how the party balances free and fair trade. Chapter Five explains American exceptionalism as a core tenet of conservative foreign policy.

Parts III and IV apply the Trump-Reagan fusion to specific foreign policy issue areas. Part III deals sequentially with the biggest threats to US national security including: China, Russia, Iran, and North Korea. Part IV addresses other foreign policy issues, including allies, energy security and climate change, and border security and immigration.

Before we dig into the details of the Trump-Reagan fusion, however, it is important to begin with the fundamentals: What is the purpose of American foreign policy?

PART I

SETTING THE STAGE

CHAPTER ONE

The Purpose of Foreign Policy

Why does the United States of America (or any other country) need a foreign policy? What are the goals of US foreign policy? And, what is the difference between a conservative and a progressive foreign policy? These are the questions this chapter will address.

America's Vital Interests

We live in an interconnected world. Some may not like that fact, but it is true. American consumers buy products from, and American companies do business, all over the world. Roughly one-quarter of US GDP comes from international trade.[22] American tourists travel to visit foreign countries. More than one-third of Americans have valid passports.[23] Americans appreciate foreign cultures and customs, including pizza, sushi, and soccer. People from other countries visit the United States, and many want to immigrate and live here. One hundred and sixty-five million tourists visit the United States each year, bringing revenue to hotels, restaurants, and museums.[24] Twenty-six percent of Americans are either foreign-born or are the children of immigrants.[25] Hostile powers, including China and Russia, interfere in US domestic politics and seek to undermine American democracy.[26] And, as we have seen throughout

3

history, hostile powers becoming too strong overseas can result in direct attacks against the US homeland. Remember Pearl Harbor and 9/11?

To paraphrase the popular advertising campaign about Las Vegas from several years ago, what happens overseas does not stay overseas.

This global interconnectedness is why the United States needs a foreign policy. The United States government needs to be engaged overseas to secure the interests of the American people. These interests derive directly from noble American values defined in the nation's founding documents. As Thomas Jefferson wrote in the Declaration of Independence, the American people have an inalienable right to "life, liberty, and the pursuit of happiness." Or, translated into today's language, they have a right to security, freedom, and prosperity. We find the same concepts in the preamble of the Constitution, which says that the purpose of the US government is to "provide for the common defence [security], promote the general Welfare [prosperity], and secure the Blessings of Liberty [freedom]."[27]

These values articulated in America's founding documents mirror the three primary goals of US foreign policy as spelled out in countless national security strategies over the years: the security, freedom, and prosperity of the American people.

Starting with this triumvirate of overarching American values, we articulate eight vital and important national interests that guide the foreign policy of the United States.

First, the United States must defend the US homeland. It needs to keep the American people safe and secure at home. It must also protect Americans and US forces when they are overseas. Providing for national defense is one of the few powers explicitly granted to the federal government in the US Constitution.

Second, Washington should seek to prevent a hostile power from dominating an important geopolitical region. Washington learned in World War II that it was a mistake to allow Hitler to dominate Europe and Imperial Japan to subjugate Asia. It was too costly to wait for the Axis powers to attack the United States and then fight a costly war to defeat them. In hindsight, America realized it would have been much better to address those threats early on. Now, Washington prevents regional rivals from becoming so powerful that they can pose a direct threat to the United States. Today, that means that the United States tries to prevent the anti-American dictators in China, Russia, Iran, and North Korea from dominating their respective regions. It should also counter their malign expansion into other regions, such as the Middle East, Africa, the Western Hemisphere, and the Arctic.

Third, Washington should maintain peace and stability in the Indo-Pacific, Europe, and the Middle East. The truth is that some regions are more important to US interests than others. Washington has rightly prioritized these three regions because they contain the greatest concentrations of wealth, power, and danger. As just noted, a US presence in these regions helps to keep its most dangerous adversaries bottled up. But stability in these regions also contributes to American prosperity. A large portion of US international trade and investment is transacted with countries in Europe (~18 percent) and Asia (~30 percent).[28] (Another 30 percent comes from Canada and Mexico.[29]) The US and allied economies depend on the free flow of oil and gas from the Middle East, which contains 48 percent of the world's proven oil reserves.[30] Even though the United States is now an energy superpower in its own right, the energy market is global, and disruptions to energy supplies in the Middle East spike the price of energy and can cause recessions in the United States. A war in any of these regions would damage the global economy and negatively impact the American people. Maintaining peace in these regions, therefore, is a vital US interest. Washington used military force, for example, in 1999 to stop Serbia's war against Kosovo in Europe. The United States would also prefer to maintain peace and stability globally, but not every conflict is a vital national interest.

To achieve stability in these priority regions, the United States has built a large network of allies and partners. Washington is not engaged in these regions primarily to help its allies. Rather, it has allies because it must remain engaged in these important regions in order to secure its own interests.

Fourth, Washington should work to stop the proliferation of nuclear weapons.[31] A rogue state, like North Korea or Iran, armed with nuclear weapons, could launch a nuclear attack on an American city, potentially killing millions of US citizens. Even if these rogue states never use their nuclear weapons, they can use the threat of nuclear attack to blackmail the United States and constrain its freedom of action. It would be much better to prevent other countries from acquiring nuclear weapons in the first place rather than to live under the constant fear of nuclear annihilation.

Fifth, the United States should counter anti-American terrorist groups globally. In the 1990s, US officials were aware that Al Qaeda harbored the intent to attack the United States.[32] But striking Bin Laden first in Afghanistan seemed too extreme to then US president Bill Clinton. After the 9/11 terror attacks, that calculus changed. The United States counters anti-American terrorist groups globally to prevent them from killing Americans overseas or conducting attacks against the US homeland.[33]

Sixth, the United States should secure the so-called global commons: the high seas, airspace, cyberspace, and outer space. When we take our family on an international vacation or go on an international business trip, we do not want our airplane to get shot out of the sky. We do not want cargo ships, which transport the products we buy from Amazon and the energy we use to fuel our cars and heat our homes, to be sunk by hostile powers or raided by pirates. We cannot access our bank accounts and investments, use email, hold Zoom calls, read digital newspapers, stream a movie, or surf the web if a hostile power has taken down the internet or hacked into our accounts. The US military and the global economy (including Google Maps, Uber, and many other daily conveniences) depend on a functioning Global Positioning System (GPS) and other satellites in space, but Russia and China have weapons designed to destroy American satellites. In short, our daily lives depend greatly on a secure global commons. It is the responsibility of the United States government to keep the seas, skies, outer space, and cyberspace free and open for the benefit of the American people.

Seventh, the United States government should advance a free and fair global economic system. Americans like to go to Walmart or Amazon and buy a wide variety of products at low prices. Many of these goods are made overseas. The socks you are wearing right now, for example, were probably made in China (58 percent of America's supply is).[34] US businesses earn more revenue and create more and better paying jobs if they can sell their products not only to 330 million other Americans but to eight billion people globally. The United States exports, for example, $27 billion worth of soybeans and $14 billion worth of financial services every year.[35] The United States would be much poorer if it were to shut itself off from the global economy. At the same time, American consumers and businesses are not doing charity work. They do not want to be ripped off by America's international trading partners. The US government, therefore, has a duty to create and safeguard a free and fair international economic system so Americans can compete on a level playing field.

Eighth, the US government should make the world safe for democracy. This is not to say that Washington should go on a global campaign to remake other countries in America's image. It should not. But it should protect America's democratic form of government. And we have seen throughout history and to the present that hostile autocratic powers are threatened by American democracy and try to undermine it. During the First Cold War, the Soviet Union supported Communist sympathizers in the United States and globally with the goal of bringing about workers' revolutions.[36] Today, Moscow and Beijing interfere in US domestic politics with the goal of turning Americans against one another and delegitimizing American democracy.[37] By promoting democracy and countering autocracy overseas, Washington can more easily secure the blessings of liberty at home.

Moreover, it is a simple fact that America's best friends internationally are other democracies like Canada, the United Kingdom, Germany, Poland, Romania, Israel, Japan, South Korea, Australia, and others. Washington shares interests and values with these nations. Political science research shows that democracies are less likely to fight wars with each other, more likely to play by the rules in the global economy, and more likely to respect the human rights of their people.[38] When there are more democracies in the world, it is easier for the United States to achieve the other important interests spelled out above.

There are, of course, caveats to keep in mind with regard to this interest. First, Washington can and should have constructive relations with cooperative nondemocracies, like Saudi Arabia, the United Arab Emirates, Vietnam, and Singapore. Second, it is often too costly, unwise, or impossible for Washington to remake the domestic political systems of other countries. But, all else being equal, and where it has the chance to make a meaningful difference at reasonable cost, Washington should encourage other countries to adopt democratic practices and respect human rights.

In sum, these are America's vital and important national interests. The order in which we listed these national interests was not accidental. There is a hierarchy, and we ordered them from the most important (defending the homeland) to least important (promoting democracy). Indeed, the first six interests are vital interests, meaning that they are so important that Washington should be prepared to use all elements of national power, including military force, to secure them. The final two interests are important, but not vital, and should be pursued with a wide range of tools short of military force, including diplomacy, sanctions, and foreign aid. Some interests are urgent and require immediate action, like stopping a terror attack, while others, like promoting democracy, can be addressed over the longer term. Critically, the effort the United States puts into pursuing each of these interests should be commensurate with its importance.

In fact, believe it or not, there has been a rough bipartisan consensus on the above interests for US foreign policy for many years. These interests have basically been recognized and pursued in one way or another by Reagan and Trump and Clinton and Obama. Major foreign policy debates between Republicans and Democrats, therefore, are mostly not over what US foreign policy interests should be but rather which to prioritize and how to pursue them.

Conservative versus Progressive Foreign Policy

What is the difference between a conservative and a progressive foreign policy? Some might argue that there is not much difference. After all, when there are changes in presidential administrations, there is generally more continuity than change in US foreign policy. Biden, for example, criticized Trump's foreign policy on the campaign trail but then mostly retained Trump's focus on competition with China when he took office. International relations scholars would argue that these broad continuities exist because much of the context of US foreign policy remains the same before and after inauguration day. The threats and opportunities facing the country do not drastically change because America had a presidential election. Every US president since Truman had to worry about Russia's nuclear weapons, for example.

The available tool kit of American power also does not suddenly change when there is a new occupant in the Oval Office. Republican and Democratic presidents alike have a restricted set of options (diplomacy, sanctions, military force, and so forth) to address international problems. New administrations repeat much of the policies of their predecessors because the policies were working or because they were the least bad options available. At other times, the Washington foreign policy "blob" follows a wrongheaded approach, and it takes a major crisis to reveal that their past policies were mistaken.[39] Ten years ago, for example, almost everyone thought Washington should engage Beijing, but Chinese president Xi Jinping's threatening behavior eventually made it clear that a new, tougher approach was needed.[40]

Still, despite these broad continuities in US foreign policy, there are consistent differences between Republican and Democratic foreign policies, and these are rooted in the differences in conservative and progressive ideologies.

This is not primarily an argument about partisan politics but about worldview. There are conservative Democrats, liberal Republicans, and many moderates and centrists in both parties. Still, on balance, the Democratic Party tends to be shaped by its progressive wing, while Republican administrations tend to reflect a more conservative perspective.

Jonathan Haidt is an American social psychologist who has categorized the fundamental moral beliefs of all human societies. He identifies five fundamental moral principles: (1) fairness; (2) caring for, or at least not harming, others; (3) respect for authority; (4) sanctity and religious tradition; and (5) in-group loyalty.[41] His research shows that progressives and conservatives both value the first two principles. Nobody believes that it is right to harm others or treat them unfairly. But, Haidt argues, the list of progressive values stops there, whereas conservatives have a broader set of moral beliefs (Haidt describes himself as a centrist who empathizes with both perspectives). Progressives, therefore, are more willing to place fairness and caring above all else. They are more willing to subvert authority, defy tradition, and betray their in-group if it advances the causes of fairness and caring. Conservatives, on the other hand, according to Haidt, try to find a balance among all five competing virtues.

Political science scholarship supports this assessment. In 1957, the late Harvard professor Samuel Huntington provided an enduring political science statement of what it means to be conservative.[42] He argued that there are several fundamental conservative beliefs. First, the world is dangerous. Second, established traditions have stood the test of time and are valuable. Third, religion is an important glue for society. Fourth, hierarchy is natural, and human attempts to eliminate it will fail. Fifth, community interests are important, and, while not stated, it is implied that "our" community's traditions and beliefs are superior to "theirs."

These moral foundations can help explain the most important differences between conservative and progressive worldviews and foreign policy. Let us begin with religion and traditional values. Christians (64 percent of the US population) believe that the world and humankind are fallen. They believe that there is good and evil. Human action alone will never eliminate evil from Earth. The best humans can do is strive to be virtuous themselves and to guard against the dangers of evil. Christian theologians, like Reinhold Niebuhr, have argued that it is the job of the state to defend its citizens from evil in a fallen world.[43]

Progressives, on the other hand, have a worldview that is more secular and heavily shaped by the European enlightenment. They believe that past evils were the result of poor human understanding, but with advances in science and education, humans can apply reason to make the world a better place. Progressives, therefore, are more likely to see the state as a tool to ameliorate the human condition.

Let us now turn to the principle of in-group loyalty. Conservatives tend to value loyalty to one's own family and nation. Familial loyalty is taught as a virtue in many major religious traditions. Biologists have also noted evolutionary advantages for groups that help their kin in times of need.[44]

Progressives, on the other hand, are more likely to want to treat people equally regardless of the circumstances. After all, we are all human beings with similar wants and desires and are capable of reason. Progressives do not believe it makes sense to treat another human being differently simply because they were born into another family, religion, or country. They want to help people in need everywhere.

To be sure, the above discussion presents a clear but overly simplistic typology. The real world is more about shades of grey than black and white distinctions. But, still, there are foundational, philosophical differences that distinguish a conservative and progressive orientation to the human condition and, relatedly, to global affairs. Let us consider how these fundamental differences shape some of the major partisan debates in contemporary US foreign policy.

Sources of International Conflict

Why does the United States come into conflict with other countries or groups like China, Russia, or ISIS? Conservatives are more likely to see international conflict as a clash between good and evil. Reagan saw America as a "shining city on a hill" in contrast to the "evil empire" of the Soviet Union.[45] George W. Bush declared the US's major enemies of Iraq, Iran, and North Korea to be an "axis of evil" in 2002.[46] Trump talked about "rogue regimes developing nuclear weapons and missiles to threaten the entire planet." There are fundamental conflicts of interest between the United States and its dangerous adversaries. The United States, therefore, needs to be strong to defend itself. And it would be naïve to be too optimistic about possible cooperation with these enemies. For conservatives, the friend-enemy distinction is an important one.

Progressives, on the other hand, are more likely to see international conflict as resulting from misunderstanding. Americans, Russians, and

Chinese are all rational human beings with similar wants and desires. Conflicts, therefore, must result from a breakdown in communication. If only we could get to the negotiating table and have meaningful dialogue, surely we could come to a reasonable agreement that satisfies everyone. Progressives do recognize the existence of real conflicts of interest. But they put much more faith in diplomacy and international agreements and cooperation with adversaries. As Barack Obama pursued rapprochement with longstanding US rivals Iran and Cuba, one colleague joked that Democrats see two categories of countries in the world: US friends and potential US friends.

The Purpose of US Foreign Policy

These basic moral differences have important implications for how conservatives and progressives view the purpose of US foreign policy. Conservatives believe the basic purpose of US foreign policy is to advance American interests and protect the American people in an inherently dangerous world. Perfecting a fallen world is impossible and a fool's errand. Washington cannot bring about paradise on Earth. It should be modest about its ability to improve the human condition. Moreover, its responsibility is to its in-group, the American people, not to humanity writ large.

Progressives, on the other hand, are more likely to see US foreign policy as a tool to advance the enlightenment project. Washington should pursue global cooperation and strive to create a better world for all of humanity.

Donald Trump championed an "America First" agenda. Many Republicans thought the slogan was an obvious articulation of the priorities of any American president and a truism: Should not any government put the interests of its own people first? But many Democrats decried it as blasphemy. How dare Trump chauvinistically proclaim American interests to be above the interests of other nations? In contrast, Biden's national security strategy (NSS) declared that Washington's foremost goal was to advance a "free, open, prosperous, and secure *international order*" (italics added for emphasis).[47] The difference in word choice may seem subtle, but it is meaningful. The stated goal of Biden's strategy was not to advance the freedom, prosperity, and security of the American people but of the entire world order.

To be sure, conservatives see value in promoting international peace, prosperity, and freedom but as a nice-to-have so long as it is consistent with American interests—not as an objective in and of itself.

The Value of American Power

Conservatives and progressives also view American power differently. Conservatives believe that American power is necessary to keep the country safe in a dangerous world. They believe in "peace through strength" (the subject of Chapter Three). When America is strong, its adversaries will not mess with it. But a weak America invites aggression. Moreover, the exercise of US power in the form of sanctions or military strikes is sometimes necessary to advance American interests. Yes, this can lead to the suffering and even death of people in other countries. This is undesirable, but, at the end of the day, protecting American lives and advancing American interests is the foremost objective of the US president.

Contrariwise, progressives are more likely to be wary of American power. To put it more bluntly, they are more likely to believe that American power is the problem. If the United States is too strong, they argue, this can be threatening to other countries. Military buildups can lead to unnecessary arms races and cycles of hostility. Given that conflict often results from misunderstanding, perhaps other countries are threatened by aggressive US actions, leading to poor relations. It is this tendency to empathize with US adversaries that led Ronald Reagan's UN ambassador Jeane Kirkpatrick to lambast Democrats as the "Blame America First" party.[48] By voluntarily restraining American power, progressives believe the United States can show goodwill and make the world safer for others. Moreover, the wielding of American power through, for example, sanctions or military strikes harms innocent people. For progressives, not doing harm to others is often more important than advancing American interests.

When it was revealed that China was engaging in a massive nuclear arms buildup in the summer of 2021, for example, conservatives assessed that Beijing was motivated by a desire to challenge the United States and its allies, and the solution was a corresponding strengthening of America's nuclear forces.[49] Progressives argued that China's arms buildup was an understandable response to protect itself from American power; they saw the solution as dialogue and arms control.[50]

Indeed, national security debates in Washington, DC, often boil down to whether one views international relations theory through the spiral model or the deterrence model. Progressives are more likely to believe in the spiral model theory of international relations. When the United States strengthens its military or uses military force, progressives worry that this might threaten other nations that then need to respond with their own military buildup or retaliate to protect themselves, leading to arms races and unnecessary cycles of hostility.

Conservatives, on the other hand, are more likely to believe in the deterrence model. They see adversary military buildups or aggression as part of a deliberate strategy to threaten the United States and its allies. A strong American military and judicious applications of American military power, therefore, are necessary to protect the United States and its allies. US arms buildups deter conflict; they do not stoke it.

International Institutions

How do conservatives and progressives view international institutions? Institutions are rules prescribing and proscribing acceptable standards of behavior and written down in the formal charters of international organizations, like the United Nations, and in international treaties and agreements, like the Iran nuclear deal.[51]

Conservatives tend to view international institutions as a tool like any other. Other instruments of foreign policy, like trade, alliances, sanctions, or military force, are not inherently good or bad. They should be judged according to whether or not they advance US interests. Sometimes working through international institutions and signing treaties can help the United States get what it wants. At other times, the terms of the deal do not advance American interests, and the United States should avoid signing the agreement or pull out if it is already a signatory. Moreover, international rules sometimes constrain American power and sovereignty, which for conservatives is generally undesirable. If the United States needs to use military force to defend itself, for example, it should do so, regardless of what some foreign diplomats think. Why should France (or Russia or China) have a veto over US foreign policy? American interests, not global rules, come first.

Progressives, on the other hand, believe that all nations, including the United States, should work through multilateral institutions and be constrained by their rules. For progressives, a system in which all countries cooperate within, and are bound by, a similar set of rules is a step toward perfecting the human condition. Progressives tend to see international treaties as evidence of progress, sometimes regardless of the details of the agreements, because they represent adversarial nations cooperating to address shared global challenges. They like international bodies that give all countries a seat at the table, because if all people are fundamentally good, or can be made so, then all countries deserve equal consideration. They are more tolerant than conservatives when the UN Security Council gives autocratic countries guilty of human rights violations, like China and Russia, a vote, just like the United States and France. They believe it would be wrong for the United States to use force against another country in general but especially without a UN Security Council resolution (UNSCR) authorizing the action.

This fundamental difference can be seen in many intense partisan fights in recent memory, including over the Iran nuclear deal, the Paris climate treaty, the International Criminal Court, and more. In each case, Democrats are more eager to sign on to and comply with global rules. In each case, Republicans were skeptical if they could not see how the agreement benefited the American national interest more narrowly defined.

American Exceptionalism

These moral foundations also shape the way America's major political parties view American exceptionalism. Republicans are more likely to

15

see America as a unique nation with a special, even divinely granted, role in the world. Democrats are more likely to see America as just one country among many others. As President Obama put it, "I believe in American exceptionalism, just as I suspect that the Brits believe in British exceptionalism and the Greeks believe in Greek exceptionalism."[52]

Conservatives are more likely to believe that it is better for the United States to be the world's most powerful country. Progressives are more likely to believe that the world (and America) would be better off if there were a more equal global distribution of power and if the United States could share global leadership with others. For example, 74 percent of Republicans say the United States should remain the world's only military superpower, and only 23 percent say it would be "acceptable" for another country to become as militarily powerful as the United States. Progressives are divided. The corresponding numbers for Democrats are 51 percent and 46 percent, respectively.[53]

These moral foundations also explain the different orientations behind the isolationist wings in both parties. Conservative isolationists want America to come home because America is too pure for the world. Progressive isolationists want America to come home because the world is too pure for the United States.

Progressives are uncomfortable with aspects of US global leadership that seem to come at the expense of fairness. Progressives are more likely to endorse statements like: What gives the United States the right to tell other countries what to do? Why should the United States lecture other countries on their human rights practices when America has problems at home and imperfections in its own history? Is it not hypocritical that the United States possesses nuclear weapons even as it tells Iran to give up its nuclear program? To progressives, these are obvious points of fairness. To conservatives, the answer to these questions is also self-evident but leads to the opposite conclusion. The United States is not just one country among many. It plays a special role in the world and needs to prioritize its own interests.

Enlightened Self-Interest

Conservatives put American interests first, but this is not to say that conservative foreign policy is narrow-minded or isolationist. Past Republican presidents, including Trump and Reagan, pursued an ambitious international agenda. But they did so for different reasons than progressives. Progressives are often internationalists because they want to ameliorate global conditions. Conservatives are internationalists out of an enlightened self-interest. They know that only an active and engaged United States can secure the vital American interests outlined above.

In the next chapter, we will examine the execution of a progressive American foreign policy in action by reviewing the foreign policy record of the Biden administration.

CHAPTER TWO

Biden's Foreign Policy

The United States faces a challenging international security environment—perhaps the most dangerous in its history. This is in no small part because China is the most powerful adversary the United States has ever faced. Washington needs a clear foreign policy vision to guide the country in the New Cold War with China.

Unfortunately, the Biden administration has not delivered. While we have nothing against President Biden or his team personally, we have not been impressed by the results of their foreign policy. The American people are, on balance, less safe today than before Biden took office in January 2021. As this chapter will show, the failings were not idiosyncratic but rather often symptomatic of a progressive orientation to international affairs.

Biden's Foreign Policy Record

Joe Biden has "been wrong on nearly every major foreign policy and national security issue over the past four decades." So said Robert Gates, respected former defense secretary to both George W. Bush and Barack Obama. When later pressed on this statement, Gates doubled down, saying, "I think he's gotten a lot wrong." As evidence, Gates cited Biden's opposition to Reagan's military buildup and his opposition to George H.W. Bush's successful 1990 Gulf War that ousted Sandam Hussein from Kuwait.

We would add to the list that Biden voted for the 2003 Iraq War, and then later proposed breaking Iraq up into three separate countries. He was among the minority in Obama's cabinet who opposed the raid to take out Osama Bin Laden. Before taking office, it was not clear that he understood the significance of the China threat, saying "China is going to eat our lunch? Come on, man." He continued, "they're not bad folks, folks. But guess what? They're not competition for us."

But, these are backward looking statements. How has Biden performed as president?

The Multiple Biden Doctrines

What is the Biden foreign policy doctrine? It is not entirely clear. The foreign policy of the Biden administration has been confusing and inconsistent.

Biden campaigned on pursuing a "foreign policy for the middle class," but he never explained what that means.[54] It appeared to be little more than a campaign slogan designed to appeal to working-class Trump voters, and, at the time of writing, there has been little follow-through on this agenda since he took office. Indeed, this concept is not even mentioned in the Biden administration's own NSS, published in October 2022.[55] In practice, his economic policies, such as large spending packages, have contributed to high levels of inflation that risk sending the US economy into a recession.

Another candidate for the Biden doctrine is the idea that the world is at an "inflection point" in a global battle between democracy versus autocracy and that democracies need to demonstrate that they "can still deliver" for their people.[56] At one level, this is not a bad bumper sticker to describe the geopolitical cleavage between the United States and its allies in the Free World on one hand and Washington's revisionist, autocratic adversaries on the other: China, Russia, Iran, and North Korea.

But bumper stickers do not make for nuanced foreign policies capable of dealing with the real world. America's concern is not with all autocracies but with aggressive, revisionist autocracies that threaten American interests. Indeed, Biden's NSS recognizes this and points out that America needs to work with nondemocracies, but the president's speeches are still laced with refrains to the "fundamental choice…between democracies and autocracies."[57] Some Biden administration officials tell us privately that they think the president is wrong to talk about the world this way, but he is the boss.

The simplistic rhetoric is a problem because it has a direct, negative impact on US interests. The United States needs to partner with pro-American nondemocracies, like Saudi Arabia, to advance its foreign policy interests. But Biden needlessly alienated this important Middle Eastern partner early in the administration, making it harder to get its cooperation when it was needed later. As a candidate, Biden threatened to make Saudi Arabia a "pariah" state.[58] An enlightenment worldview might imagine a perfect world occupied solely by democratic states, but the reality is different. While in office, Biden realized this was a mistake and went to Riyadh to meet Saudi crown prince Mohammed Bin Salman to patch things up.[59] But it was too little, too late, and Americans paid for this mistake. When, in the fall of 2022, for example, Biden asked Riyadh to increase oil production to help ease inflation in the United States, the Saudi monarchy snubbed him. Saudi Arabia cut oil production instead, keeping prices high and hurting the US economy.[60]

Moreover, in practice, Biden has often used the democracy versus autocracy rhetoric to advance a partisan domestic political agenda. In the 2022 midterm elections, for example, he argued that the Republican Party is a threat to democracy and that voters who value democracy should cast their ballots for Democrats.[61] Ironically, therefore, Biden was essentially arguing that a free and fair election representing the will of the American people was only democratic if the people voted the way he wanted them to.

A final overarching theme of Biden's foreign policy is the idea that Biden restored America's alliances.[62] This is usually paired with an explicit criticism that Trump alienated US allies. It is true that many Western European governments prefer Biden to Trump, but the feeling is not universal. Other allies and partners, including America's close partner Israel, were more comfortable with Trump in the Oval Office.

Moreover, sometimes America's allies need tough love. Trump was correct to remind Germany, for example, that Berlin needed to increase defense spending and diversify its energy supply away from Russia.[63] In contrast, in the name of restoring relations with allies, Biden gave Berlin a pass, allowing Germany to complete the Nord Stream 2 pipeline, which only deepened the Western alliance's economic dependence on Russia.[64] In February 2022, following Russia's further invasion of Ukraine, Germany decided to do exactly what Trump had recommended years earlier; it promised to drastically increase defense spending and sever its energy ties with Moscow. Allowing allies to persist in geopolitical mistakes is not doing the ally or the United States any favors.

Coming down from high-level rhetoric to the daily practice of foreign policy, the Biden administration's NSS was premised on the notion that Washington would focus on competition with China. To pursue that objective, Biden planned to divest US strategic attention and resources from other regions of the world. He wanted to exit from the war in Afghanistan, put relations with Russia on a "stable and predictable" footing, and quickly reenter the nuclear deal with Iran.[65] These bets were mostly based on a progressive optimism that America's adversaries would agree with America's reasonable objectives and cooperate.

The world had other ideas.

A Say-Do Gap on China

One of Trump's greatest accomplishments was making the tough decision to confront China after decades of a failed US engagement policy. Biden, to his credit, has kept this basic orientation in place, but his policies are confusing, and he has not followed through with action, resulting in a dangerous say-do gap.

Let us begin with the confusing policy. President Biden has said multiple times that the United States would fight if China attacks Taiwan.[66] This is the right policy. But his own White House has walked back his statements every time. Who is in charge? What accounts for this confusing disagreement between Biden and his own staff? Is he uninformed, and his staff needs to correct his misstatements? Is he clear what

21

the policy should be, but he cannot control his own staff? Is this some carefully orchestrated master plan to keep the Chinese guessing? No one knows the answer, and everyone, likely including Chinese president Xi, is confused about America's policy toward Taiwan. This lack of a clear commitment to defend Taiwan is dangerous. It could invite the very Chinese attack that America wants to ward off.

Perhaps most troubling is Biden's say-do gap on China. He talks a big game about defending Taiwan, but he is not building the military that would be necessary to do that. Defense experts and politicians on both sides of the aisle believe that the United States must increase defense spending, but, in fiscal year 2022, Biden requested only a 1.6 percent nominal increase, meaning that after inflation, Biden's request would have actually cut the Pentagon's budget.[67]

Instead of making China the biggest defense priority, as it should be, the Biden administration has been distracted by the war in Ukraine. Biden is right to help Ukraine defend itself, but not at the expense of America's more important defense priorities. As China engages in a massive nuclear buildup, many experts believe that Washington should be strengthening its own nuclear deterrent.[68] Instead, for ideological reasons, Biden vowed to "reduce the role of nuclear weapons in national security strategy" and cut a nuclear weapon, the sea-launched cruise missile (SLCM-N), demanded by US military leaders.[69] Biden's defense policy for China turns Teddy Roosevelt's maxim on its head; speak loudly and carry a small stick.

Biden's say-do gap also plagues his economic policy with China. For years, China has been stealing intellectual property. For years, American companies have been allowed to sell advanced technologies to China for profit, harming American security.[70] To his credit, Biden has taken steps to address this problem, including a sweeping China ban on high-end semiconductors and chip-making equipment.[71] But broader and more consistent action is needed. Biden's Commerce Department continues to wave through exports. In one recent study, it was revealed that more than 90 percent of technology export licenses to China are still granted, including to firms, such as Huawei, known to work closely with China's defense and intelligence agencies.[72] Biden talks tough on China but continues to allow Beijing to tilt the economic playing field to its advantage.

Consistent with a progressive worldview, the Biden administration is also overly optimistic about the prospects for cooperation with China. Biden's NSS promises to cooperate with China on global challenges like climate change, public health, and arms control.[73] It is difficult if not impossible, however, to confront China in its malign geopolitical objectives and deepen cooperation with China at the same time. Moreover, China is not interested in cooperating with the United States in these areas. Beijing is the world's largest greenhouse gas emitter, its poor public health practices turned a local COVID-19 outbreak into a global pandemic, and it engages in a massive nuclear buildup while refusing to come to the arms control negotiating table.[74] Saying we should cooperate with China to solve global challenges is like saying we should cooperate with arsonists to stop house fires.

We will articulate a better China strategy in Chapter 6.

The Afghanistan Withdrawal

The Biden administration's chaotic withdrawal from Afghanistan in August 2021 was a national humiliation. There is reasonable debate as to whether the United States should have stayed or remained in Afghanistan, but it is obvious that Biden botched the withdrawal.[75]

Biden had promised for months that the withdrawal would be responsible and safe and pushed back on the notion that a Taliban takeover of the country was inevitable.[76] Instead, the Afghan government and military collapsed in the face of a Taliban offensive even before US forces had left the country.[77] The United States abandoned Bagram Air Base and tens of billions of dollars' worth of high-end military equipment to the Taliban. US forces were reduced to depending on the Taliban's good graces to complete the evacuation of US soldiers and diplomats.[78] In the rushed evacuation, the Biden administration failed to provide adequate security at Kabul's airport, creating an opening for ISIS to conduct a devastating terrorist attack that killed sixty Afghans and thirteen US troops.[79] Then, in an attempt to prevent follow-on attacks, Biden ordered a drone strike on a van carrying an innocent Afghan family, killing all ten occupants, most of them children.[80] For years, Washington had promised loyal Afghans on the ground—people who had served as translators and otherwise aided the US war effort—that they would be protected. Instead, the Biden administration abandoned many of them to the mercy of their new Taliban rulers.[81]

With the rise of a new Taliban government in Kabul, Afghanistan has once again become a safe haven for terrorists.[82] Biden promised that he would be able to combat terrorism in the country by conducting "over the horizon" drone strikes on terror training camps and suspects.[83] But without boots on the ground, the United States lacks access to the kind of actionable intelligence that would make this strategy effective. As a result, the Biden administration has conducted few such strikes since the withdrawal.[84]

The Biden administration vows to advance democracy and human rights, but their precipitous evacuation from Afghanistan returned the country to a theocratic autocracy that tramples on human rights. Women and girls, for example, are again prohibited from going to school.[85]

Biden claimed that exiting Afghanistan would enable Washington to prioritize strategic competition with China, but, instead, the botched evacuation weakened America's position in Asia and its standing globally.

Finally, according to America's then top general in Europe, the Afghan withdrawal led directly to Vladimir Putin's invasion of Ukraine.[86] Putin took Biden's measure in Afghanistan. The dictator in Moscow assessed, correctly, that he could start the largest land war in Europe since World War II and that Biden would not intervene to stop him. As Trump and Reagan understood, weakness invites aggression.

Russia's Invasion of Ukraine

When Russian forces mobilized for an invasion of Ukraine in the fall of 2021, instead of deterring Putin, Biden inadvertently gave him a green light by assuring him that a direct US military response was off the table.[87] This was consistent with a progressive worldview that saw American power as part of the problem. Biden may have hoped that by removing the US military threat, Putin would feel safe and do the right thing. This was the wrong approach. Biden was right to rule out sending American troops to fight in Ukraine, but it was foolish to alert Putin of the decision. We should want Putin to be afraid of going too far, not reassure him that he can invade his neighbors with relative impunity.

Instead of threatening the use of US military power, Biden thought Washington could deter Putin with "integrated deterrence," the centerpiece of Biden's National Defense Strategy. It is a novel and confusing concept that seems to maintain that military power is less important than it used to be, and the United States can use other tools of statecraft, like diplomacy and sanctions, to stop dangerous enemies. Consistent with this theory, Biden threatened that if Putin invaded Ukraine, Washington would respond with sanctions, arms to the Ukrainians, and by strengthening NATO.[88] The threats and the strategy of integrated deterrence failed. Putin invaded Ukraine despite Biden's threats.

Not only did the Biden strategy for deterring a Russian invasion of Ukraine fail, his strategy for dealing with the war was also misguided. In a major intelligence failure, the Biden administration assumed that Kyiv would fall to Russian forces within days. Instead of standing up to Putin as he promised on the campaign trail, Biden was willing to capitulate to Russian aggression almost immediately, offering to exfiltrate Ukrainian president Volodymyr Zelensky to exile in the United States. Zelensky rebuffed the American president with his now-famous line, "I need ammunition, not a ride."[89]

Even when it became clear that the Ukrainian will to resist was stronger, and the Russian military weaker, than previously understood, the Biden administration never articulated a clear strategy for the war. At the time of writing, one year and a half after the war began, Biden has yet to articulate clearly to the American people what he hopes to achieve in Ukraine and his plan for reaching those goals. It is no wonder that many Republicans became skeptical of aid to Ukraine. They did not want to provide a "blank check" to the Biden administration when they lack confidence in Biden's ability to prosecute a decisive strategy to end the war quickly on terms that advance American interests.[90]

Some conservatives criticize Biden for sending arms to defend Ukraine's borders while doing very little to defend America's southern border.[91] It is an understandable point but also a false dilemma. The United States is a superpower. It can and should defend its own borders even as it confronts dangerous adversaries abroad. In a speech at the Hudson Institute, for example, Trump's secretary of state Mike Pompeo convincingly explained why all Americans benefit from stopping Putin in Ukraine.[92] Reagan would have relished the opportunity to destroy the Russian military without risking the lives of American troops. The question is not whether the United States should help Ukraine, but rather to what end, at what cost, and for how long.

We will provide a better Russia strategy in Chapter 7.

Biden's Delayed National Security Strategy

The Biden administration was so surprised by the Russian invasion of Ukraine that they had to significantly delay their NSS. The US Congress requires that every presidential administration publish an NSS to explain to the American people the threats facing the country and the administration's plan to address them. The document also serves as a guide to the sprawling executive branch about its role in executing the president's strategy. Finally, the public document serves to communicate America's position to the world, assuring US allies and deterring US enemies. The Trump administration, for example, published its NSS in its first year in office in December 2017.[93] Trump's document marked a major shift in US foreign policy, declaring that after decades of focus on counterterrorism and wars in Iraq and Afghanistan, the United States would shift to prioritize great power competition with China and Russia.

Biden, on the other hand, did not publish his administration's NSS until October 2022, almost two years after he took office.[94] Its lateness is itself a condemnation of Biden's foreign policy. The administration had it ready to go in February 2022, and then, they realized they did not give adequate attention to Russia as Putin was launching the biggest land war in Europe since the end of World War II. So, they had to go back to the drawing board. It would have been embarrassing to release a strategy that downplayed the Russia threat at a time when Russia was marauding through Europe. But not publishing an NSS until the middle of the presidential term was also embarrassing.

It has been obvious to everyone that Russia posed a major threat to US interests, even before its 2022 further invasion of Ukraine. Then presidential candidate Mitt Romney named Russia as the United States' greatest geopolitical foe back in 2012.[95] Atlantic Council Strategy Papers have warned about the need to deal with Russia and China at the same time for years.[96] The first drafts of the Biden NSS did not even list Russia among the top national security challenges to the United States, ranking it behind things like COVID-19, climate change, and economic recovery. A good strategy would have accounted for the Russia threat from the beginning. This late strategy, therefore, is a serious condemnation of the Biden administration's strategic foresight and competence.

The world was left without a definitive guide on Biden's foreign policy for nearly two years. The delay of the NSS meant that subsequent reviews on specific but important elements of US security policy (such as the National Defense Strategy, Nuclear Posture Review, and Missile Defense Review) were also needlessly delayed.

Misreading Iran

Russia was not the only dangerous adversary that the Biden administration misjudged. The Islamic Republic of Iran is the world's leading state sponsor of terror.[97] It possesses the Middle East's largest stockpile of ballistic missiles. It conducts malign activities throughout the region that pose a threat to US interests and partners, including Israel. It also has an advanced nuclear fuel making capability that puts it within days of a dash to a nuclear weapon. Iranian officials lead their people in frequent chants of "death to America." Despite these stubborn facts, American progressives continue to believe they can win over the clerics in Tehran.

The original sin of America's recent Iran policy was the Obama-Biden decision in 2015 to sign a nuclear deal with Iran. The deal provided Tehran with billions of dollars of sanctions relief in exchange for temporary limits on Iran's nuclear program. The deal did not solve the problem as many of its champions claimed. It merely kicked the can down the road and made it harder for the United States to solve the problem in the future.

Trump was correct, therefore, to pull out of the agreement and re-impose a "maximum pressure" campaign on Iran.[98] When Biden took office, however, he was determined to reenter the nuclear deal with Iran. Iran smelled weakness and drove a hard bargain. Several times the Biden administration thought it was close to a deal, and every time Tehran demanded more concessions, leading to a new round of negotiations. Tehran was probably not genuinely interested in a deal. Rather, it was pretending to negotiate as it marched toward a bomb.

Meanwhile, the Iranian nuclear program continues to expand. Many Democrats argue that Iran's nuclear program was halted by the Iran nuclear deal but accelerated again when Trump pulled out. If one looks at the timeline of Iran's nuclear developments, however, one can see that Iran's most significant nuclear developments, such as moving to 60 percent enriched uranium, occurred during Biden's time in office.[99]

With diplomacy failing, Biden should have turned to other options. But he put all his eggs in the diplomacy basket and had no plan B. Obama, Trump, and Biden all vowed that they would use force, if necessary, as a last resort to stop Iran from going nuclear. Trump likely meant it.[100] Biden appears to be bluffing. Several consecutive presidents from W. Bush to Trump to Biden declared an Iranian nuclear weapon "unacceptable," but the Biden administration appears to be accepting the unacceptable.

Biden's overall Middle East policy was also misguided. The Trump administration achieved a remarkable peace in the Middle East. Trump was able to work with traditional US partners in the region (such as Israel, Saudi Arabia, the United Arab Emirates, and others) against Iran. In so doing, Trump was able to bring Washington's partners closer together.[101] In the Abraham Accords, Bahrain and the United Arab Emirates established full diplomatic relations with Israel after decades of refusing to acknowledge the existence of the Jewish state. The Abraham Accords opened new economic and diplomatic opportunities that are transforming the region.

Instead of building on this successful legacy, Biden flipped the script. He sought to find an accord with America's enemy Iran, while alienating America's traditional friends. Now, the Gulf states are pursing closer relations with America's enemies, China and Russia.[102]

In Chapter 8, we will provide a better strategy for confronting Iran and advancing US interests in the Middle East.

Other Challenges

There are other threats to US interests that have also been mismanaged or left unattended. North Korea has become only the third US enemy with the ability to conduct a nuclear attack on the continental United States. It is estimated that North Korea has dozens of nuclear warheads and intercontinental ballistic missiles.[103] Instead of addressing this challenge head on, however, the Biden administration has placed it on the back burner, where it simmers and threatens to boil over. We address this problem in Chapter 9.

Energy security is national security, but, following a progressive and unrealistic dream of eliminating greenhouse gas emissions in the short term, the Biden administration declared war on fossil fuels and set unrealistic expectations for the advancement of new green energy technologies.[104] As a result, energy companies have curtailed exploring and drilling for new wells, unnecessarily constraining US energy production. When US energy supplies ran low, Biden was reduced to becoming a supplicant to US adversaries, like Venezuela and Iran, in the hope that these countries would export more oil and gas.[105] Biden's war on fossil fuels means that Americans paid higher prices that enriched America's enemies, when the alternative could have been energy independence and jobs in the United States. We take up this problem in Chapter 11.

Biden's immigration policies have contributed to a sharp increase in illegal immigration and a humanitarian catastrophe.[106] These policies are also motivated by a progressive worldview that places all humans, including illegal immigrants and US citizens, on the same plane. Cartels bring narcotics and violence into the United States. US border towns are overrun and suffer economic dislocation. Central American governments are destabilized by the mass migrations across their borders. We provide a better approach in Chapter 12.

Biden's profligate spending has contributed to considerable increases in the US national debt and annual deficits to the point that they are undercutting US national security. "The most significant threat to our national security is our debt," warned Joint Chiefs of Staff Chairman Adm. Michael Mullen in 2010.[107] It is estimated that larger than necessary spending by the Biden administration has added more than $4.8 trillion to US deficits between 2021 and 2031.[108] The Congressional Budget Office projects that by 2031, interest payments on the national debt will exceed defense spending.[109]

To be sure, the Biden administration has also overseen foreign policy accomplishments. Perhaps most notable was the unexpected unity of the Free World in response to Putin's invasion. Sweden and Finland applied to join NATO. Germany, Poland, Romania, and other major European powers announced significant plans to increase military spending. US allies in the Indo-Pacific, such as Japan, Korea, and Australia, joined in the sanctions against Russia. Many of these developments, however, were as much an obvious response to Putin's aggression as they were the result of skilled diplomacy orchestrated by the Biden administration.

In sum, our assessment is that the Biden administration's foreign policy has been disappointing. The Biden administration's policies made more likely the largest land war in Europe since the end of World War II. In the Middle East, the Biden administration lost the war in Afghanistan in a humiliating fashion and is standing by as Iran becomes a nuclear-armed power. And, in the Indo-Pacific, US defense officials testify that their conventional military advantages against China have eroded.[110] Biden's economic policies caused an economic slowdown, which top economists say was "totally avoidable."[111]

These are troubling developments that have left the American people less safe and less prosperous. But there is an alternative available. We will begin to articulate a conservative approach to foreign policy in the next chapter by explaining the Trump-Reagan Fusion in the domain of defense and national security policy.

PART II

THE
TRUMP-REAGAN
FUSION

CHAPTER THREE

Peace through Strength

The Ancient Romans said *sī vīs pācem, parā bellum*—if you want peace, then prepare for war.[112] This is the origin of peace through strength, the foundation for conservative American foreign and defense policy today.

This chapter will do three things. It will explain the concept of peace through strength and compare it to other approaches to national security. It will show how peace through strength successfully guided Presidents Reagan and Trump and how other presidents (both Republican and Democrat) fared less well when they strayed from this principle. Finally, it will outline what a US defense policy of peace through strength should look like today given the threat from China and Russia and the other challenges the country faces.

Peace through Strength in Theory

International relations scholars maintain that the world is anarchic.[113] By this, they do not mean that it is chaotic but rather that there is no world government. Instead, the world is composed of roughly two hundred sovereign nation states (e.g., the United States, China, France, Djibouti, and the like) that are equal according to international law. There are international institutions, like the United Nations, but these are not world governments. Rather, the UN is a series of buildings headquartered in New York where diplomats meet to discuss and sometimes even agree on issues but only rarely act in a consequential manner to manage international matters. When the UN acts, that is shorthand for saying that the United States, Russia, China, Britain, and France agreed to act. When these powerful countries disagree, which is usually the case, the UN cannot take meaningful action.

International anarchy makes the world a dangerous place. After all, imagine what US city streets might look like after a few days if there were no local government and no police forces. Remember Portland's failed experiment with an "autonomous zone" in 2020? Philosopher Thomas Hobbes argued that international anarchy necessarily results in "war of all against all."[114]

When a country is threatened, like when Japan attacked the United States at Pearl Harbor, what recourse is available to the victim nation? It cannot call an international 911. There is no world police. Rather, the country must find ways to protect itself. The lack of a world government means that international politics is a self-help system.

Much of international relations theory examines how countries maintain security in an anarchic international system. One of the proposed mechanisms for maintaining peace and stability in an anarchic world is the balance of power. Countries build up their own military power or form alliances to balance against dangerous rivals. When a country becomes too powerful and threatening, like Napoleon's France in the 1800s or Hitler's Germany in the 1940s, then other countries form coalitions to balance against them to prevent them from dominating the world.

International relations scholars assume that states are rational. This does not mean that they do not make mistakes. Rather, they assume that, for the most part, leaders are weighing the costs and benefits of various courses of action and are trying to do what is best for their country. Since there is no world police to prevent countries from going to war, leaders make decisions on war and peace by weighing the costs and benefits.

To deter a threatening country, a defending country needs to persuade its dangerous rival that the cost of aggression outweighs any likely benefit. In essence, leaders need to be able to say to their rivals, "You might think that you can benefit from attacking me and my friends, but actually, I will defeat you on the battlefield and impose very high costs on your society. It is not in your interest to mess with me. Do not even think about it."

This is the concept of peace through strength. If you are thinking that the balance of power reasoning of government officials sounds similar to mafia bosses, you would not be the first to make that connection.[115] Ganglands and international politics are both dangerous environments, and in order to be safe, one must be strong.

If Washington wants to maintain peace with dangerous adversaries like Russia, China, Iran, and North Korea, then the US military must be powerful. US leaders must be able to persuade the leaders of potential aggressor nations that the US military is so capable that they could not possibly prevail in a war with the United States. They need to persuade them that war with the United States would mean disaster for themselves, their governments, and their societies.

In addition to capability, Washington needs credibility. A powerful US military has no deterrent value if the rest of the world does not believe the US president would ever employ it. A US president must ensure that the rest of the world believes their military threats and promises.

A strong United States leads to peace because America's dangerous adversaries are cowed. On the other hand, a weak America tempts its adversaries to try their luck.

Peace is the goal in peace through strength. This approach recognizes that military power is most effective when it is not used. Ronald Reagan's secretary of defense Caspar Weinberger articulated the canonical Weinberger Doctrine for when and how the United States should employ military force.[116] The Weinberger Doctrine is sometimes also referred to as the Powell Doctrine after Reagan's national security advisor who later become Bush 43's secretary of state, Colin Powell. The Weinberger/Powell Doctrine states that the United States should only use military force when several key conditions are met: (1) the vital national interests of the United States or its allies are at stake, (2) there are clearly defined military and political objectives that the use of military force can achieve, and (3) the United States is prepared to apply overwhelming force with a clear strategy for victory.

Recognizing the importance of a powerful US military, therefore, is not to say that the United States should go around threatening and invading other countries. On the contrary, military force is a blunt instrument. It is necessary for deterring and, if necessary, defeating dangerous adversaries in armed combat. It is not well suited for many other foreign policy goals. It is difficult, if not impossible, for example, to remake other societies at the barrel of a gun. Because it is so capable, there is always a temptation to rely on the US Department of Defense for missions beyond its core competencies. Some US presidential administrations on both sides of the aisle have tried to use the Department of Defense to advance less than vital interests, such as to stop humanitarian disasters or for nation building. But this is generally a mistake.

Peace through strength is a powerful maxim, but it is not the only way to conceptualize US defense strategy and policy. The clearest alternative to peace through strength might be labeled peace through appeasement and accommodation. As shown in Chapter One, progressives often believe that American power is part of the problem. By voluntarily constraining American power, they hope to signal goodwill to other nations and assure them that America will not harm them. Progressives are also often eager to cut defense spending in trade-offs between guns and butter; they cut the Pentagon's budget so they have more to spend on domestic social programs. As discussed previously, they also believe in the Enlightenment ideal of human progress and see international conflict as the result of misunderstanding. They tend to empathize with US adversaries and hope that they can accommodate adversaries' legitimate demands and achieve a fair and peaceful outcome. At their most ambitious, they hope to transform enemies into friends through dialogue and international agreements.

Peace through appeasement is a logically coherent body of thought, but it usually does not work in practice. If the primary danger to international peace were American power, then this approach might make sense. But the United States is generally not the problem. Rather, America is, on balance, a force for good in the world. As we will discuss at length later in the book, the greatest threat to international peace and security today comes from revisionist autocracies, like China, Russia,

Iran, and North Korea. They do not like the world the United States and its allies have built since World War II, and they want to challenge it and tear it down. The problem is not misunderstanding. We understand each other quite well. It is just that we have inherent conflicts of interest that will not be resolved through toothless diplomacy. Diplomacy works best when it is backed by military force. As Teddy Roosevelt said, "Speak softly and carry a big stick."[117]

Peace through Strength in History

How have these competing approaches to defense policy worked in practice? This section will review the foreign policies of several administrations to show that peace through strength typically delivers positive results.

Ronald Reagan was a practitioner of peace through strength.[118] As he said at the 1980 Republican National Convention, "We know only too well that war comes not when the forces of freedom are strong, but when they are weak. It is then that tyrants are tempted."[119]

When Reagan took office, the prevailing Cold War strategy was *détente*. There was a sense that the Soviet Union was a rising power, the United States was in a relative decline, and the two rival superpowers would have to learn to peacefully coexist. Throughout the 1970s, Washington and Moscow entered into a series of arms control agreements, mutually agreeing to cap the sizes of their strategic nuclear forces.

Reagan saw things differently. He believed the United States possessed inherent strengths, that the Soviet Union's communist system was riddled with fundamental flaws, and that the best strategy for the First Cold War was to get tough and force Moscow to compete. As noted above, when asked about the goals of his Cold War strategy, he famously said, "We win, and they lose."[120]

Reagan began a vaunted defense buildup. When Reagan took office, the US defense budget was $325 billion. By 1987, it reached $456 billion, a stunning 43 percent increase.[121] Moreover, much of defense spending goes to paying people (the salaries, health care, retirement benefits, and the like of DoD civilian and military employees). This is important, but the biggest improvements to military capability usually come from procurement spending—buying new weapons. Under Reagan, procurement spending more than doubled from $71 billion to $147 billion.[122]

Much of that money was invested in strategic forces. Reagan resurrected the B-1 bomber and MX missile programs, which had previously been canceled by Jimmy Carter. The contract for the B-2 stealth bomber program was also awarded by Reagan. He deployed nuclear-armed intermediate-range Pershing missiles in Europe that could strike Moscow within minutes.

Perhaps even more important was Reagan's vision, unveiled in 1983, for a space-based missile defense system. The Strategic Defense Initiative, or "Star Wars," promised to render the Soviet Union's nuclear weapons obsolete.

It did not bother Reagan that his critics fretted that he risked starting a dangerous new arms race with Moscow. He retorted that "the Soviet Union cannot possibly match us in an arms race."[123]

His detractors claimed that his reckless policies would start WWIII. Instead, they led to peace. Carter tried unsuccessfully to negotiate limits on the Soviet Union's intermediate-range nuclear-armed missiles for years.[124] These missiles were threatening America's European allies. But it is hard to trade something for nothing. Once Reagan deployed Pershing missiles in Europe, Moscow was suddenly willing to talk. In 1987, Reagan and Gorbachev negotiated the Intermediate-Range Nuclear Forces (or INF) Treaty, banning the deployment of all intermediate-range missiles in Europe. The INF Treaty is often considered the most successful arms control treaty in history because it banned an entire class of nuclear weapons. It remained in place for thirty years.

Most importantly, however, Reagan's defense buildup led directly to Cold War victory. His hunch was correct; the Soviet Union could not keep pace in an arms race with the United States. His plans for Star Wars were particularly worrisome to Gorbachev and a new generation of Soviet leaders. They understood that they were being outcompeted. They sought to reform their system internally and seek accommodation with the West. The result was the collapse of the Soviet Union and the end of the First Cold War.

The value of Reagan's defense buildup did not end there, however. Instead, it set the stage for the unipolar moment.[125] Thanks to Reagan's investments, the United States maintained military dominance throughout the 1990s and 2000s with stealth technology, cruise missiles, precision-guided munitions, and more.

While Reagan practiced peace through strength, he was also willing to use force when necessary. In 1983, Reagan ordered the invasion of the small Caribbean island-nation of Grenada. Strife within the Marxist-Leninist government threatened regional stability and the lives of US citizens on the island. Reagan invaded with an overwhelming force of seven thousand US troops with superior training and equipment compared to about 1,500 in Grenada's military and six hundred Cubans on the other side.[126] The operation was completed within four days, and new elections were subsequently held in Grenada—the country remains a full democracy to this day.

In 1986, Reagan launched retaliatory military strikes against Libya. At that time, Libyan dictator Colonel Muamar Qaddafi was one of the world's leading state sponsors of terror. He financed and encouraged attacks on US and Western interests around the world. On April 5, 1986, terrorists bombed a nightclub in Berlin, known to be frequented by Americans, killing two US soldiers and wounding hundreds of others.[127] On April 14, Reagan responded with more than one hundred US aircraft conducting strikes on Libyan military facilities and command centers, including Qaddafi's personal headquarters, killing his daughter Hana. As Reagan explained, "When our citizens are attacked or abused anywhere in the world on the direct orders of hostile regimes, we will respond so long as I'm in this office."[128]

In 1988, Reagan launched Operation Praying Mantis against Iran, the largest US naval surface warfare operation since World War II. During the Iran-Iraq War, Iran mined the Persian Gulf. When a US warship struck an Iranian mine and was damaged, Reagan responded, sinking six Iranian naval vessels.

While Reagan was an effective national security leader, he was not perfect. In 1983, he sent in the US Marines to Lebanon with the amorphous goal of trying to stabilize an ongoing civil conflict. Hezbollah terrorists attacked the Marine barracks in Beirut, killing 241 US ser-vicemembers. Reagan withdrew US forces shortly thereafter. He did not persist in his mistakes.

Reagan also mobilized the resources of the Free World to counter the aggressive actions of the Soviet Union. The Free World comprised formal treaty allies like NATO members and allies in Asia like Japan and Australia. It also included nondemocracies around the world that helped the United States counter the Soviet Union.

Like Reagan, Trump also practiced peace through strength.[129] On the campaign trail, and in office, he frequently used the term. In his speech to the UN General Assembly in 2020, for example, Trump told his audience that America was "fulfilling its destiny as peacemaker, but it is peace through strength."[130]

Trump launched a systematic effort to rebuild American military power. His first defense budget of $738 billion was the largest since World War II, even after accounting for inflation.[131] Obama aimed for "a world without nuclear weapons," reducing the size of the US nuclear arsenal and cutting legacy nuclear systems. In contrast, Trump called for a US nuclear arsenal "at the top of the pack" and for a "state of the art" missile defense system. He continued the US nuclear modernization program and called for two new low-yield nuclear weapons to deter Russia and China. When it was revealed that Russia was cheating on the INF Treaty, Trump withdrew from the accord and began building American inter-mediate-range missiles. He created the first new US armed service since 1947, the US Space Force, to defend US assets in space—a critical mili-tary mission in the twenty-first century.

When critics raised concerns that Trump's policies would start an arms race, he did not seem bothered. Channeling Reagan, he responded, "Let it be an arms race. We will outmatch them at every pass and outlast them all."[132]

Like Reagan, Trump was skeptical of drawn-out American military interventions with no clear resolution in sight. He sought to close out US military missions in Syria, Africa, and Afghanistan.

But Trump was far from a pacifist. He was willing to flex American military muscle to advance US interests. He inherited the US war against

ISIS, but he lifted Obama-era restrictions on US military commanders and accelerated the war effort. Trump quickly cleared ISIS from the battlefield in Iraq and Syria.

In Syria, dictator Bashar al-Assad used chemical weapons against his own people in a civil war. President Obama drew a "red line" regarding chemical weapons use in Syria but then backed down, undermining American credibility. In contrast, shortly after taking office, President Trump ordered US cruise missile strikes against government and military targets in Syria to demonstrate to the world that there would be serious consequences for violating the global taboo against using weapons of mass destruction. When, under the Trump administration, US service personnel came into conflict with Russian mercenaries fighting for Assad, the US military killed hundreds of these Russian troops.

Most notably, Trump ordered a drone strike killing Iranian general Qassem Soleimani. Soleimani had the blood of many Americans on his hands and even plotted a terror attack on a popular Washington, DC, restaurant. Many Trump critics predicted that, after the strike, Iran would engage in large-scale retribution and worried about World War III. Instead, Iran was afraid to start a major conflict with the United States. Tehran engaged in token retaliation, and the crisis quickly de-escalated. The event reminded the world that the United States was still an unmatched military superpower.

Trump also updated peace through strength for the twenty-first century. As we will discuss in subsequent chapters, he was correct to demand that US allies do more for their defense and to insist that border security be considered part of national security.

Other recent presidential administrations were wrong when they strayed from peace-through-strength principles. Bill Clinton pursued drastic cuts to US military power and the defense industrial base seeking to gain from the post-Cold War "peace dividend."[133] He was sometimes unwilling to use military force to defend vital US interests, including passing on an opportunity to take Osama Bin Laden off the battlefield.[134] Had he chosen differently, 9/11 might have been prevented. Clinton also got bogged down in several amorphous nation-building and peacekeeping campaigns, including in Somalia, leading to the "Black Hawk Down" tragedy.

The George W. Bush administration came into office promising to focus on China and to avoid nation building.[135] Instead, after the 9/11 attacks, the administration became engulfed in two open-ended nation-building operations in Afghanistan and Iraq. To be clear, Bush was right to retaliate after 9/11, but the lack of a clear strategy meant that the twenty-year war effort did not accomplish its objectives. The Taliban is now back in power in Kabul, and Afghanistan is once again a safe haven for terrorism.

Obama believed that by curtailing American military power and "leading from behind," he could make the world a more peaceful place.[136] Instead, Russia invaded Ukraine in 2014, and China took territory from its neighbors in the South China Sea through military coercion. Obama sought to end the war in Iraq by precipitously withdrawing US troops, but ISIS quickly filled the vacuum, establishing a large terrorist caliphate in the Middle East.

In sum, this brief review of recent US presidential administrations shows that peace through strength tends to work better than the alternatives, but what does peace through strength look like today and tomorrow?

Peace through Strength Today and Tomorrow

Peace through strength is the mantra of leading Republican politicians. Speaking in South Carolina in January 2023, Trump said, "Through weakness and incompetence, Joe Biden has brought us to the brink of World War III...As president, I will bring back peace through strength."[137]

In 2017, then vice president Mike Pence tweeted, "Peace only comes through strength. @POTUS believes we must be strong, able to confront all who would threaten our freedom & way of life."[138]

In 2021, Mike Pompeo tweeted, "Peace is achieved through strength, something this [Biden] Administration has yet to show."[139]

WE WIN, THEY LOSE

In November 2022, former UN ambassador Nikki Haley tweeted, "I want peace—& that's why I want to renew our strength. A strong America doesn't start wars. A strong America prevents wars!"[140]

Speaking at the Reagan Presidential Library in 2022, Senator Tom Cotton said, "This is a foreign policy, above all, of peace through strength. Because only the strong can survive in a dangerous world. Only the strong can preserve their freedom. Only the strong can protect the weak. And only the strong can afford to be merciful."[141]

As we will discuss in the coming chapters, the United States faces a daunting international security environment. Trump was correct to assess that the United States may be on the brink of World War III. Adm. Philip Davidson, former commander of US Indo-Pacific Command, predicted China could invade Taiwan by 2027.[142] Some of his colleagues think it will happen even before then.[143]

Russia's war in Ukraine could spill across international boundaries threatening NATO allies and immediately drawing the United States into the conflict.

Iran is a nuclear threshold state, and several consecutive presidents have warned that all options are on the table to stop Iran from building nuclear weapons. If Tehran dashes to the bomb, therefore, a US president might be compelled to launch air strikes to degrade Iran's nuclear facilities.

North Korea could decide to attack America's allies South Korea and Japan or US forces and bases in those countries. Posters at the US military base Camp Humphreys, in Seoul, South Korea, remind American service personnel they must be ready to "fight tonight."

Moreover, China, Russia, Iran, and North Korea are increasingly working together. Russia, China, and Iran have conducted joint military exercises, and Iran and North Korea are supplying weapons for Putin's war against Ukraine.[144] These dictators could coordinate simultaneous attacks on the US alliance structure or opportunistically seize on the distraction provided by the others' aggression. In other words, there is a serious risk of simultaneous major power wars in Europe, the Middle East, and the Indo-Pacific.

The most consequential defense question of the twenty-first century, therefore, is: How can the United States and its allies develop a defense strategy to deter, and if necessary defeat, this New Axis of Evil?[145] These dictators have not signed a formal treaty alliance with each other, and they have real conflicts of interest among themselves. It is unlikely that they will form a deep and trusting partnership, like the US-UK special relationship, for example. Still, they are deepening their strategic partnership in the military and national security domains in ways that are deeply concerning for US national security.

The Biden administration's defense strategy documents correctly recognized this problem, but then put forward a defense strategy that simply will not work. The Biden administration's force-sizing construct is predicated on the notion that the Pentagon needs to be able to fight only one major power war at a time. Unfortunately, Washington does not get to choose how our enemies sequence their aggression. If Russia attacks NATO and China invades Taiwan at the same time, Biden's defense strategy has no answer. It is literally planning to fail.

There is healthy debate on this problem within the Republican Party. Those in the "Asia first" camp argue that the Pentagon should prioritize the major threat from China and devote less attention to Europe and the Middle East.[146] Those in the "walk and chew gum" camp argue that the United States is still a global superpower, and it cannot afford to abandon other geopolitical regions.[147] In reality, this is mostly a semantic debate, and the vast majority of the Republican Party supports what could be called an "Asia first, but not only" defense strategy. Yes, China should be the priority, but Washington has important interests globally. Furthermore, China has conducted military exercises in Europe and the Middle East. Competing with China militarily means competing globally, not just in Asia. Moreover, China is aligned with Russia and Iran, and weakening China's allies undermines China's position. In addition, Xi is gauging US resolve, and a weak position in Europe or the Middle East might make a Chinese move on Taiwan more likely.

A good strategy starts with clear goals, and, as we argued in Chapter One, Washington has a vital national interest in developing a military that can maintain peace and stability in Europe, Asia, and the Middle East.

To be sure, developing such a strategy will be challenging, but there are a number of ways to begin to square the circle. First, Washington should increase defense spending. In fact, a bipartisan congressional commission recently recommended increases to the topline defense budget in real terms.[148] Unfortunately, the Biden administration's defense budget is barely keeping up with inflation, meaning that it is holding steady, if not cutting, US defenses. Contrary to those who claim that constrained resources will force tough choices, the United States can afford to outspend all of its adversaries at the same time. The United States is not France; it is not compelled to make gut-wrenching strategic choices about its national security due to constrained resources. In 2022, the United States spent $778 billion on defense compared to only $310 billion in Russia and China combined.[149] Moreover, the United States could go so far as to double defense spending (currently 3 percent of GDP) and still remain below its First Cold War average (close to 7 percent of GDP). Indeed, given that this New Cold War is every bit as dangerous as the last one, a meaningful increase in defense spending is in order.

Second, as Trump correctly argued, the allies must do more. The United States can actively lead its allies in Europe and the Indo-Pacific to develop a Free World defense strategy. Just as during the First Cold War, the United States must lead the Free World countries that oppose the revisionist and expansionist aims of the New Axis of Evil.

The United States and its formal treaty allies possess nearly 60 percent of global GDP, and together, they can easily marshal the resources to maintain a favorable balance of military power over both China and Russia. Existing formal alliances like NATO in Europe and bilateral alliances in Asia can be supplemented with new arrangements, such as AUKUS and the Quadrilateral Security Dialogue.

Allies do need, therefore, to step up and do more for their defense, but they will not do it on their own if the United States threatens to abandon them. US interests in Europe are too significant to let them be worked out solely between Putin and the United States' European allies. Instead, Washington should actively lead, designing the necessary Free

World force posture, explaining to allies how they fit in, and demanding that allies make the necessary contributions. This should include incorporating key allies into military planning, sharing responsibilities, and devising a rational division of labor for weapons acquisition. The United States should prioritize high-end strategic capabilities like nuclear weapons; global conventional strike capabilities; and intelligence, surveillance, and reconnaissance. European allies should invest in armor and artillery, while Asian allies buy naval mines, anti-ship missiles, and submarines. In addition, wealthier allies can purchase advanced weapons systems, like hypersonic missiles and air and missile defenses, while smaller allies stock up on larger quantities of less sophisticated weapons, like dumb bombs, which will be necessary but in short supply just weeks into a major power war.

Finally, Washington will likely need to take a page from its playbook for the First Cold War and rely more on nuclear weapons to offset the local, conventional advantages of its rivals. The presence of US tactical nuclear weapons in Europe helped deter the massive Soviet Red Army for decades. Similarly, the United States could rely on nuclear weapons to deter and, as a last resort, thwart a Chinese amphibious invasion of Taiwan or a Russian tank incursion into NATO. To be sure, there are risks associated with nuclear deterrence, but nuclear weapons have played a foundational role in US defense strategy for three-quarters of a century—and will likely continue to do so for decades to come.

The United States should use this strength to promote peace by deterring its dangerous enemies. It should refrain from starting wars of choice to pursue amorphous nation-building or humanitarian ends. And it should use force only to defend the vital national interests spelled out in Chapter One, consistent with the principles in the Weinberger Doctrine.

Deterring all the geographically disparate members of the New Axis of Evil at the same time will not be easy, but it is better than pretending Washington can deal with one major power rival at a time at its convenience. Thank goodness former US president Franklin Roosevelt did not choose victory in only one theater during World War II. The next US president should follow his example and plan to defend US global interests at the same time.

CHAPTER FOUR

Free and Fair Trade

America's international economic policy matters for the standard of living of all Americans and as an engine of growth for the global economy. Since economic power is also a key determinant of military power, it also buttresses national security. But how should the United States go about conducting trade and investment with other countries? What is the best international economic policy in theory? How have past presidents, especially Reagan and Trump, managed US economic policy? And what is the conservative American trade policy that the next president should pursue? These are the questions this chapter will address.

Free and Fair Trade in Theory

Modern international trade theory begins with Adam Smith and David Ricardo.[150] Writing in the 1700s, these British economists explained that countries are better off when they pursue free trade with other countries. The concept of comparative advantage holds that it makes sense for countries to specialize in the economic domains for which they are best equipped and trade for other goods and services. It would be foolish for Germany to grow unappetizing coffee beans and Colombia to build subpar helicopters. Rather, it is better for Germany to produce world-class rotorcraft and Colombia to cultivate tasty java and then trade, so both can have the best products. By pursuing free trade, individuals and companies can offer their goods and services to consumers in a global market. (We hope to sell this book to many readers residing outside of the United States!) In addition, American consumers and firms can buy quality products from all over the world at lower prices.

Moreover, political economists argue that the United States, the world's most powerful country, benefits most from an open trading system.[151] As the world's wealthiest country, the United States has among the most talented workforces and the best companies that can compete effectively in global markets.

Further, there is also a US strategic argument for free trade. By increasing trade and investment with friendly countries, Washington can draw them closer and keep our adversaries out. International relations scholars also believe that countries bound by trade are more likely to have cooperative relations generally and less likely to come into armed conflict with each other.[152] During the First Cold War, for example, Washington increased economic exchange with Europe and many other countries in the Free World following such a geopolitical logic.

Given these benefits of free trade, you might be asking: Why is anyone opposed? The other side of the equation is that free trade creates winners and losers. The most competitive companies and workers benefit from a global market. Everyone around the world aspires to consume American entertainment, German automobiles, and French wine. But those that are less able to compete globally lose out from global competition. Every BMW purchased in the United States is a sale that does not go to Ford or Chevrolet. If American automobile producers cannot sell cars, then they cannot hire American workers. Countries sometimes protect (usually less competitive) domestic industries to insulate them from international competition.

Most economists, however, believe that protectionism is counterproductive.[153] It artificially props up less competitive companies and makes it more expensive for citizens to purchase superior international goods and services. A tariff (really a tax on imports) on cars to protect Ford, for example, means that Americans must pay a higher price to purchase a BMW. Moreover, protectionism also hurts American global businesses. If the United States puts up trade barriers against foreign products, then foreign countries can retaliate with barriers of their own, making it harder for US companies to access international markets. Instead of protecting unproductive sectors, economists argue that governments should assist those workers and firms to transition to other more productive sectors where they can flourish.[154]

There are at least four circumstances, however, when it makes sense for governments to put up barriers to trade. The first and most important reason is national security. The United States is good at making B-21 bombers, but it would be foolhardy for Washington to sell stealth technology to North Korea in search of profit. The United States has, therefore, put in place measures, like export controls, to prevent the spread of sensitive military equipment and technology to enemy nations. Similarly, the United States has often protected domestic steel manufacturing. Steel is needed to produce tanks and other weapons. It would be dangerous for the United States to buy all of its steel from an enemy nation that could cut off the supply during a war. Washington ensures, therefore, that it has secure supply chains for goods relevant to national security.

Second, governments also inhibit trade due to safety and quality concerns. To protect the American people, for example, the United States prohibits the import of foreign toys made with lead paint or foreign beef tainted with mad cow disease. Quality barriers, however, can easily bleed into protectionism. The European Union has introduced strict regulations regarding the sale of genetically modified organisms (GMOs), citing safety concerns.[155] This restricts US sales to Europe. The US government insists that GMOs are safe and that Europe is simply trying to shield its farmers from international competition.

Third, it makes sense for governments to put up barriers if another country is cheating. If one country's government is giving its companies an unfair leg up through protective measures, then it would be foolish for other countries to allow that country's companies unfettered market access. Rather, the victim nation can retaliate with countervailing measures, including tariffs, of their own. In fact, the World Trade Organization (WTO) is premised on reciprocity and includes mechanisms to permit countries to employ countervailing measures to punish cheating trading partners that break global rules.

Fourth, and finally, governments might engage in protectionism for domestic political reasons. International trade creates winners and losers. If a political party's constituents are disproportionally made up of the losers from globalization, then that political party can win at the ballot box by promising to protect those voters' jobs, even if it is counterproductive for the country's economy overall. In decades past in the United States, labor unions and manufacturers tended to vote Democrat, and the Democratic Party attempted to protect its constituents' jobs from international competition. Big business has tended to support the Republican Party, which generally pursued free trade to expand Americans' international business opportunities.

Free and Fair Trade in History

The United States was founded partly on free trade. In 1776, the Declaration of Independence charged the British with several offenses, including "cutting off our Trade with all parts of the world."[156]

Jumping ahead to the years after World War I, the global economy was reeling from war and later the Great Depression. To protect American workers, the United States put in place high tariffs. The 1930 Smoot-Hawley tariffs instituted a 20 percent tax on most foreign goods. This meant that Americans were strongly incentivized to buy American-made products, and American companies had a ready consumer base for their products in the United States. The problem was that other countries retaliated, putting in place high tariffs of their own, hurting US exports. Global trade and investment came crashing down, exacerbating the Great Depression.

Following World War II, the United States and its allies assembled at a hotel in Bretton Woods, New Hampshire, to redesign the global economic system.[157] They were determined to avoid repeating the protectionist mistakes of the interwar years. They envisioned a more open global economy that would benefit both the United States and the rest of the world. They also paved the way for international institutions, like the 1947 General Agreement on Tariffs and Trade (which later became the World Trade Organization), to ratchet down trade barriers and encourage free trade. Trade and investment flourished among the United States and its allies in the Free World.

During the First Cold War, Communist countries behind the Iron Curtain chose to cut themselves off from this globalized economic system. Their economies were centrally planned, and they did not participate in free trade. But, after the end of the First Cold War, formerly Communist countries rushed to reform their economic systems along market principles to join the global economy.

Overall, the system worked. From 1945 to the present, levels of international trade and investment—and standards of living—soared. As we can see in Figure 1, global imports and exports as a share of global GDP (a common measure of globalization) increased sixfold from roughly 10 percent to 60 percent over the past seventy-five years.

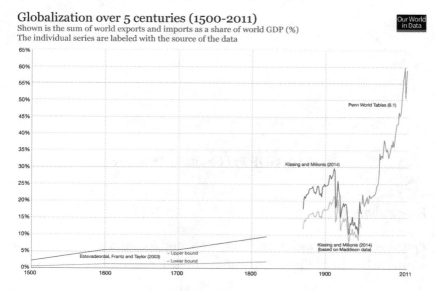

Globalization over 5 centuries (1500-2011)
Shown is the sum of world exports and imports as a share of world GDP (%)
The individual series are labeled with the source of the data

Figure 1. Globalization over Five Centuries (1500–2011)[158]

This expansion of international trade and investment directly contributed to a reduction of poverty and to increased standards of living. In 1945, 66 percent of the world's population lived in poverty. Today, that number is 10 percent.[159] As we can see in Figure 2, US and global GDP per capita increased more than fourfold in this time period, even after controlling for inflation. In 1940, US GDP per person was $12,000. In 2018, the corresponding figure was $55,000 in constant dollars. The same numbers globally are $3,000 in 1940 and $15,000 in 2018.

In short, free trade worked.

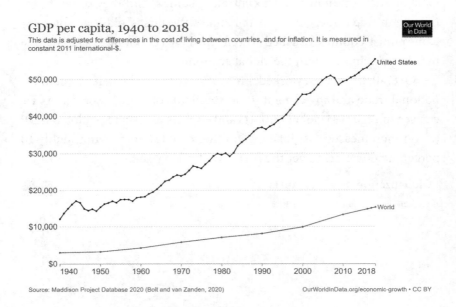

GDP per capita, 1940 to 2018
This data is adjusted for differences in the cost of living between countries, and for inflation. It is measured in constant 2011 international-$.

Source: Maddison Project Database 2020 (Bolt and van Zanden, 2020)   OurWorldInData.org/economic-growth • CC BY

Figure 2. GDP Per Capita, 1940–2018[160]

Reaganomics

President Reagan passionately supported and led on the free trade consensus of his time.[161] In a 1988 radio address he stated:

> *Over the past 200 years, not only has the argument against tariffs and trade barriers won nearly universal agreement among economists, but it has also proven itself in the real world where we have seen free trading nations prosper while protectionist countries fall behind.[162]*

WE WIN, THEY LOSE

In his 1980 presidential campaign, Reagan proposed the creation of a North American Free Trade Agreement (NAFTA). He began to make progress on this promise in his second term. In 1985, the United States signed its first-ever free trade agreement with Israel. In 1986, his administration initiated the Uruguay Round of multilateral trade negotiations, which lowered global tariffs. In 1988, he signed the US-Canada Free Trade Agreement, which would later expand to include Mexico and become NAFTA. He also promoted the Caribbean Basin Initiative. And when Congress put forward protectionist bills in 1985 and 1988 that would have placed quotas on foreign textiles, Reagan vetoed them.

Reagan added, however, a crucially important qualifier to his support for free trade. In a 1985 meeting with business and trade leaders, he argued that American companies can compete effectively when all follow the rules of free trade. American business, he pointed out, "is as innovative, efficient, and competitive as any in the world," and "the American worker is as good and productive as any in the world."[163]

What matters, though, is that "all must abide by the rules" because "free trade is, by definition, fair trade."[164] He gave examples of trade violations: the closing of domestic markets to foreign exports, government subsidies that allow companies to export their goods at prices below their production cost, and theft of intellectual property.

He added that "if trade is not fair for all, then trade is free in name only." He then announced that, for the first time in US history, he had instructed the US Trade Representative to initiate several unfair trade practice investigations. The initial targets were US friends and allies like Japan, South Korea, Brazil, and the European Common Market.

Reagan made clear, however, that he remained committed to free trade. The "ultimate purpose" of his punitive measures was "the expansion of free and open markets everywhere."

Reagan paid particular attention to the trade violations of Japan, a rapidly growing, export-oriented country that had surpassed the Soviet Union to become the second-largest economy in the world. The Japanese government's mercantilist policies included: subsidies for strategic industries selected by the government, such as automobiles, electronics, and steel; low-interest loans and tax breaks; protection of domestic industries from foreign competition through tariff and non-tariff barriers; limits on internal competition; and government deals with trade unions to pacify workers.[165] These policies reflected "Japan Inc.," the idea that government, business, and trade unions should act in unison to advance the country's economic interests.

Reagan imposed punitive tariffs on Japanese equipment and electronics as retaliation for Japan's "dumping" of computer chips at below-market prices, while closing off American chip exporters' access to the Japanese market.[166] He raised tariffs on Japanese motorcycles by forty-five percentage points. He imposed a 100 percent tariff on Japanese computers, televisions, and power tools. And, after considerable arm-twisting, he convinced Japan to enact "voluntary export restraints" on automobile exports to the United States.

Reagan's actions to level the playing field were not limited to Japan.[167] He also levied a 15 percent tariff on Canadian lumber. He negotiated textile quotas with Taiwan, South Korea, Hong Kong, Brazil, India, and Pakistan. He imposed sugar quotas on Brazil, the Dominican Republic, Mexico, and the Philippines. Reagan required eighteen countries, including Brazil, Spain, South Korea, Japan, Mexico, South Africa, Finland, and Australia, as well as the European Community, to accept "voluntary restraint agreements" to reduce their steel exports to the United States. He also demanded that Taiwan, West Germany, Japan, and Switzerland restrain their exports of machine tools to the United States.

Still, the general direction of the Reagan presidency remained strongly pro-free trade. US imports increased from $334 billion in 1980 to $663 billion in 1988.[168] The annual income of the average American rose more than 20 percent in the same time period from $29,000 to $36,000.[169]

The China Mistake

Following Reagan's presidency, America continued to pursue a policy of expanding international trade. In 1994, the United States finalized NAFTA. In 1995, the GATT became the WTO. The most consequential trade question of the 1990s, however, revolved around what to do about the People's Republic of China, led by the Chinese Communist Party.

WE WIN, THEY LOSE

The First Cold War had ended. The Soviet Union collapsed, and a newly independent Russia seemed to be moving toward democracy and capitalism. Eastern European countries previously behind the Iron Curtain rushed to adopt free markets and politics and join the European Union and NATO. Francis Fukuyama famously argued that it was "The End of History."[170] He claimed that ideological fights over types of political and economic systems were over, and all countries would soon adopt democratic-capitalist systems.

While China remained under strict CCP rule, it began selectively opening its markets in what some experts labeled a new state-led, capitalist model. Still, there remained serious distortions in the Chinese economy. The CCP was heavily involved in the economy, and it engaged in egregiously unfair trading practices. The global economic system had been set up by free-market democracies that, for the most part, played by the rules. From a purely economic perspective, China did not fit.

But, under President Clinton, Washington made a strategic bet. Its hope was that if China became enmeshed in the global economic system, the CCP would adopt freer markets over time. China would become wealthier. As China reformed and grew economically, the argument went, China's politics would become less oppressive. Beijing would adopt a democratic form of government and respect the human rights of its people. Proponents of engaging China further argued that a democratic-capitalist China would also become more peaceful and cooperative internationally. Persuaded by these arguments, President Bill Clinton welcomed China into the WTO in 1999.[171]

Unfortunately, the bet did not pay off. China did become wealthier and more powerful through trade with the West. But the CCP did not change its ways.[172] It continued to engage in unfair trade practices, including massive technology theft from the United States. Contrary to WTO rules, it forced foreign firms that wanted to do business in China to partner with local Chinese firms and transfer technology. Despite these unfair Chinese practices, American businesses flocked to China seeking to exploit China's cheap labor pools and manufacture products at lower cost. Millions of American manufacturing jobs were lost, and the US trade deficit with China soared.[173]

To be sure, there were economic benefits from trade with China. Many American companies did profitable business in China, but the CCP's restrictions meant that business opportunities in China were never as great as many had hoped. The American people benefited from lower interest rates as the CCP used income from its trade surpluses to buy US Treasuries. US consumers also benefited from lower prices for cheap, Chinese-made products.

Still, on balance, the economic dimension of this arrangement was one-sided. From 1999 to 2020, China's share of global GDP grew from 3 percent to 18 percent, while America's share remained steady at about 25 percent.[174]

Not only was this economic arrangement one-sided, but the strategic bet was also not paying off. Instead of liberalizing its economy and politics and becoming more cooperative on the international stage, China was moving in the opposite direction. Under Xi Jinping, China backtracked on promised economic reforms and reasserted state control over the economy.[175] China became less free as Xi cracked down on domestic opponents and committed gross human rights abuses. Most worrisome, China became more aggressive overseas, taking territory from its neighbors in the South China Sea through military coercion and engaging in a massive military buildup designed to defeat the United States in armed conflict.

Still, the bipartisan consensus to engage China remained in place. The hope was that Clinton's bet would eventually pay off. The solution was always more engagement. Eventually, many thought, China would come around and become a "responsible stakeholder" in the US-led system.[176]

It took a disrupter to put an end to this counterproductive policy.

Trumpanomics

President Trump had had enough. He had long criticized American trade policy as providing a raw deal for all Americans.[177] Trade with China might have brought benefits for some, but it also hollowed out industries and resulted in job losses and stagnating wages for many working-class

Americans. As a successful businessman, he argued, he could negotiate a better outcome for the American people. His administration announced that they were moving from an international economic policy based on free trade to one premised on fair and reciprocal trade. The United States would engage in free trade with any country that played by the rules, but it would no longer be played for a sucker.

In a 2018 speech to the World Economic Forum, Trump was very clear: "We cannot have free and open trade if some countries exploit the system at the expense of others. We support free trade, but it needs to be fair and it needs to be reciprocal."[178]

Trump took aim at the PRC, the principal mercantilist violator of international trade of his time. China had rapidly increased its economy to become the second largest in the world. It took courage and toughness to upend a bipartisan approach to China that had been in place for two decades, but Trump enjoyed flouting conventional wisdom. Within months of taking office, he placed stiff tariffs on China. His administration then engaged in trade negotiations with China with the goal of producing a fairer arrangement that could reduce America's trade deficit and provide more economic benefits to the American people. Despite years of negotiations, and a provisional trade agreement, Trump was unable to achieve a breakthrough, and the tariffs remained in place.

Trump also complained about unfair trade arrangements with America's allies. It is true that during the First Cold War and after, the United States sometimes intentionally entered trade arrangements that benefited US allies more than itself. Washington wanted its allies to be wealthy enough to withstand the temptations of Communism and to afford a military buildup to counter Soviet expansionism. And greater economic engagement would pull these countries toward the United States and the Free World and away from the Soviet Union.

But Trump believed that these agreements had become unnecessary geopolitically and an unfair economic burden on the American people. To level the international trade playing field, Trump imposed tariffs to bring other countries to the negotiating table and create leverage for his negotiators. In 2018, for example, Trump imposed tariffs on steel and aluminum imports from several countries and the European Union.[179]

He argued that these industries were essential for national security and that they were under pressure from unfair foreign competition. The EU retaliated, and there was fear of a trade war.[180] He also imposed tariffs on other US friends, including Canada, Mexico, and Japan.[181]

But, like with Reagan, Trump viewed protectionism as a temporary measure to create a freer trade environment. Jean-Claude Juncker, the president of the European Commission, flew to Washington in July 2018 to negotiate a solution. In advance of the negotiations, Trump tweeted a bold proposal, "Both the U.S. and the E.U. drop all Tariffs, Barriers and Subsidies! That would finally be called Free Market and Fair Trade!"[182]

In a Rose Garden ceremony, Trump and Juncker announced a deal to avoid a trade war.[183] The EU promised to buy more American petroleum, soybeans, and manufactured goods, and Trump approved talks to resolve the auto and steel tariffs. Trump also announced that the two sides had "agreed today, first of all, to work together toward zero tariffs, zero non-tariff barriers and zero subsidies on non-auto industrial goods."[184]

In addition, Trump used leverage from the threat of tariffs to renegotiate two important trade deals. The KORUS agreement with South Korea was updated, and NAFTA became the new US-Mexico-Canada Trade Agreement (USMCA).[185] In both cases, the terms were adjusted, and the deals were modernized to account for aspects of the global economy, like digital trade, that did not exist when the initial deals were struck.

Many criticized Trump's trade policy as protectionist and isolationist. On balance, however, Trump deserves credit for upending a failed, twenty-year, bipartisan consensus on China. Trump's updates to trade agreements with several US allies were also steps forward. Indeed, after criticizing Trump on the campaign trail, Biden left almost all of Trump's trade policies intact.

The approach started by Trump, however, remains incomplete. The challenge with China is not primarily the trade deficit. A new trade deal in which China agrees to purchase more American soybeans does not solve the problem. The problem is more fundamental; China under the CCP is not a market economy. Absent a fundamental change in China's political and economic system, unfettered free trade with China is not in the American interest. In addition, Trump could have addressed the trade balance with other countries, including US allies, only after making substantial progress on the priority problem of China.

So, what is the best approach for the next Republican president?

Free and Fair Trade for Today and Tomorrow

The next American president should continue the Trump transition from a trade policy based on free trade to one premised on fair trade. The United States and other market-based economies should selectively decouple from China. At the same time, Washington should seek to expand fair and reciprocal trade that benefits the American people with countries that are willing to play by the rules.

How to Selectively Decouple from China

The United States must continue to selectively decouple from China. The selective part of this phrase is important. Some argue that China is a threat, so the United States needs to sever completely economic ties with China. Others argue that the US and Chinese economies are so intertwined that decoupling is unrealistic. Moreover, they claim, some people and firms are getting rich from trade with China, so what is the problem? Both of these perspectives are too extreme.

Continuing the unfettered free trade of the 1990s no longer makes sense, but it is also true that a complete decoupling is unfeasible and unwise. What is needed is a selective decoupling. A synonym for selective decoupling is "de-risking." Going forward, there should be three major categories of US and Chinese economic exchange.[186] First, in sensitive national security and military domains, the United States and its allies should pursue a complete decoupling. Second, in areas where China is engaging in unfair practices, Washington and its allies should punch back with countervailing measures. Third, and finally, there are areas where unfettered trade can safely continue.

Let us consider each in turn, starting with the areas in need of a hard decoupling. A single story will illustrate the depth of the problem. *The Washington Post* reported in 2022 that the US government subsidized a Silicon Valley technology company to design software that simulates a wind tunnel.[187] Instead of designing, building, and testing new hypersonic missiles in wind tunnels, this technology allows engineers to put their missile designs through trial and error virtually before building the first prototype, saving money and time. After developing the software with taxpayer money, however, the company applied for an export license to sell the software to a Chinese company. The US Department of Commerce approved the sale. China's "civil-military fusion" policy means that the software went straight to the People's Liberation Army (PLA).[188] In short, US taxpayers subsidized a technology that China plans to use to kill Americans. This does not make sense.

Unfortunately, it is not an isolated example. Wall Street is investing pension funds in Chinese technology companies that are working with the PLA.[189] In other words, Americans' retirement accounts are being used to help finance China's military buildup. The CCP purchases national security technology companies in the United States and then exfiltrates the technology back to China.[190] Major US defense companies have supply chains with suppliers sourcing component parts from China, meaning that America's defense depends in part on the goodwill of Chinese suppliers.[191]

These types of economic transactions are detrimental to US national security and should be banned altogether. There are a number of tools Washington can employ as it pursues decoupling. It should strengthen the Committee on Foreign Investment in the United States (CFIUS) to better screen Chinese investments, including foreign purchases of American tech companies. It should ban TikTok and Chinese purchases of land near US military bases. It should tighten export controls to prevent US companies from exporting their most sensitive technologies—including those with weapons applications—to China. It should force financial companies to be transparent about their investments in China and ban investments in companies that do business with the PLA. It should prohibit the US defense industrial base from sourcing from China and encourage them to friendshore and reshore supply chains to friendly countries or to the United States.

It is not enough, however, for the United States to take these actions on its own. If the CCP is blocked by the United States, it can still go to

Europe, Japan, or other advanced economies to acquire necessary technologies and inputs. Washington must work with its allies, therefore, to ensure that they also decouple in sensitive areas. Over the past several years, Washington has worked to persuade partners, like Sweden and Israel, for example, to put in place CFIUS-like legislation to stop sensitive investments, but much work remains to be done.[192]

The United States must also decouple from China due to human rights abuses. China is engaged in a genocide against Uighur Muslims in Xinjiang province. They place men, women, and children in labor camps and force them to produce goods, including cotton, for export to the global market.[193] In one particularly gruesome example, the CCP forcibly chopped off the long hair of Uighur women and turned it into hair extensions for sale in the United States.[194] The United States and its allies should ban Chinese products made with slave labor or that otherwise violate international human rights standards.

Second, let us consider where and how Washington can respond with countervailing measures against China's unfair trade practices. Hollywood provides a good example. China places a quota on foreign films.[195] It only allows thirty-four foreign films per year to be screened. It is an unfair practice, and it is contrary to WTO rules, but Washington has not pushed back. Hollywood studios, eager to reach an audience of one billion potential moviegoers in China, goes to great lengths to make sure that their films are among the chosen. They portray China in a positive light in their scripts and avoid content that might be offensive to the CCP, such as mentions of Taiwan. They partner with Chinese studios and cast Chinese actors. When Hollywood star John Cena called Taiwan a "country," he recorded a video apology in Mandarin so as not to offend the Chinese government.[196] During the First Cold War, Hollywood was one of America's most effective forms of soft power. We are now in a situation where the CCP has more control over this font of American soft power than the US government.

These unfair practices are not limited to Hollywood. China engages in all manner of market-distorting practices from stealing intellectual property, to subsidizing domestic companies, to restricting foreign firms' market access in China.

The United States and its allies knew about these practices for decades, but they turned a blind eye due to their engagement strategy with China. But now that strategy has been abandoned, and it is time to hit back against the CCP's unfair trade practices. Indeed, WTO rules allow countries to take countervailing measures as compensation after they have been cheated in a trade relationship.[197] The United States and its allies should respond with their own tariffs, quotas, and other countervailing measures to recoup their losses and punish China for its unfair practices. This may cause China to change its ways, and, in the more likely case that it does not, at least US and Chinese companies will be competing on a more level playing field.

Third, and finally, there are areas where US and Chinese trade can safely continue. In 2022, US-China trade totaled $690 billion.[198] Bringing this to zero dollars would be unnecessary and counterproductive. It would devastate the global economy and the pocketbook of all Americans. The vast majority of economic exchange between China and the United States is unproblematic. Farmers can still sell soybeans to China, for example. And Americans can continue to purchase Made-in-China baseball caps, toys, and furniture.

The Positive Economic Agenda

Even as the United States decouples from China, it can pursue a positive economic agenda including fair trade with like-minded countries that play by the rules. The overriding objective of a new economic agenda is to enhance the general welfare of the American people.

The world is not experiencing "deglobalization" as some critics wrongly claim. Rather, global trade and investment flows, as during the First Cold War, will increasingly follow geopolitical alignments. The United States and its allies in the Free World will do less business with adversaries, like Russia and China, and trade more with friendly countries.

A positive American trade agenda should advance several objectives. The first is to secure supply chains and boost America's innovation and industrial base. Already, we are seeing reshoring and friendshoring.

As companies from the Free World move out of China, they are shifting supply chains to the United States or to other friendly countries. Critics ridiculed Trump's trade wars, arguing that US manufacturing jobs were never coming back to the United States. They were wrong. The United States is already incentivizing domestic production of key technologies, such as semiconductors, with new fabrication facilities opening in the United States.[199] Similar steps should be taken for other critical supply chains, including rare earth elements and medical supplies. In other cases, American companies can be encouraged to friendshore. Apple, for instance, has already moved some of its production out of China into politically less sensitive countries in South and Southeast Asia.[200] This trend will likely continue.

Second, US trade negotiators should ensure a level playing field at home and abroad. They should address trade imbalances caused by unfair trade practices. The United States should strengthen and enforce trade laws to ensure that US exporters are not injured by non-market trading practices. Trade policy tools, including tariffs and quotas, are legitimate instruments of economic policy and should be employed pragmatically to advance US interests.

Third, US trade negotiators should strive to open new markets for American businesses. Access to strong and open export markets is essential for US innovators, farmers, ranchers, and manufacturers. By opening new markets, a fair-trade agenda will create new jobs at home. The United States can open its domestic markets as part of new trade arrangements, but it should expect trading partners to provide reciprocal market access. These international economic policies should be paired with pro-growth policies at home that cut taxes and government regulation and incentivize US innovation, growth, and employment.

Washington should pursue new trade arrangements in either bilateral or multilateral fora. Trade negotiators should pragmatically choose the format to best advance US interests. While remaining cognizant of their limitations, Washington should work to update and reform global economic institutions, like the WTO.

Fourth, expanding international markets can enhance US global influence. Countries that depend on the United States for their economic well-being are more likely to consider Washington's requests in a broader range of economic and security issues. Twenty years ago, the vast majority of countries on Earth counted the United States as their largest trading partner.[201] Today, China holds that position. Washington should seek to reclaim US trade leadership through an updated trade promotion agenda.

Fifth, and finally, a new economic agenda should advance American values. At the end of the First Cold War, it was taken for granted that the American model of open-market democracy was the only legitimate way to organize domestic political and economic systems. Now, there is a new competitor in town. Beijing touts its state-led, authoritarian capitalist model as superior. Many dictators propagate the myth that they can provide their people economic prosperity even as they maintain strict political control. Partly as a result, global freedom has declined in each of the past seventeen years.[202] Through robust international economic engagement, Washington can also outcompete China ideologically and demonstrate the superiority of free politics and free markets. As argued in Chapter One, a freer world advances American interests and values.

But advancing American values goes well beyond economic policy. Indeed, it is this subject of values and American exceptionalism that will occupy our attention in the next chapter.

CHAPTER FIVE

American Exceptionalism

"America is the greatest country in the world." Sixty-nine percent of Republicans endorse this statement, but only 37 percent of Democrats concur.[203] American exceptionalism is the mainstream conservative position when it comes to US values and role in the world in the New Cold War with China. The United States is an exceptional country. It is the world's oldest constitutional democracy. It was founded on the noble principles of life, liberty, and the pursuit of happiness. It is a shining city on a hill and a light to the nations. American power has been a force for good in the world and for the American people. For more than seventy-five years, America has been the leader of the Free World. This chapter will explain American exceptionalism and contrast it to the realist and anti-American perspectives found elsewhere on the US political spectrum. It will examine how recent US presidential administrations have approached these issues, and it will finish with recommendations for how future Republican presidents should advance American values.

American Exceptionalism in Theory

American exceptionalism can be traced to the country's founding. America's Founding Fathers were fleeing religious persecution and heavy-handed, monarchical rule in Europe. They came to the new world to create a society where people could be free to govern themselves and practice their religion. To repeat the important language of the Declaration of Independence, the country was founded on the noble values of "life, liberty, and the pursuit of happiness."[204] America's founding documents are clear that freedom is not a favor bestowed upon people by their government, but it is included among the "inalienable rights" granted by God, never to be taken away.[205]

In a time of divine-right monarchic rulers in Europe, this was a radical concept on which to base a country. America's experiment with open government frightened autocrats throughout Europe and inspired countless democratic revolutions.

While other democracies have at times backslid into authoritarianism, or fundamentally remade their democracy, and crafted new constitutions along the way (France, for example, is currently in its Fifth Republic), the United States has endured as the world's oldest continuous constitutional democracy.

Since the United States was founded in freedom in the eighteenth century, it had no preexisting class structure, like in Europe. Enterprising people could come from humble beginnings, but with talent and hard work, they could make their fortune here. The country was more meritocratic than others and facilitated extreme upward mobility.

These unique circumstances constitute what political scientists usually mean when they refer to American exceptionalism.[206] Why did a consequential US Communist Party—or even a social democratic one—never emerge in the United States? Because it is hard to build a political party around oppressed working classes in a country where there are no oppressed working classes. In the United States, the poor did not organize in their resentment against the rich (who were often self-made). Rather, they idolized the rich and hoped that they or their children would one day reach the upper classes. They knew this was within the realm of possibility.

The United States is also exceptional for what it represents in its foreign policy. It is the world's only democratic superpower, and, as such, it symbolizes safety and freedom for billions of people around the world. Rival autocratic powers go into the world only to pursue their narrow self-interest, but Washington advances a broader, enlightened self-interest because it understands the American people are better off in a world made safe for democracy. America's example has inspired many successful transitions to democracy. Washington has also regularly promoted the spread of democracy and human rights.

The United States was founded in a revolution against colonial Great Britain, and it cannot help but recognize itself in people struggling to secure their freedom against dictators.[207] Moreover, the ideals in the US founding documents are not restricted to the people of the United States. They declare that all people have "inalienable rights"; America's founding documents enshrine a philosophy that is inherently global in its vision.[208]

But America's inclination to support freedom is not about idealism alone. It is also about advancing American interests. As argued above, democracies are less likely to fight wars with one another.[209] They are more dependable alliance partners (nearly all of America's thirty-four treaty allies are democracies).[210] They are more likely to sign and comply with international agreements that advance US interests, like the Nuclear Non-Proliferation Treaty.[211] They are more likely to engage in free trade and less likely to engage in unfair trading practices.[212]

As discussed in Chapter One, this does not mean that the United States should push democracy on other countries when it does not make sense or at any cost. Some countries do not provide fertile soil at a certain moment for democracy to take root. And forcing democracy at the barrel of a gun has usually proven to be both costly and ineffective. But when the United States can encourage freedom, democracy, human rights, and free markets consistent with US interests and at a reasonable cost, it should do so.

American exceptionalism is also rooted in the reality that America's democratic form of government is perhaps its greatest source of strength. Kroenig's scholarly research has identified democratic political institutions as a fundamental driver of a country's international power and wealth.[213] America's rule-of-law system provides a stable business environment that encourages entrepreneurs to take risks and invest in new ideas, propelling high long-run rates of economic growth. The United States' freedom and entrepreneurial culture unleashes radical innovations, like the airplane, the internet, and artificial intelligence. And America's democratic political institutions and culture increase its soft power and make it an attractive diplomatic partner. Other countries often look to the United States for leadership.

America's democratic institutions are also foundational to its military power. The above-mentioned assets of economic growth and technological innovation undergird American military strength. In addition, dictators must spend enormous resources to repress their populations, but because the US government does not fear its own citizens, it can devote more of its security resources to addressing foreign threats.

Finally, compared to unconstrained dictators, the checks and balances in the US system often hinder the executive from making rash decisions in foreign policy and on matters of war and peace. While the United States has made mistakes, they are fewer and easier to rectify than those of its autocratic rivals.

In short, America's democratic system of government, unique among the major global powers, provides it with an unending source of economic, diplomatic, and military strength that helps the United States excel in geopolitics. Given these democratic advantages, it is no surprise that the United States won the First Cold War and that the Soviet Union's autocratic system collapsed under its own weight.

America is also exceptional due to its raw power. Contrary to what one may hear, the United States is not declining. China has risen over the past two decades, but the United States remains in a class of its own. The United States has had the largest economy on the planet since the late 1800s. It currently accounts for 25 percent of global GDP compared to 18 percent for China, its closest competitor.[214] Washington has more formal treaty allies, thirty-four, than any other country. The United States also has the world's most effective military. It spends more on defense ($800 billion annually) than the next nine countries (China, India, Russia, the United Kingdom, Saudi Arabia, Germany, France, Japan, and South Korea) combined.[215] And most of those countries are US allies and partners. American economic, diplomatic, and military power remain exceptional indeed.

The final element of American exceptionalism is that the United States is a force for good in the world.[216] After World War II, the United States was left standing as the world's most powerful country with more than 50 percent of global GDP. Historically, countries in similar situations would have used that power to create an oppressive empire. Russia certainly did; the Red Army that defeated Nazi troops in Eastern Europe stayed as an occupying force for half a century. In contrast, the United States wanted its forces to come home. Washington's friends in Europe and Asia begged for American troops to stay, creating an "empire by invitation."[217] Instead of subjugating countries under US influence, Washington helped these countries' reconstruction, promised to protect them, and gave them a say in the operation of American hegemony through new institutions, such as NATO.

In essence, Washington externalized its domestic rule-of-law system into international politics, creating what has been referred to as a "rules-based international system." Washington created a dense set of international rules to govern international security (NATO, the Nuclear Non-Proliferation Treaty, and the like), economic relations (WTO, IMF, and others), and values translated into international law (e.g., the 1948 Universal Declaration of Human Rights). These institutions give other countries a seat at the table and advance American interests by creating a more stable and predictable international environment. Many do not like the term "rules-based system," but the dense set of global rules and institutions created by the United States and its allies after 1945 is historically unique and could have only been conceptualized and implemented by a democratic superpower.

On balance, the US-led, global system has been successful. Since 1945, there have been zero great power wars. From 1600 to 1945, 1–2 percent of the world's population could expect to die in armed conflict. Today that number is 0.01 percent. As mentioned in the last chapter, since 1945, global poverty rates have been reduced sixfold, and the income of the average human has increased fivefold. In 1945, there were about a dozen democratic countries in the world. Today, there are roughly one hundred. The world has been much safer, richer, and freer since the onset of US global leadership.[218]

It is completely unthinkable that if Nazi Germany had emerged victorious from World War II, or if the Soviet Union had won the First Cold War, that the world would look anything like it does today. Rather, these autocratic powers would have set up a traditional imperial system to subjugate other nations. As we will discuss below, these are the stakes in today's contest between the United States and the CCP. Communist China seeks to displace the US-led system and create a traditional imperial system centered in Beijing.

This brief review underscores how America is exceptional with regard to its founding principles, foreign policy values, raw power, and role in the world. Still, some observers see things differently.

Blame America First

There are other approaches to thinking about America's role in the world, but they do not make much sense. At the other extreme is what has been called the "Blame America First" position.[219] This is a view often found in the progressive wing of the Democratic Party. It sees the United States as a fundamentally flawed nation at home and a force for evil abroad. When looking at the history of American society, people in this camp do not highlight America's positive values and accomplishments but its flaws. They focus on the period of slavery in America's history, the poor treatment of Native Americans, and what they claim is continued systemic racism and sexism in American society today. They see hypocrisy in America's admiration for founding documents that state that all men are created equal, combined with toleration for continued inequalities within the United States.

Turning to America's role in the world, they obsess over its mistakes. They highlight the failed military interventions in Vietnam, Iraq, and Afghanistan. They remind us of American colonialism in the Philippines and elsewhere. America claims to be a force for good in the world, they argue, but it used nuclear weapons on Japan in World War II and props up dictators in the Middle East today.

The Blame America First view is woefully misguided. It is selective in its use of evidence. It cherry picks the most controversial elements of American history, society, and foreign policy and downplays or overlooks mountains of evidence on the other side of the equation. To be sure, America's history and foreign policy have not been perfect, but they have been pretty good. Just look at the evidence reviewed above analyzing the results of the US-led international system.

Moreover, what is the relevant baseline for comparison? Blame America First implicitly compares the United States to a utopian, progressive dream that has never existed in world history and never could exist in reality. It then argues that the United States does not live up to this abstract progressive ideal and, therefore, is irredeemably flawed.

But, this is obviously the wrong standard. Let us instead look at the plausible alternatives to US global leadership today. The CCP engages in genocide against its Uighur Muslim minority. Russian troops, many recruited from prisons, commit atrocities in Ukraine and their leader, Vladimir Putin, is wanted by the International Criminal Court. Iran is the world's largest state sponsor of terrorism and executes homosexuals.[220] North Korea holds political prisoners in work camps.[221] These countries are hardly paragons of diversity, equity, and inclusion.

American exceptionalism compares the United States to every other major power that has ever existed in world history and finds the competition lacking. It recognizes that the United States does not always live up to its lofty ideals but that it takes these ideals seriously and continuously strives to achieve them.

Realism

Realism is another misleading approach to thinking about American values. Realism is a theory that holds that international politics is a dangerous place, so countries need to do whatever it takes to protect themselves.[222] It is OK, they argue, if this means using military power in unprovoked wars, spying on allies, and other immoral (or amoral) actions that advance national interests. Some countries might talk about pursuing noble ideals or values, but, at the end of the day, realists claim, major countries are all the same, self-interested, amoral, power seekers.

For realists, the United States is not exceptional. It is merely one great power like all the others, including Russia and China, ruthlessly pursuing its interests in a dangerous world. They would argue that what really matters is power, not ideology, and that it would be a mistake for

Washington to take its eyes off the balance of power by focusing on fluffy subjects like democracy and human rights.[223]

Realism is often a useful guide for thinking about defense policy, but it is misapplied when it comes to thinking strategically about American foreign policy more broadly because it does not pay due respect to American values. The First Cold War was an ideological rivalry between democratic capitalism and totalitarian communism. Trying to superimpose a realist academic theory on this reality does not change the facts. Similarly, the US-PRC struggle today is also an ideological rivalry, whether or not this reality fits with academic theories. The United States is a democracy that favors the global system it has built and that has brought peace, prosperity, and freedom to the American people and to many others around the world. China is a genocidal dictatorship that wants to overthrow the US-led system and create a new world order safe for dictators and centered around Beijing. These are the stakes.

We ignore the ideological aspects of the confrontation at our peril. If the United States is just one ruthless great power, like any other, then why should the rest of the Free World align with the United States? If America and China are the same, then why should anyone outside of the United States care who wins the New Cold War? It is true that China and Russia are mostly ruthless and immoral. But the United States stands for universal ideals greater than its immediate self-interest. Like-minded allies that share America's values are better off in a US-led system than in one designed by Vladimir Putin or the CCP.

Ironically, therefore, in emphasizing power and downplaying ideology, realists overlook the important ideological aspect of American power. As a result, realists often make the mistake of assuming America is weaker and its rivals stronger than they really are. This leads to bad policy. In the 1970s, realists thought the United States was declining and the Soviet Union was rising. They concluded that Washington had no alternative other than *détente*. They were wrong as Reagan (who properly understood the ideological sources of American strength) demonstrated years later when he led America to outcompete the Soviet Union and end the First Cold War.

Realists today risk making the same mistakes by incorrectly conclud-ing that the United States is not strong enough to take on its autocratic rivals. They urge Washington to make radical and risky trade-offs in its foreign policy, such as abandoning major world regions.[224]

But an accurate assessment of America's position and recommenda-tions for its foreign policy can only be based on a complete evaluation of all relevant factors, including the fact that America's ideological superi-ority is an important strategic asset.

Wilsonian Idealism

Another flawed approach for thinking about American values is Wil-sonian idealism. At the Paris Peace Conference following World War I, President Woodrow Wilson attempted to impose his liberal vision for global order.[225] He set up the League of Nations in the hope that nations could resolve their differences through negotiations rather than armed conflict. He also promoted the concept of "national self-determination" and broke up several large, multinational European empires into smaller nation-states.

Wilson's vision failed and contributed to igniting World War II. The League of Nations lured many into a false sense of security, but it could not stop Mussolini and Hitler from attacking their neighbors and launching World War II. Moreover, by creating small and indefensi-ble nation-states, Wilson provided easy targets for Hitler's subsequent aggression.

Still, even today, many US foreign policy thinkers and leaders find Wilsonianism attractive. They rightly agree that the United States is exceptional, but they wrongly conclude that the purpose of US foreign policy should be to remake the international system into a liberal utopia. All problems should be solved through multilateral institutions. Global-ization and expanding commerce invariably lead to peaceful relations among states. The United States should use its foreign policy to advance human rights around the world. Often this means pushing controver-sial progressive policies, such as woke ideology, onto unwilling foreign countries.

Neoconservativism, a variant of Wilsonianism, agrees that America has a duty to spread freedom and is generally held to believe that, if necessary, this goal should be achieved through the exercise of American military power.

But these are the wrong lessons to derive from American exceptionalism. The United States is a force for good in the world, but it cannot transform the world into utopia. It is, therefore, a poor use of US resources and against the national interest to pursue such a fool's errand.

Moreover, Wilsonians often believe that working through multilateral bodies is good in and of itself and that these institutions can facilitate global cooperation on their own with minimal US involvement. But, as stated above,, international institutions are a tool like any other. Sometimes they are helpful. Other times, they are not. Moreover, these bodies rarely work in America's interest unless actively led by the United States and backed by American power and influence.

The commercial peace argument also has it mostly backward. Countries that enjoy good relations can become good trading partners. But trade cannot transform enemies into friends, as Washington learned from its failed attempt to make the PRC a responsible stakeholder in the US-led international system. Finally, the United States is right to promote democracy and human rights but only when consistent with US national interests.

It is also a mistake to push progressive social policies—many controversial even within the United States—on other countries with even more traditional values.[226] In contrast, the next Republican president should reinstate Ronald Reagan's Mexico City Policy, which prevents US government funding for foreign nongovernmental organizations that promote abortion. Since Reagan, this policy has been reversed by every Democratic president, and then reinstated by every Republican president.

American Exceptionalism in History

As with many aspects of conservative foreign policy, the clearest expression of American exceptionalism can be found in Ronald Reagan. As he said in his farewell address:

> I've spoken of the shining city all my political life... it was a tall, proud city built on rocks stronger than oceans, wind-swept, God-blessed, and teeming with people of all kinds living in harmony and peace; a city with free ports that hummed with commerce and creativity. And if there had to be city walls, the walls had doors and the doors were open to anyone with the will and the heart to get here. That's how I saw it, and see it still.[227]

He understood that the United States was a shining city on a hill in contrast to the "evil empire" of the Soviet Union. He had an intuitive grasp of the strengths of America's system of government and was confident that it would ultimately prevail in a competition with the Soviet Union's brittle autocracy. He pragmatically promoted American values. Due to Reagan's influence, several major US allies in Asia, such as the Philippines, Taiwan, and South Korea, peacefully transitioned from autocracy to democracy in the 1980s. Moreover, by ending the First Cold War, Reagan's foreign policies were a major force for good in the world. He brought down the Soviet Union and the communist bloc and in so doing helped to spread the US-led system and its attendant peace, prosperity, and freedom to countries formerly captive behind the Iron Curtain. These gains were pragmatically locked in by the administration of George H. W. Bush, Reagan's vice president.

Bush 43, however, is an example of how trying to impose American values by force does not work. He was correct in concluding that America was a force for good in the world engaged in a contest with an "Axis of Evil": Iraq, Iran, and North Korea. But instead of promoting American values by example and at the margins, he made the "freedom agenda" a central element of his foreign policy platform. He believed that through military occupation, he could transform Iraq and Afghanistan into functioning democracies. Tragically, he was mistaken.

It is difficult for a US president to fully embrace the "Blame America First" position, but Obama came closest. He believed that US power and intervention had often made things worse. He was criticized during his presidential campaign because his pastor (and someone Obama lauded as a close, personal mentor), Jeremiah Wright, had publicly preached about the terror attacks of 9/11 being "America's chickens coming home to roost."[228] In other words, America deserved it. Obama began his presidency with a global "apology tour," expressing contrition for America's past mistakes and promising to pursue a restrained foreign policy going forward.[229] He believed that if the United States pulled back from the world, other responsible powers would step up and do more. He was mistaken. As his administration "led from behind," hostile powers China, Russia, and ISIS filled the resulting power vacuum in ways that were detrimental to US interests. As noted above, when asked about American exceptionalism, Obama emphasized that Greeks think they are exceptional too.[230]

The Trump administration practiced a unique mix of American exceptionalism and realism. Trump's vice president, Mike Pence, said, "I believe that the ideals that America has stood for throughout our history represent the highest ideals of humankind."[231] He argued that the US Constitution "will forever be the greatest charter of liberty our world has ever seen. It has fostered our nation's unparalleled success. And it is, to this day, the greatest bulwark against tyranny in history."[232]

Trump's secretary of state, Mike Pompeo, declared, "America is the most exceptional nation in the history of civilization."[233] UN Ambassador Nikki Haley asked, "Is our nation perfect? Of course it's not, but the principles at the heart of America are perfect." She also stated that "America is the greatest nation on earth."[234]

Trump's "America First" slogan was essentially a vision of restoring what, in his view, was a lost American exceptionalism. He believed that the United States had a remarkable past and deserved to be respected in the world. He believed that recent US presidential administrations did not live up to America's potential and that he alone could "make America great again." As he said in 2016, "America first will be the major and overriding theme of my administration. But to chart our path forward, we must first briefly take a look back. We have a lot to be proud of."[235]

When asked about American exceptionalism specifically, Trump turned to recent US failings, especially in economic policy. "First of all, Germany is eating our lunch. So, they say, 'Why are you exceptional? We're doing a lot better than you.'"[236] He continued, "We may have a chance to say it in the not-too-distant future. But even then, I wouldn't say it because when I take back the jobs, and when I take back all that money and we get all our stuff, I'm not going to rub it in."[237]

Trump also has some realist tendencies. Democracy and human rights were not a major theme in his foreign policy. He was willing to engage directly with anti-American dictators. When asked about Russia's human rights record, for example, he said, "Well, you think our country is so innocent?"[238] But Trump is clearly not a Blame America Firster. He believed that the United States deserved to be placed first. He is also clearly not a Wilsonian; he was definitely not interested in placing the amelioration of global society above US interests.

In sum, the Trump administration included a dose of realism but was at its best when it embraced American exceptionalism.

Biden is an old guard Democrat who probably believes in a version of American exceptionalism himself, but his administration has been pulled to the Left by an ascendant progressive wing of the Democratic Party that embraces Blame America First. *The Washington Post*, a paper in tune with the Democratic Party's progressive wing, describes American exceptionalism as "a kind of 'magical thinking' that clouds wise strategy."[239] It argues that "America is not particularly exceptional. Compared to numerous other societies in the developed world, its citizens are less healthy, less secure, and less educated. Its political system is seen increasingly for its anachronistic flaws."

The Biden administration subscribes to the view that America is systemically racist and sexist and otherwise oppressive.[240] Biden's State Department pushes woke ideology on unwilling allies and partners. It flies gay pride flags that offend more conservative societies.[241] It uses tax payer money to fund drag shows in Ecuador.[242] The State Department said the purpose of the drag shows is "to advance national interests, and enhance national security."

This is clearly not the best way to advance American interests and values. But what is?

American Exceptionalism for Today and Tomorrow

How should Republican Party leaders deal with America's role in the world and American values? Like Ronald Reagan, they should be un-apologetic supporters of American exceptionalism. They should proudly declare the United States to be a force for good in the world. They should also proudly contrast America's values and record against those of our dictatorial adversaries. And they should include a place for the pragmatic promotion of democracy and human rights in their foreign policy.

These principles are highly relevant in the New Cold War with the CCP. As the US-China confrontation heats up, one key question is whether this contest is primarily about power or ideology. Some prominent thinkers have argued that China poses a threat because it is a rising power and that it would be a "catastrophic mistake" to view the current confrontation primarily through an ideological lens.[243]

They contend that the United States would be worried about China's rise even if it were a democracy and that a focus on the ideological dimension of the challenge complicates Washington's ability to court non-democratic allies and paints the contest in unnecessary absolutist terms. They conclude that an "insistence on ideological concordance or total victory is a fool's errand—and quite possibly an invitation to disaster."

But it would also be an invitation to disaster if Washington were to overlook the important ideological element of this confrontation. This is not a contest with a generic China but with the People's Republic of China that is under the dictatorship of the Chinese Communist Party. The differences in governing systems between a democratic United States and an autocratic China matter not just for idealistic reasons like defending democracy and human rights (though they are important) but also for practical, hard-power concerns.

That's because the nature of the threat China poses abroad stems from its autocratic politics at home. Moreover, formulating the best US and allied strategy for addressing the challenge requires a clear-eyed assessment of the strengths and weaknesses of autocratic versus democratic systems.

An "either-or" framing makes for good debate, but power and ideology both matter when it comes to the US-China contest.

It is true that the China challenge is to a large degree about power. China possesses the world's second-largest economy. Its military investments have shifted the balance of power in the Indo-Pacific region, leading former US defense officials to warn that a World War III pitting the United States against China is possible and that the United States might very well lose.[244] These threats are not primarily about ideology. After all, many autocratic countries, including Egypt and Saudi Arabia, have poor human rights records, but they are not among Washington's national security concerns because they are neither hostile nor great powers.

But it is the CCP's ideology that determines what China does with its great power—and, therefore, the threat that it poses. This ideology is heavily shaped by its domestic political system. Contrary to the power-centric argument, the foremost economic concern is not that China is growing wealthy but that it is systematically preying on the global economic system.

The CCP engages in unfair trading practices, including intellectual property theft, state subsidies to Chinese firms, and restrictions on foreign firms operating in China. This is not just normal great-power politics but behavior peculiar to an autocratic nation. Economists have shown that open markets and free politics tend to go hand in hand.[245] Further, political scientists have found that democracies are more likely to enter into and abide by fair international economic agreements.[246]

The current global economic system and the World Trade Organization were set up by democratic countries that, for the most part, play by the rules and expect other countries to do the same. But the CCP has not done so. Instead, it systematically violates the rules to achieve an unfair advantage. Indeed, it will be difficult for China ever to come into full compliance with global trading standards without fundamentally altering its domestic political and economic model.

The same is true of the military threat. The CCP is currently involved in territorial and maritime disputes with most of its neighbors, including Taiwan, India, Japan, the Philippines, and others. Beijing is employing military coercion in these disputes, and all are possible flash points for armed conflict. It is unlikely that a liberal democratic China would behave in this way. Lacking institutionalized sources of legitimacy, the CCP stokes nationalist sentiment to maintain domestic support, giving assertions of territorial claims against foreign enemies an outsized role in Chinese foreign policy. There is a real risk that China's disputes with its democratic neighbors will turn violent, largely because Beijing is governed by the autocratic CCP.

It should go without saying, but it is hard to imagine that a liberal democratic China would engage in the ethnic cleansing of its minority populations, develop twenty-first-century tools of autocratic control that it exports to other dictators, or employ economic coercion and disinformation in an attempt to undermine democratic practices in the Free World. But the CCP is doing exactly that.

Unfortunately, as Chinese power has grown, global freedom has retreated, with the number of democracies globally declining in each of the past seventeen years.[247]

China's sharp-power practices are working, including by silencing free speech critical of China in the United States and other established democracies.[248] This is a problem.

To recognize that the growing Chinese military, economic, and governance threat is heavily shaped by Beijing's autocratic political system is not to engage in abstract moralizing but, rather, is essential for a clear-eyed understanding of the challenge. "Realists" urge analysts to focus on power, but it would simply be unrealistic to ignore the ideological component of the China threat.

Understanding the ideological dimension of this struggle is also necessary for developing a sound strategy. The US national security community often obsesses over adversaries' strengths and Washington's weaknesses, but good strategy often begins by leveraging one's own strengths against the enemy's weaknesses.

As Kroenig argued in a recent book, America's democratic system provides it with many advantages, while China's autocratic form of government hinders its effectiveness.[249] To be sure, there are autocratic strengths and democratic weaknesses as well, but the US system's special ability to generate enormous wealth, power, and influence on the global stage more than outweighs these liabilities.

Democratic systems tend to produce sound economic institutions that spark innovation and generate high, long-run rates of economic growth. America has been the world's largest economy since the 1890s and its innovation leader since the time of Thomas Edison. Companies listed on Wall Street and US Treasuries remain the world's safest investments, placing the United States at the center of the global financial system.

Democracies are better at building alliances and partnerships, and America's global network of friends, including thirty other members of NATO, Japan, South Korea, Australia, and others, combine to make up 59 percent of global GDP. Democracies also tend to win the wars they fight, and the United States remains the world's only military superpower with global power-projecting capabilities.

At the same time, the CCP is undermining China's effectiveness. Dictators usually prioritize political control over economic performance. To reassert the primacy of the CCP, President Xi Jinping is renationalizing parts of the Chinese economy and backtracking on promised economic reforms, even though this stalls China's growth.

Dictators like Xi struggle to forge enduring international partnerships, and unfavorable views of China have reached all-time highs around the world.[250] Finally, autocracies' greatest weakness is domestic insecurity. China spends more on internal repression than on its military. If you follow the money, the CCP is more afraid of Uighurs and protesters in Hong Kong than of the Pentagon.

These US strengths and Chinese weaknesses should be understood and exploited in any successful competitive strategy. Ignoring ideological differences would cause Washington to overlook some of its most significant competitive advantages.

Those who dismiss the ideological nature of the contest argue that viewing China through an ideological lens would restrict America's strategic options, but they are mistaken. They claim that Washington must work with autocratic countries like Vietnam and Singapore, whose interests are also threatened by China's revisionism and expansionism, but that the United States will alienate them if it emphasizes China's autocratic politics.

This is a false choice. Washington can recognize the ideological dimension of the China challenge and emphasize it to rally the Free World even as it maintains pragmatic security partnerships with friendly autocratic governments. Indeed, US foreign policy has followed just such an approach for decades with great success, including during the First Cold War.

Those who minimize the threat of CCP ideology also claim that an ideological competition requires that Washington pursue maximalist goals like dismantling the CCP, but this does not follow. The United States and its allies and partners can recognize and exploit the ideological dimensions of this rivalry even as they set modest goals. Indeed, the primary goal of great-power confrontation should be to change the intent and capability of China's leaders, regardless of whether they stand behind the CCP banner in the years to come.[251]

Finally, critics charge that taking ideology seriously requires believing that overthrowing the CCP and spreading liberal democracy throughout the world will end all of our problems. But this is also a non sequitur. Conflicts of interest would certainly remain between a democratic China and the United States, but they would be different, and most likely less severe, than those that exist today. The resulting relationship would be more akin to present US frustrations with India or the European Union, or economic tensions with Japan in the 1980s, than to a global death match.

There is an undeniable ideological dimension to US-CCP competition, and Washington should embrace it. If these were just morally equivalent great powers jockeying for position, then other nations, even traditional US allies in Europe, would be reluctant to choose a side.

But the United States and China are not morally equivalent. The United States is the leader of the Free World and the principal architect of a global system that has brought the world seventy-five years of unprecedented peace, prosperity, and freedom. China, under the CCP, is a revisionist and expansionist autocracy that wants to disrupt and displace this system. If it succeeds, the consequences could include increased conflicts and decreased standards of living and human rights within the CCP's sphere of influence and, over time, globally. This competition is about more than power politics—and freedom-loving people worldwide should recognize they have a direct stake in its outcome.

PART III

NATIONAL SECURITY THREATS

CHAPTER SIX

China

This section of the book considers the greatest national security threats facing the United States: China, Russia, Iran, and North Korea. These countries are threatening in their own right, but they are increasingly working together in a New Axis of Evil. These chapters will put forward a conservative deterrence and diplomacy strategy for addressing these threats and securing America's interests. We will start with the most significant threat to US interests: the New Cold War with the Chinese Communist Party.

The China Threat

Under dictator-for-life Xi Jinping, the CCP has become more threatening in the use of its economic, diplomatic, and military power to challenge US interests. He promises that by 2049, the one hundredth anniversary of the Communist Party's takeover of China, China will be at the center of the international system in the dominant position.[252] In short, Xi seeks to overturn the US-led international system and replace it with a new system led by Beijing. If China succeeds, the consequences would be devastating for the security and well-being of all Americans.

As noted in the introduction, there are important differences between the First Cold War and New Cold War. This contest is primarily with the PRC, not the Soviet Union. Beijing is a much more serious economic and technological competitor than Moscow ever was. The First

Cold War was a global competition centered in Europe. The New Cold War is a global competition centered in Asia. The United States is economically interdependent with the PRC, whereas the Free World and the Communist Bloc were economically isolated.

Still, as also noted in the introduction, there is a key similarity. This is a contest for global mastery between the United States and a revisionist dictatorship. The stakes could not be higher. Moreover, we should hope that this contest will remain a *cold* war and, like the First Cold War, never turn into a hot, shooting war.

Before we turn to Washington's strategy for victory in the New Cold War, let us consider the serious threats Beijing poses in the economic, technological, governance, diplomatic, and military realms.

Economic

China possesses the world's second-largest economy, with 18 percent of all global economic activity occurring in China (compared to 25 percent in the United States).[253] Economists used to project that China would overtake the United States to become the world's largest economy, but that looks less likely now. As Xi centralizes power, he is undermining China's once successful development model and ruining China's economy.

Still, China remains an economic threat. China systematically preys on the global economic system and through its unfair trading practices has caused the loss of millions of American jobs. It steals intellectual property from the United States through cyberattacks and other means at an estimated value equivalent to the GDP of the Commonwealth of Virginia every year.[254] China subsidizes its companies, like tech giants Huawei and ByteDance, giving them an unfair market advantage over US tech firms like Google and Amazon. Another way it gives its companies an unfair economic advantage is through lax environmental and labor rules. Complying with these global standards is a cost that US companies must pass on to consumers, whereas PRC companies can sell at a lower price because they do not have such compliance costs. China restricts market access to American firms that want to do business in China. When an American company wants to open a factory in China, for example, Beijing requires the American firm to partner with a Chinese company that retains a majority ownership. China also requires the company to transfer its technology. After a few years, the Chinese partner kicks the American company out and sets up shop on its own. PRC companies also have an advantage in many global markets because they can pay bribes to procurement officials, something that is rightly illegal for American companies. China has engaged in these unfair practices for decades, but Washington turned a blind eye, hoping that China would become a responsible member of the international community as it became wealthier. That hope did not pan out. It is time to fight back.

Technology

The United States has been the world's innovation leader for more than a century. This technological edge has given the United States enormous economic, diplomatic, and military advantages. American technological innovations from the airplane to the internet have been a major source of US economic growth and worldwide economic leadership. America's cutting-edge technology made it the envy of the world, giving the United States enormous soft power. And its technological innovations propelled America's military dominance from nuclear weapons to precision-guided munitions.

The PRC wants to seize this technological dominance for itself. Through a plan formerly known as "Made in China 2025," the CCP plans to dominate the most important emerging technologies of the twenty-first century, including: 5G, artificial intelligence, quantum computing, hypersonic missiles, and more.[255] To achieve these ambitions, China is using many of its customary, unfair economic practices, such as intellectual property theft. But it is also coming straight through the front door. It is buying US technology in transactions that are approved by Biden's Commerce Department. Most of China's best technologists were trained in US universities. Millions of American teenagers download China's TikTok app on their phones, giving China access to their user data—and data is the new oil of the twenty-first century. China is trying to install its Huawei 5G technology all over the world, including in countries allied with the United States, allowing Beijing to control the digital infrastructure of the twenty-first century. The PRC is already ahead of the United States in several critical technologies, including: 5G, quantum computing and satellites, certain applications of AI, and hypersonic missiles. Losing the new tech arms race to China would mean ceding long-standing US economic and military advantages to its Communist rival.

Democracy and Human Rights

Communist China has abhorrent human rights practices. It censors the internet because it is afraid that if its citizens learn the truth from X or *The Wall Street Journal*, they will rise up against the Communist regime. It spies on its citizens using facial-recognition technology and other tools. It then assigns all citizens an Orwellian "social credit score."[256] People who have low social credit due to even minor infractions, such as jaywalking, are denied basic rights, like the ability to purchase a plane ticket. China harvests and resells organs from prisoners, killing many in the process. Most concerning, however, is that China is engaging in genocide and systematic crimes against humanity against an entire segment of its population: the Muslim Uighur minority. It has moved millions of them into concentration camps in Xinjiang province where women are sterilized, men and women are pressed into slave labor, and children are indoctrinated to forget their Muslim heritage.

The CCP is also promoting these abhorrent practices beyond China's borders because it wants to create a world safe for autocracy. The CCP is threatened by democracy anywhere. It is afraid that if democratic ideals are emulated in China, the CCP would fall, and its leaders would be brought to justice.

The contest with the CCP, therefore, has a clear ideological dimension regardless of Washington's preferences, because Xi believes he is in an ideological competition.[257] It is also global in scope. Xi is promoting China's state-led capitalist model as an alternative to open-market democracy and is assisting other dictators by, for example, providing them with technologies to better repress their populations. Xi believes that

China's Communist system is superior and that democracy is feeble and in decline.

But Xi's fight against democracy does not end there. He is even interfering in American democracy. The CCP has set up police stations within the United States to spy on Chinese Americans. It requires all Chinese in the United States (including students and workers on temporary visas) to spy for Beijing. The FBI has made Chinese counterintelligence in the United States one of its top priorities, and it opens a new China-related counterintelligence case about every ten hours.[258]

The PRC also uses its power in attempts to curtail the free speech of American citizens in the United States. When American private citizens or corporate representatives say things that offend the CCP, Beijing retaliates by threatening to close them out of China's market. The result is that Americans censor their speech to avoid offending Communist China. Hollywood will not portray China in a negative light in their films, for example. As noted earlier, actor John Cena offered an abject apology in Mandarin Chinese for calling Taiwan a "country."[259] United Airlines changed its maps to remove references to Taiwan.[260] NBA star LeBron James slam dunked a Houston Rockets executive for condemning China's brutal crackdown on protestors in Hong Kong. LeBron said the executive was "not educated on the situation" and issued a bizarre warning that "so many people could have been harmed, not only financially but physically, emotionally, spiritually."[261] American free speech is being undermined by a combination of Chinese ruthlessness and American greed.

Diplomacy

Communist China is also increasing its diplomatic influence at America's expense. To a large extent, this is due to the PRC's increasing economic heft. As noted above, twenty years ago, the United States was the top trading partner for most countries in the world. Today, that position belongs to China. Perhaps most notably, China is a major global purchaser of natural resources and commodities, including oil and gas from the Middle East, rare earth elements from Africa, and agricultural products from Latin America. Moreover, China's Belt and Road Initiative (BRI) promises to build infrastructure, such as roads, ports, and bridges, for counties in the developing world. In many of these deals, China pays bribes to local officials to ensure they are beholden to Communist China. Even worse, many of these investments are not economically sound and had been previously rejected by prudent investors. The PRC demands that the recipient country provide as collateral its most valuable assets and threatens to seize them when the deals go sour. Beijing used this "debt trap diplomacy," for example, to seize a port in Sri Lanka that may be turned into a Chinese naval base.

China uses its economic influence for geopolitical leverage. Many countries around the world kowtow to Beijing because their economic well-being depends on it. If they do not, China makes an example of them. When US ally South Korea deployed US missile defenses despite Chinese objections, China retaliated economically by shutting down Chinese tourism to South Korea, a major income source, and closing a prominent South Korean grocery chain in the PRC. The message was clear: defy Beijing and suffer economic consequences. Other countries learned the lesson and are careful to do Beijing's bidding.

China's malign diplomatic influence also extends to multilateral institutions. The UN system was set up with the ideal that all countries of the world could come together to discuss global problems and solutions. Instead, the PRC is using its influence in international bodies to turn them against their original purpose. It vetoed UN Security Council resolutions that condemned Russia for its invasion of Ukraine in 2022. It prevents the UN Human Rights Council from addressing China's grave human rights violations in Xinjiang and elsewhere. And it stopped the World Health Organization from conducting an effective investigation into COVID-19's origins, thereby making subsequent outbreaks more likely.

The CCP's aggressive "wolf warrior" diplomacy has turned off many of its erstwhile friends. This style of diplomacy is based on a popular nationalist Chinese action hero. In a display of newfound confidence, PRC diplomats taunt foreign governments that dare to stand in China's way. When Australia criticized aspects of Chinese policy, for example, the PRC's foreign ministry belittled Australia as "chewing gum on China's shoe."[262] Similarly, when France was critical of the CCP's response to COVID-19, China's ambassador to Paris said, "They howl with the wolves, to make a big fuss about lies and rumors about China."[263] "Western egotism and white supremacy" is how China's ambassador to Canada dismissed Ottawa's concerns over the wrongful detention of Canadians in China.[264]

China has historically shunned alliances, but in recent years it has been the leader of a New Axis of Evil, linking China to Russia, Iran, and North Korea. These anti-American dictatorships share fierce opposition to the US-led order and are working together to bring it down. The China-Russia link is the most concerning. Xi and Putin have declared that their friendship has "no limits."[265] During the First Cold War, Moscow was the senior partner, but, in recent years, those roles have been reversed with Russia becoming a de facto vassal state to China. As the West sanctions Russia in an attempt to stop Russia's aggression in Ukraine, China gobbles up cut-rate Russian oil and gas, providing Russia with a much-needed economic lifeline that Russia uses to finance its war. The CCP shields Russia from consequences from its invasion of Ukraine, while still trying to portray itself as a neutral party to the conflict. There is also military cooperation. They have conducted joint military exercises in Europe, Asia, and the Middle East. The greatest fear of many US military planners is that China and Russia could conduct coordinated attacks on the US alliance systems in Asia and Europe, forcing the United States into a two-front war against two major power rivals.

Military

Some argue that, unlike the First Cold War, which was heavily militarized, the New Cold War will primarily play out in the economic and technological domains. That is wishful thinking. The enemy also gets a vote. While China would prefer to "win without fighting," it is also preparing for war.[266]

For the past several decades, China has gone to school on the American way of war and has developed a defense strategy designed to defeat US forces in armed conflict. Its so-called "anti-access, area denial" strategy threatens to conduct large-scale attacks on US bases and forces in the Indo-Pacific using surface-to-surface and surface-to-air missiles. China's plan is to force the United States to pull back its military from the region and thereby give the PRC a free hand to attack Taiwan and other vulnerable neighbors.

It is supporting this strategy with a massive military buildup. According to the Pentagon, China will quintuple the size of its nuclear arsenal by 2035 to reach 1,500 nuclear weapons—nuclear parity with the United States.[267] It is also investing in conventional capabilities to blunt American military power in the Indo-Pacific, including thousands of conventionally armed missiles. These missiles would be used to destroy US forces and bases in the region. The DF-21 "carrier killer" potentially renders US aircraft carriers—a key element of American power-projection capabilities since WWII—obsolete. The PRC is investing in naval power, including hundreds of amphibious ships that would enable it to launch an invasion of Taiwan. The CCP now has the world's largest navy with more ships than the United States. As noted above, China is also leading the United States in several emerging defense technologies, such as hypersonic missiles.

Unfortunately, there are many possible flash points for conflict since the PRC has border and maritime disputes with nearly all of its neighbors. In the South China Sea, China is occupying disputed islands through military force. Several other countries, including US treaty ally the Philippines, claim the same islands. The United States and allied militaries conduct "freedom of navigation operations" near the islands, but China warns that it may one day shoot down US aircraft or sink US ships if they continue to violate what Beijing claims are its sovereign waters and airspace. How would a US president respond if the PLA shoots down an American warplane in anger?

The PRC and Japan nearly went to war over the disputed Senkaku Islands in 2012. Washington subsequently clarified that its defense treaty with Tokyo extends to the islands and that another clash could trigger US military involvement.

China and India fought a border war in 1962. The dispute remains unresolved and has reignited with skirmishes in 2020 with tens of soldiers killed on each side. It is unlikely that this dispute could escalate into a broader conflict that draws in the United States, but it is possible.

The PRC and the United States last fought each other in large-scale war in the Korean War (1950–1953). A future Korean war could also lead to a direct Sino-US conflict. If the regime of Kim Jong Un collapses, US and South Korean military forces would march north to stabilize the country, secure Pyongyang's nuclear weapons, and reunite the Korean Peninsula. The PLA has plans to march south to secure its border, seize the WMD, and ensure that a North Korean buffer state remains between China and US forces in South Korea. With few mechanisms of military coordination between Beijing and Washington, this scenario could lead to a major conflict.

The greatest war fears, however, are over Taiwan. China considers Taiwan a renegade province that must eventually be reunited with mainland China. The United States and the Free World see Taiwan as a thriving capitalist democracy that does not want to be subjugated by Communist China. America's complicated "One China policy" recognizes Beijing as the official government of China, while maintaining robust unofficial ties with Taipei. Washington is happy with the status quo. It discourages a declaration of independence by Taiwan but also opposes PRC's use of force to conquer the island. To support the latter objective, the Pentagon sells weapons to Taiwan every year.

If the PRC attacked, would the United States intervene militarily to defend Taiwan? Washington maintains a formal policy of "strategic ambiguity." That means Washington does not say whether or not it would go to war to defend Taiwan. Biden has said four times that he would fight for the island, but, each time, his own White House walked his comments back. Ambiguous indeed.

Washington has a strong interest in preventing the CCP from conquering Taiwan. Let us also examine a map of East Asia from Beijing's point of view, looking out to the Pacific Ocean. China is bottled up by a string of US allies in the First Island Chain running from Japan in the north to the Philippines in the south. Taiwan is the cork of this bottle. If the PRC takes Taiwan, it could turn it into a large aircraft carrier. It would be in a much better position to threaten other US allies and US forces in Japan, South Korea, the Philippines, and elsewhere. It could also build major bases in Taiwan and project power directly into the Pacific Ocean threatening Hawaii and the West Coast of the United States. If the PRC dominates Asia militarily, it might be tempted to even attack the United States homeland.

A Chinese attack on Taiwan would also devastate the US economy. China and Taiwan are both top ten US trading partners. A war between them could crash the global economy and the standard of living of all Americans. If China succeeds in dominating Asia or the world, it could also be in a better position to threaten US trade routes and economic well-being more broadly.

There is also the question of values and the US-led order. If America stands aside while a genocidal dictator like Xi conquers its vulnerable democratic neighbors, why would he stop there? Would other dictators also try their luck at foreign military adventurism? We would replace the rule of law for the law of the jungle, and none of us relishes this prospect.

A Chinese-Led System

Ultimately, the New Cold War between China and the United States is about what kind of world we want to live in. The US-led system since 1945, inspired by democratic principles and based on respect of international rules, has not been perfect, but it has been better than any system in world history. It has also greatly benefited all Americans to live in the world's wealthiest and most powerful country.

If China wins the New Cold War, that will all come to an end. China would use its power to economically coerce the United States, like it has done with other countries that are vulnerable economically. It would use its influence to further interfere in US domestic politics and society, undermining America's freedoms. And it would be in a better position to militarily attack the United States and its global interests.

In short, if China runs the world, all Americans will be less secure, prosperous, and free. How do we prevent that outcome?

A Strategy for Victory in the New Cold War

The United States needs a strategy to win the New Cold War with China. A good strategy starts with clear goals. After all, if you do not know where you are going, any path can take you there. The United States declared the return of "great power competition" with China in 2017, but, since then, it has struggled to articulate a clear goal. What does victory look like?

To identify a goal for the New Cold War with China, we take our inspiration from Ronald Reagan: "We win and they lose."[268] That is what Reagan famously said about the First Cold War with the Soviet Union. By envisioning it, he made it happen.

Winning the New Cold War with China would mean getting to a point where the Chinese government no longer has the will or the capacity to threaten core US interests. There are many different paths to victory. The CCP might mellow over time. A new generation of Chinese leaders might change their minds. They might decide that Xi's aggressive approach failed. They may conclude that challenging the United States and its allies is too difficult and too costly for Beijing and try a more cooperative path. China may be so thoroughly outcompeted that it loses the capacity to seriously threaten the United States. The CCP might collapse. Autocratic regimes are brittle, and they often collapse, especially at times of leadership transition.[269] The new PRC regime might be a less threatening autocratic one or—less likely but possible—a peaceful, liberal democracy. It might also become a dysfunctional inward-looking state. Finally, a CCP collapse might lead to the PRC's breakup into many pieces as China's multinational empire crumbles with Tibet, Xinjiang, and other restive regions tired of Beijing's harsh rule declaring independence.

Any of these outcomes would be a victory for the United States and the Free World. These possibilities are not mutually exclusive. Indeed, the First Cold War ended in a mix of the above outcomes for the former Soviet Union.

Deterrence and Diplomacy

To achieve this goal, Washington should follow a conservative, dual-track, deterrence and diplomacy strategy. First, it should systematically pressure and impose costs on the CCP everywhere it challenges US interests. Second, it should employ diplomacy to build a pro-freedom, anti-CCP coalition and to hold out the prospect of engagement with a future, reasonable government in Beijing.

This was essentially Reagan's strategy for victory over the Soviet Union. He was confident that America's free-market democracy system was inherently stronger than the Soviet Union's totalitarian system and that by forcing Moscow into an unrelenting competition, he could defeat the Communists and bring to power a reformer in Moscow who would negotiate the Soviet Union's peaceful surrender.

DETERRENCE

The first element of the strategy is deterrence. This is the hard-hitting part of the strategy. The United States needs to confront the CCP. In response to illegal and aggressive behavior, Washington needs to make life as difficult as possible for Xi and the CCP to show them that challenging the United States and its allies is a losing cause.

Many describe the US-China relationship as a "competition." For example, Biden's White House press secretary Jen Psaki said, "We welcome stiff competition" with China.[270] This is naïve. This is not a tennis match where both sides compete politely while observing common rules. Does Washington really "welcome" cheating on trade, genocide, and territorial aggression? Describing such systemic violations of accepted international standards as mere "competition" is misleading and confusing. This is not just semantics. Using the right term to define how we engage the CCP has practical implications: it tells the American people, our adversaries, and the entire world that we understand the stakes and the seriousness of the matter. "Confrontation" rings truer.

The most important aspect of this confrontation is military deterrence. The United States needs to ensure that it has a strategy to deter, and if necessary defeat, a Chinese military attack on US allies and partners, including Taiwan. To maintain deterrence, Washington should change to a policy of "strategic clarity" and be crystal clear that it would defend Taiwan if China attacks. The most likely path to war is that Xi miscalculates and thinks it will be easy. Washington needs to persuade Xi that he would lose any war over Taiwan and that he would be better off not to try. To make this policy work, the United States should achieve a favorable balance of power at every level of military conflict, starting with strategic forces.

This is a major difference between Republicans and Democrats in defense policy. Democrats believe that the United States should aim for mutual nuclear vulnerability and mutually assured destruction (MAD) with our adversaries. They argue that so long as the United States and China can both destroy each other in a nuclear war, then neither side has an incentive to fight one, resulting in peace.

This is foolish. It is foolish strategically to take off the table an important area of competition where the United States has an inherent edge. And it is foolish morally to choose a policy of intentionally leaving the American people vulnerable to a Chinese nuclear attack. This policy boils down to outsourcing the very survival of the United States as a functioning society to the whims of Xi Jinping. If he decides to launch a major nuclear attack on the United States, for whatever reason, he could destroy the country in a matter of minutes. This is intolerable.

Reagan and Trump agreed that the answer lies elsewhere. Reagan engaged in a massive strategic forces buildup in the 1980s to force the Soviet Union to compete in this area. He also announced his Strategic Defense Initiative (SDI) missile defense system with the dream of protecting the United States from a Soviet nuclear attack. Trump declared that the United States needed a nuclear weapons capability "at the top of the pack" and a "state of the art" missile defense system. He introduced new nuclear weapons into the US arsenal for the first time since the end of the First Cold War.

Future Republican presidents should follow their lead and prioritize strategic forces with the goal of achieving strategic superiority over China (and Russia). They should invest in a nuclear weapons and missile defense buildup to make it clear to Moscow and Beijing that they are outgunned in strategic forces. This will leave our adversaries two undesirable options. They can either accept their vulnerability. This will make them more cautious in challenging the United States and more likely to back down in high-stakes crises. Alternatively, they can attempt to arms race the United States. But, arms racing with the United States—the wealthiest, most technologically advanced nation throughout the nuclear era—will not be easy. The Soviet Union failed trying, and the same fate might await China.

Next, the United States needs to strengthen its conventional military forces, with a special focus on denying China the ability to successfully attack Taiwan.[271] To invade or blockade Taiwan, the PLA would likely rely heavily on naval and air power, including large numbers of amphibious ships and helicopters to bring large numbers of Chinese military personnel across the Taiwan Strait to occupy the island. To counter China, the Pentagon needs the ability to sink the Chinese navy in seventy-two hours.[272] The United States should invest in anti-ship missiles, surface-to-air missiles, long-range bombers, submarines, smart naval mines, and other capabilities to blunt China's naval and air forces. It should also disperse forces in the Indo-Pacific and invest in missile defenses to render US forces in Asia less vulnerable to China's anti-access, area-denial (A2/AD) capabilities.

Allies are among the US's greatest strengths, and Washington should enlist its friends to ensure a favorable military balance in Asia. The Pentagon should speed weapons deliveries to Taiwan and ensure that Taipei is purchasing the right types of weapons, like anti-ship missiles, that are most relevant to a Taiwan Straits contingency. It should help other regional allies, like Japan, Australia, South Korea, and the Philippines, to develop their own A2/AD capabilities to defend themselves and contribute to the defense of Taiwan. Washington should encourage expeditionary European allies, like the Brits, the French, the Germans, the Dutch, and the Danes, to contribute symbolic shows of force in Asia to make it clear to Beijing that an attack on Taiwan is an attack on the entire Free World. Finally, Washington should negotiate basing and overflight agreements with friendly countries in the region, such as India, to enable access in a major war.

Economic deterrence must be used as much as military deterrence. The United States should make it clear to the CCP that they will pay a steep economic price for an invasion of Taiwan.

An anti-CCP coalition should hold public economic sanctions exercises much like defense ministries hold joint military exercises. They should practice how to put in place sanctions swiftly in response to Chinese aggression. The CCP should understand that if it invades Taiwan, then the United States and the Free World will respond with broad economic retaliation that will come fast and hard, and that would have a severe impact on the Chinese economy.

Washington also needs to economically de-risk. As was explained in Chapter Four, the United States needs to decouple economically from China in a selective fashion and encourage its allies to do the same. This will mean export controls, bans on outbound investment, more stringent foreign investment screening, enhanced cyber defenses to protect IP, and other restrictions for trade in areas of national security concern. In tandem, Washington and its allies should reshore and allyshore production of sensitive products. This can be facilitated by new policies, including government subsidies and tax breaks, to incentivize American and allied production of key technologies and components, such as semiconductors, pharmaceuticals and medical equipment, and critical mineral mining and reprocessing. The United States and its allies must also impose countervailing measures in areas where China is cheating on the global trading system in less sensitive areas, such as the film industry. This will ensure secure supply chains for the Free World. It will help reinforce the Free World's technological leadership, as China's innovation model has been parasitic on the West. It will also help to choke China's economic growth, technological development, and power potential. The CCP attained 10 percent growth rates for decades only because the West had a strategic plan to help China develop. Now, Xi's aggressive foreign policy is antagonizing all of his trading partners and undercutting the export-led model that fueled China's rise over the decades.

The final area in which the deterrence element of strategy must be applied is in domestic politics and values. China is interfering in US domestic politics and undermining America's traditional freedoms. The

United States should implement several new measures designed to limit and deter Chinese malign activity in the United States. It should require industries, companies, nonprofits, and politicians—from Hollywood to universities to big banks—to disclose the funds they receive from, and the investments they make in, China. These industries inadvertently undermine America's national security interests to make a buck. At a minimum, they must be transparent about their practices. This transparency would be a first step toward subsequent government restrictions or bans. The FBI should step up counterintelligence investigations into Chinese spying and shut down Chinese police stations and spy rings operating out of Chinese consulates in the United States. TikTok, Confucius Institutes, Huawei, and other means the CCP uses to harvest data from Americans and to sow disinformation in the United States should be banned outright.

Moreover, and importantly, Washington should fight fire with fire. China is messing around in America's domestic political system. The United States should do the same in China. Domestic political stability is an autocrat's Achilles' heel. Yet, the Biden administration has given the CCP a pass in this critical vulnerability. Instead, Washington should force the CCP to play defense in this area. The US government should identify what the CCP considers the pillars of its regime stability and put them at risk. For example, the CCP controls the internet with a "Great Firewall" because it believes that the Chinese people's access to free information would destabilize the regime. US Cyber Command should make it a daily mission to bring down the Great Firewall and provide access of information to the Chinese people. The US government should send a daily text message to all Chinese cell phone users about the corruption of Xi and other CCP elites and so on. Such measures would be morally justified, contributing to the freedoms of the Chinese people despite the efforts of the CCP to repress them. They would also carry strategic benefit. At a minimum, these measures will force the CCP to focus its energy and resources on domestic repression, reducing its ability to threaten the United States and its allies. At best, these measures could contribute to the mellowing or collapse of the CCP and the end of the New Cold War.

DIPLOMACY

The other major pillar of the strategy is diplomacy. But this is not naïve diplomacy. The Biden administration has promised to cooperate with China to solve shared global challenges. As we will explain below, this is wrongheaded.

Instead, the primary focus of the diplomatic component should be to grow and strengthen an anti-CCP coalition. If the United States must combat China on its own, the tale of the tape is a bit too close for comfort. Together with US formal treaty allies, however, the Free World possesses a preponderance of power able to shape decisively global outcomes. US efforts to cut off China from sensitive technology on its own, for example, would be futile, because Beijing could simply go to Europe or Japan for tech acquisition. To be effective, the United States needs to use its diplomatic skill to build the largest and most effective anti-China coalition across a broad range of issues: technology, economics, military, human rights, and so forth. Fortunately, China's aggressive diplomacy has alienated many countries and pushed them into the US camp, proving the old adage that only the CCP can contain China. Washington should build on this momentum to expand and strengthen the Free World coalition.

Next, Washington should seek to win over hedging states. The 2022 Russian invasion of Ukraine showed that the world is divided into three blocs. The US and its formal treaty allies in the Free World have proven to be more united than many thought. Opposing them, the New Axis of Evil (China, Russia, North Korea, and Iran) are increasingly working together. But there has emerged a third camp. Major powers in the Global South, like India, Indonesia, South Africa, and Brazil, do not want to choose sides. We call this grouping the hedging states. They sympathize with the Free World, but they also want to continue profitable relationships with Russia and China. India used the opportunity from the war in Ukraine to purchase cut-rate Russian oil. And China is the largest market for Brazil's agricultural exports. The United States and its allies need a strategy to give these countries an alternative to economic vassalage to the revisionist autocracies—a plan to pull them into the Free World camp.

The diplomatic strategy should also focus on competitive multilateralism with China. No longer can Washington allow China to spread its malign influence in the multilateral institutions created by and for the Free World, such as the United Nations, the World Health Organization, the World Bank, and so on. Washington should reassert its influence in these bodies by, for example, actively supporting the candidacy of US and Free World nationals for leadership positions and spotlighting publicly Chinese and Russian hypocrisy when they turn these institutions against their founding purposes.

The strategy must also include a role for direct engagement with China, but not the way the Biden administration thinks about it. Cooperating with China on shared challenges is mostly a fool's errand. This is increasingly a zero-sum relationship. But, Washington should still engage with the CCP to deliver tough messages. The State Department can detail for China the long list of its behaviors that it finds unacceptable. It can explain its strategy of ensuring that the CCP pays a severe price when it engages in threatening behavior. American diplomats can make clear to Beijing and the world that the CCP's aggressive strategy to run the world by 2049 is bound to fail. They can also hold out the prospect for a more cooperative relationship if a future Chinese government is willing to change its stripes.

The United States should also engage directly with the Chinese people to separate them from their government. Washington must be clear that its grievances are not with the Chinese people but with the CCP. Americans admire China's history and civilization and Chinese ingenuity. It can also sympathize with the Chinese people, including Uighurs, Tibetans, Hong Kongers, and others, as they are often the greatest victims of the CCP's predations.

Finally, is there any role for cooperating with China on shared challenges? There is a narrow but useful path. The Biden administration claims that they will cooperate with China to address shared global challenges, like climate change, public health, and arms control. But China is not part of the solution in these areas; it is the biggest part of the problem. On climate change, China is the world's largest greenhouse gas emitter, accounting for 28 percent of global emissions—nearly double

WE WIN, THEY LOSE

the amount of the United States and more than all the developed countries combined.[273] As Washington and other powers cut their emissions, Beijing promises to continue *increasing* emissions until 2030. In global public health, China's initial delay in reporting COVID-19 turned a local breakout into a global pandemic. Beijing blocked a meaningful investigation into the disease's origins, making a future reoccurrence more likely. The story is similar in arms control. China is engaging in a massive nuclear arms buildup and refuses to even come to the table to talk about arms control.

Saying, therefore, that we must "cooperate" with China on the very challenges that China itself is causing greatly stretches the meaning of the term.

Still, Washington should visibly attempt to cooperate with China in the above areas. When China inevitably refuses to cooperate sincerely, Washington should use this as part of its diplomatic strategy. It should continually point out that Washington is making a good faith effort to cooperate and that China is the problem. This will place the blame on the PRC and help build the anti-CCP coalition mentioned above.

In addition, Washington can keep alive a few remaining areas of genuine cooperation. Washington would like Beijing to continue purchasing American agricultural products and US treasuries, for example. And Beijing wants Washington to retain its commitment to a "One China" policy with regard to Taiwan.[274] Cooperation in these areas contributes to the long-term strategy outlined above because it can show future Chinese leaders that Washington can be a constructive partner when China reciprocates.

The words we use have real effects on how we think about the China challenge and what we should do about it. The US government, the American public, US businesses, and US allies and partners need to fully understand that the US-China relationship is an increasingly confrontational one, and it is likely to get worse before it gets better. They need to prepare for this reality by getting tougher with China when it breaks the rules and by looking to disentangle themselves from China's malign influences. Presenting the US-China relationship as a recipe with equal parts cooperation and above-board competition creates misperceptions with potentially counterproductive results.

This is not to say that Washington desires confrontation with China. It has shown through its actions over the past decades that it would prefer a cooperative relationship. But that does not appear possible so long as Xi (and perhaps the Chinese Communist Party) remains in power. The United States and its allies, therefore, should push back hard on China's rule breaking to defend their interests and to show China's leaders that challenging the United States and the Free World is too difficult and costly for Beijing and ultimately not in China's own self-interest.

Achieving cooperation with China in the future, therefore, requires confrontation now. Washington and its like-minded allies and partners should do more to confront China on its unfair trade practices, abysmal human rights record, military aggression, pollution, poor public health record, and nuclear arms buildup. Xi will find cooperation more attractive when he learns that his confrontational approach has backfired.

Some will argue that confronting the CCP will lead to more aggressive Chinese behavior and an increased risk of military conflict. They have it backwards. A resolute policy of confrontation now is the United States' best hope of eventually convincing Beijing to change course and put us on a path toward a better future.

CHAPTER SEVEN

Russia

Putin's Russia is in a de facto alliance with Xi Jinping and the PRC and poses a significant threat to US interests. The PRC threat should remain the top priority of US NSS, but Washington also needs to lead its allies and partners to counter the serious challenges posed by Moscow.

The Russia Threat

While much of the world and the American people have benefited from US global leadership, Xi and Putin fear it. Since they are dictators, they feel threatened by an international system built on the sovereignty of nations, free markets and fair trade, and democracy and human rights. This freedom-based vision of the world stands in stark contrast to their despotism at home and military aggressiveness abroad. They perceive the very existence of this free world vision as an existential threat to their regimes. As a result, the two dictators are working closely together to undermine US interests and the US-led system.

Since Xi took power in 2012, Xi and Putin have met forty times in one-on-one meetings, twice as often as either has met with any other world leader.[275] During a visit in Beijing on the eve of Russia's invasion of Ukraine in 2022, Xi and Putin declared a partnership with "no limits."[276] In Moscow a year later, Xi told Putin that "right now there are changes—the likes of which we haven't seen for 100 years—and we are the ones driving these changes together."[277]

Putin responded, "I agree."

Russia and the PRC have a close economic partnership, and Russia is a major supplier of oil and gas that fuels China's economy. Russia is also a major source of advanced weaponry to China, including helping to build up its nuclear forces.[278] As noted above, Russia and the PRC have participated in joint military exercises in Europe, Asia, and the Middle East.[279]

China is aiding Putin's war in Ukraine by providing Moscow with economic assistance, non-lethal military equipment, and diplomatic support. Xi wants Putin to prevail in Ukraine. A strong Russia is part of the CCP's geostrategic plan because a strong Russia is better able to threaten US interests in Europe, keep the United States distracted there, and give Xi a freer hand in Asia. Xi also suspects that if the United States and its Free World allies cannot stop Putin in Ukraine, then they will not be able to stop him in Taiwan either.

The emerging Xi-Putin alliance is a top US national security concern. Indeed, among the biggest fears of US military planners is that Xi and Putin could mount simultaneous attacks on America's allies and partners in Europe and Asia, forcing the United States into a two-front war.

Putin is Russia's de facto dictator for life and has controlled Russia continuously as president or prime minister since 1999. He wields power using a small group of cronies, most of whom are personal friends and veterans of the Soviet military, security, and intelligence apparatus. Some have become owners or managers of state assets. Others control the security services or the judiciary. All have become fabulously rich. They only keep their wealth and, indeed, their lives, however, if they remain loyal to Putin.

The Russian people are impoverished by Putin's kleptocratic regime. The corrupt and arbitrary application of law has discouraged domestic and foreign investment. Many talented Russians have fled the country in a massive brain drain to escape the country's political and social pathologies.[280] As a result, Putin's Russia lags behind the advanced economies. In 2022, Russia's GDP per capita was $15,345. This compares to $43,261 or 182 percent higher, in Organisation for Economic Co-operation and Development (OECD) member countries.[281]

The Russian people also lack freedom. The political system in Putin's Russia is rigged, with sham elections and a playing field heavily slanted against opposition parties and politicians. Putin and his cronies control all the major media outlets. The police and the judiciary are supine tools of Putin's autocratic rule employed to stifle dissent. Those who dare challenge Putin's rule end up in jail, in exile, or dead.

Since Putin cannot give the Russian people prosperity or freedom, he is serving up generous portions of nationalism. Like many dictators, Putin is promoting an ideology of national victimhood and revisionism. In his false telling, Russia is under threat from NATO, and Moscow, therefore, needs to occupy and control neighboring countries to protect Russian national security and regain its past glory.

Putin seeks to reestablish the Russian empire through military force. He invaded Georgia in 2008, and Russian forces continue to occupy parts of that country. He invaded Ukraine in 2014 and again in 2022, launching the biggest war in Europe since the end of World War II. He stations Russian troops in a breakaway region of Moldova.[282] He has turned Belarus into a vassal state and used it as a launching pad for his war in Ukraine. He deployed "peacekeeping" troops in Azerbaijan in 2020 during its war with Armenia.[283] He used military force to quell domestic unrest and prop up a friendly dictator in Kazakhstan in 2022.[284]

This brief history illustrates two important points. First, Putin is sane. Some people question the rationality of his 2022 invasion of Ukraine.[285] After all, given Washington's recent history in Iraq and Afghanistan, large-scale military invasions seem like a bad idea. But, from Putin's perspective, past military interventions had always achieved their purpose. He assumed that the Ukraine invasion would be as successful.

Second, it shows that the war in Ukraine was not provoked by NATO expansion as some wrongly argue.[286] Rather, it is part of Putin's plan to occupy and dominate his neighbors by military force. In fact, Putin has used military force in almost every former Soviet republic that is not a member of NATO. In contrast, he has not used military force against any former Soviet republics that are NATO members, like Estonia, Latvia, and Lithuania. He would have invaded Ukraine at some point—and likely even earlier—without NATO expansion into Eastern Europe. If

Ukraine had joined NATO earlier, like Estonia, Putin would not have invaded. If anything, the problem is not too much NATO but not enough.

At the time of writing, Putin was struggling in the war in Ukraine, but he could still succeed in subduing the country. Ukraine's defense depends on heroic Ukrainian resistance and massive Western aid, but, if either of those falters, Russian military fortunes could drastically improve. If Putin succeeds in occupying Ukraine, why would he stop there? He could seek to subjugate Moldova and even smaller NATO members, like Estonia, Latvia, or Lithuania. Some see Russia's failure to easily defeat Ukraine as evidence that Russia is not a threat to NATO, but within days of Russia's 2022 invasion, Russian forces were able to take Ukrainian territory roughly the size of Estonia and Latvia.[287] This is not very reassuring to US allies in Tallinn and Riga.

While Putin understands that an attack on a NATO ally would be risky, it may still be tempting to him.[288] Putin may gamble that NATO does not have the stomach for a major war. If he could succeed in occupying a NATO ally without triggering a NATO reaction, he could break the alliance and open the way to expanding his new Russian empire and revising Europe's security architecture in his favor. This is the very result he demanded in his ultimatum on the eve of invading Ukraine in 2022.

The United States has an interest in preventing this outcome. Washington has always sought to prevent a hostile state from dominating important geopolitical regions. Europe remains America's largest trade and investment partner, so peace and stability in the region are important to the pocketbook of all Americans. Moreover, there are strong cultural and values-based ties between the United States and Europe.

In addition to the danger it represents to Europe, Russia also poses a direct military threat to the United States. Russia possesses the world's largest nuclear arsenal. If he so decided, Putin could end the United States as a functioning society before you finish reading this chapter.

Putin is also projecting Russia's malign influence around the world. He intervened militarily in the Syrian civil war in 2015, reestablishing Russia as a power broker in the Middle East for the first time since the 1970s. Russia interferes in the domestic politics of the United States and European countries, seeking to discredit democracy and weaken the

NATO alliance. It props up anti-American dictators in Cuba and Venezuela. It supports obsessively anti-American Iran. Russian mercenaries are providing military assistance to dictators throughout Africa, increasing Russian influence on the continent to the detriment of US interests.[289]

Fortunately, the power base to support Putin's expansive aims is limited. At less than 2 percent of global GDP, Russia's economy is smaller than Italy's. Italy is a lovely country, but it is not a superpower. Russia sits on some of the world's largest oil and gas reserves, and this has been a major source of its strength. It played pipeline politics, exerting influence over countries dependent on Russian energy supplies. As the saying goes, it is a gas station with nuclear weapons.[290] As much of Europe transitions away from Russian energy supplies following Russia's 2022 invasion of Ukraine, however, even this source of power and influence is waning.

In short, Russia is weak but dangerous. How should the United States handle this threat?

Misguided Approaches

Before turning to our preferred strategy, we will review several commonly proffered solutions and explain why they will not work.

Split Russia from China

During the First Cold War, President Nixon and Henry Kissinger partnered with Communist China against the Soviet Union. Some argue that we should do a reverse Kissinger today and partner with Russia against China. This will not work.[291]

Putin is currently waging the largest war in Europe since the end of World War II and committing crimes against humanity. He is not an ideal partner to say the least. Furthermore, Putin has no reason to help Washington confront the PRC. While Russia does not want to subordinate itself to the PRC, it does not want to be adversarial toward it either. Xi and Putin are in a deepening strategic partnership with "no limits." In addition, Putin will not want to bolster the United States, the country he sees as his foremost enemy.

Moreover, in exchange for giving China a cold shoulder, Putin would almost certainly demand unpalatable concessions, such as granting Russia a sphere of influence in Eastern Europe and limiting US nuclear weapons and missile defenses. That would be unacceptable.

Further, even if Putin did promise to work with the United States, it would be a mistake to believe him. Putin cannot be trusted to abide by arms control agreements or cease-fires in eastern Ukraine. Why would Washington stake its strategy for the most important national security challenge of the twenty-first century on Putin's word?

Finally, Russia does not bring much to the table. It is a declining power with a small economy and a shrinking population. Winning Russia over does not solve America's China problem.

Fortunately, the United States has other potential partners. Democracies excel at building effective alliances, and the United States enjoys a large formal alliance system with economic might three times larger than the combined GDP of Russia and the PRC.

Washington can work with its allies in the Free World to simultaneously counter Russia and China. The United States and its allies already enjoy the economic, military, and political power needed to prevail in this new era of great-power confrontation. Beijing and Moscow, not Washington, should worry about powerful and ideologically hostile adversaries aligning against them.

Asia First

Others argue that Washington needs to prioritize the bigger threat from China over that from Russia.[292] They maintain that the United States does not have the ability to take on two near-peer, nuclear-armed powers at the same time. They claim that Washington should, therefore, pivot away from Europe and let wealthy European allies, like Germany, step up to defend Europe from Russia.

This strategy has several shortcomings. First, the United States has an important interest in maintaining peace and stability in both Europe and Asia. A major strategic loss in either region would be devastating to the security and prosperity of all Americans. After all, the United States intervened in Europe twice in the twentieth century to end wars and shape the post-war balance of power. It would be much better for the United States to maintain a military presence in Europe and deter war rather than to withdraw, allow Russia to attack its neighbors, and fight its way back in later.

Second, if the United States withdraws, it is uncertain how Europe will step up and defend itself. "Europe" does not exist as a coherent entity in security and defense matters. The United States is the leader of the transatlantic alliance. Without US leadership, thirty smaller European countries will make thirty different decisions. There is no telling what they might do. Some European states might take steps to defend themselves, to be sure, but this might be in ways that are contrary to US interests, such as building independent nuclear weapons arsenals. The United States does not benefit from a runaway nuclear arms race in Europe. More worrisome, some European states may conclude that, with America gone, their best bet is to appease Putin. They could sell out the Free World in exchange for cheap Russian oil and gas. They could cut side deals with Moscow, which would allow Russia to greatly expand its influence throughout Europe at America's expense. Do we really trust Paris and Berlin to always look after America's best interests?

NATO allies do need to step up and do a lot more, as we argue below, but the United States is better off leading this process rather than retreating from Europe and letting our European allies figure it out for themselves in ways that are potentially contrary to US interests.

Third, the PRC threat is global. The United States needs to counter it everywhere, not just in the Indo-Pacific. If the United States builds a strong defense only in Asia, then the PRC can simply increase its malign influence in regions abandoned by the United States. The PRC is already enhancing its power in Europe, including through its economic and military partnership with Russia. A comprehensive strategy for countering the PRC requires countering the PRC-Russia alliance in Europe.

Fourth, and finally, the United States and its allies do have the ability to maintain peace and stability in both Europe and Asia simultaneously. As noted above, US and allied economic potential is more than three times that of China and Russia. The United States spends more than twice as much on defense annually than China and Russia combined. And so on. A look at objective numbers shows that resource constraints do not force the United States to make gut-wrenching trade-offs.

A variant of this difficult-trade-offs argument holds that the United States should not spend resources to defend Ukraine's border because it must focus on its own southern border with Mexico.[293] This variant of the argument also presents a false dilemma. To be sure, America's southern border is important, but there is no reason why the United States must choose. It is a global superpower with the ability to both enhance border security at home and protect its interests in Europe.

Biden's Approach

The final approach that has not worked is the Biden policy towards Russia and Europe. As we argued in Chapter Two, Biden has been too soft on Russia. His premature eschewal of force was an invitation to Putin to invade. He even suggested that a "minor incursion" into Ukraine will not trigger much of a reaction from Washington.[294] He has also telegraphed his fear of Russia's nuclear weapons for the world to see, only inviting further Russian nuclear saber rattling and attempts at blackmail. Biden has neither laid out a clear objective for his intervention in the war nor articulated a coherent strategy. His incremental approach to providing weapons to Ukraine has given the Ukrainians enough to keep fighting but not enough to win. He was against long-range artillery to Ukraine, and then he was for it. He was against tanks for Ukraine, and then he was for it. He was against aircraft for Ukraine, and then he was for it. This half-hearted approach has made the war longer, costlier, and deadlier than necessary.

Many congressional Republicans are skeptical of Biden's approach to Ukraine, not because they are isolationists, but because they do not want to give a "blank check" when they are not confident the president knows what he is doing.[295]

As countries around the world rightly sanction Russian oil, they are looking for other suppliers. But Biden's war on fossil fuels has reduced

US energy production and made it harder for other nations to reduce their dependence on Russian exports. A better approach is needed.

A Deterrence and Diplomacy Strategy for Russia

To address the threat from Putin's Russia, the United States should pursue a deterrence and diplomacy strategy. It should deter Russian aggression to prevent a major war and use diplomacy to strengthen the transatlantic alliance and seek an improved relationship with a post-Putin Russia.

Deterrence

The first step in deterring future Russian aggression is to help end Putin's war against Ukraine. Unlike the Biden administration, Republicans should define a clear goal for US involvement in the war in Ukraine. Washington should aim to bring the war to a rapid conclusion, and Ukraine should emerge from the war as a sovereign state capable of deterring and defeating future Russian aggression.

Instead of cowering in fear of Russian nuclear weapons, the United States should deter Russian nuclear escalation by making it clear that any Russian nuclear attack would lead to a decisive US response and catastrophic consequences for Russia.[296]

After victory, Ukraine will need to be rebuilt, and Washington should insist that this will be primarily the responsibility of our wealthy European allies.

Next, the United States should lead the design of an effective defense strategy and force posture to deter future Russian aggression against NATO. The United States should provide the advanced capabilities that it alone can contribute, like nuclear deterrence and intelligence, surveillance, and reconnaissance. It should also keep significant US Army units in Europe. They cost the same whether deployed overseas or kept at home, but their value as a deterrent for Russia and source of reassurance for allies is far greater in Europe than in Texas. Asia is the more important military theater, but it is an air and maritime theater, so there is no place to station large ground units there. They are better positioned in Europe.

Next, Washington should insist that its NATO allies step up and provide the nuts and bolts for a European conventional force posture: tanks, artillery, aircraft, personnel, air and missile defense, and the like. Instead of general hectoring, it should work with NATO to design country-specific regional plans. For example, it should say, "Germany, to defend Europe, we need you to deploy X tank divisions to Lithuania. France, we need you to deploy Y aircraft to Romania." And so on.

A European defense buildup is also a major opportunity for US defense exports. Washington should reform its antiquated arms transfer restrictions to make it easier to sell cutting-edge defense technology to friends. Many allies are already doing a lot. For example, Finland recently purchased sixty-four F-35 stealth fighter aircraft from the United States.[297] Many countries still have much to do, and Washington should set clear and high standards and hold them accountable.

Diplomacy

America's Russia strategy should also contain an important element of diplomacy. Washington should, as argued above, use diplomacy to strengthen the NATO alliance, develop a defense strategy and force posture for Europe, assign roles and responsibilities with a greater share of the burden borne by European allies, and to hold allies accountable for meeting their defense targets.

In addition, Europe should assist the United States in confronting the CCP. Much of the Free World's contest with China is in the realm of economics and technology. The European Union, which makes up roughly 25 percent of global GDP, is a superpower in these areas. Washington should work with European allies as they selectively decouple from China in the economic and technology domains. As they do so, and reshore and friendshore to allies, they can also enhance the trade and technology cooperation among the Free World. Europe should leverage its moral standing to call out the CCP's many and grave human rights violations and join Washington in levying sanctions on the perpetrators.

Washington and Brussels can negotiate standards for new technology, such as AI, that are consistent with the Free World's interests and values. This will force China to conform to these standards or be forced out of key global technology markets. The United States and Europe should plan the economic sanctions that would be levied against China should it invade Taiwan and publicize them ahead of time as a deterrent.

NATO should continue to issue statements supporting peace and stability in the Taiwan Strait. Moreover, Washington should encourage NATO allies to engage in symbolic shows of force in the Indo-Pacific region. Such shows of force will demonstrate to the PRC that an attack on Taiwan would create a rupture between Beijing and the entire Free World.

Washington should also engage in energy diplomacy. Instead of waging a war on energy, Washington should expand domestic energy production and offer its energy exports to the world. This will create jobs in the United States and help European allies to transition away from Russian oil and gas. Lithuania is a model in this regard. At the time of Russia's first invasion of Ukraine in 2014, Vilnius was heavily dependent on Russian energy. After the invasion, it quickly built an LNG terminal at its port in Klaipeda to import energy from the United States and the Middle East.[298] By the time of Russia's further invasion of Ukraine in 2022, Lithuania was energy independent from Moscow.

There is little role for direct engagement with Putin in this diplomatic strategy. FDR did not meet with Hitler during WWII. Putin is a war criminal and should be ostracized. But there is a role for direct negotiations between the United States and Russia at other levels of government to negotiate an end to the war in Ukraine and to discuss risk reduction measures to prevent unintended escalation and war.

The final and most important role for the diplomatic strategy is to prepare for a post-Putin Russia.[299] He and his highly personalized regime will not last forever. He could have a heart attack tonight. He could be removed from office by his generals or the Russian people, especially if he loses the Ukraine war. Autocratic regimes are most brittle at times of leadership transition. It is possible that a future Russian government could be worse than Putin's regime, but that is hard to imagine given that Putin has already launched most significant conflict in Europe in decades. The United States would desire a Russian leadership that is more cooperative or, at a minimum, less hostile. It should formulate a plan to engage with Russian opposition figures now and during a regime transition to support pro-Western forces and to set the stage for more cooperative future relations between Washington and Moscow.

CHAPTER EIGHT

Iran

In addition to the revisionist, autocratic great powers, China and Russia, the United States also faces threats from regional rogue powers, Iran and North Korea. This chapter will consider the Islamic Republic of Iran and the subsequent chapter will deal with North Korea. While not as capable as the great powers, Iran and North Korea pose serious challenges, and they should be addressed with a deterrence and diplomacy strategy.

The Iran Threat

For decades, the United States and Iran enjoyed constructive relations when Tehran was ruled by Shah Reza Pahlavi.[300] Iran was a secular and pro-Western country and cooperated with the United States in its First Cold War struggle with the Soviet Union. That changed, however, after the 1979 Iranian revolution. Ayatollah Ruhollah Khomeini returned to Tehran, and the shah was forced to flee. Khomeini designated himself the supreme leader of a new Islamic Republic of Iran, and he imposed a body of radical clerics to govern the country.

At home, they drastically changed almost all aspects of the daily life of Iranians by introducing strict rules derived from their interpretation of Islam. Abroad, the new Islamic Republic made similarly drastic changes. The Islamic Republic was founded on resistance to the United States and the West. During the revolution, activists captured and held hostage fifty-two American diplomats for 444 days at the end of the Carter administration. They were finally released the day Reagan assumed office.

Since the revolution, the Iranian regime has declared itself a sworn enemy of the United States. Iran's clerics lead congregants in chants of "Death to America." They call the United States "the great Satan" and refer to Israel, America's closest partner in the region, as "the little Satan."

As noted above, in 1983, Iranian-backed Hezbollah terrorists attacked the US Marine barracks in Lebanon killing 241 marines and sailors. In 1988, the US Navy fought its largest battle since World War II when Reagan sunk the Iranian navy in retaliation for Iran's mining of the Persian Gulf during the Iran-Iraq War.

Today, Tehran is a member of the New Axis of Evil and often acts in concert with China and Russia. Revisionist dictators are trying to create a parallel international order to rival the system built by the United States and the Free World. In making this choice, Iran's leaders are revealing their religious hypocrisy. They preach for Islamic fundamentalism, but the Muslim clerics are cozying up to an atheist China that kills and persecutes Muslim Uighurs and to avowedly Christian Orthodox rulers in the Kremlin who led a devastating war against Muslims in Chechnya.

With Chinese assistance, Tehran has provided weapons to Russia for use in its war against Ukraine.[301] In addition, China, Russia, and Iran have conducted joint military exercises, such as the Maritime Security Belt naval drills in the Indian Ocean and the Gulf of Oman in 2019, 2022, and 2023.[302] For years, Russia and China have opposed and watered down sanctions against Iran.[303] In the Syria civil war, the New Axis of Evil supported Bashar al-Assad, the Butcher of Damascus, diplomatically, financially, and with arms deliveries; Russia and Iran also sent troops.[304] There is collaboration between hackers from the three countries. Russia and Iran have expressed support for China's claims in the South China Sea.[305] Also, Tehran is in the final stages of joining the Shanghai Cooperation Organization, a political and security bloc founded and dominated by China and Russia.[306]

The most significant threat posed by Iran comes from its nuclear program. Iran is a near-nuclear power. Indeed, on current trajectories, it may be a nuclear-armed state by the end of the Biden administration. The most difficult part of building a nuclear weapon is producing the fuel, and Iran has an advanced ability to enrich uranium. At the time of this writing, Biden's Pentagon estimates that if Iran's supreme leader decides to sprint to a bomb, Iran could enrich enough weapons-grade uranium for its first bomb in only twelve days.[307]

Note, this is a conditional timeline. It is like saying that the authors could run a mile in eight minutes. We will not run a mile in the next eight minutes because we are writing this book. But we could do so any time we choose. Moreover, this timeline shrinks every day as Iran continues to ramp up its enrichment program. The world is running out of time to solve this problem.

The Biden administration and the intelligence community like to say that there is no evidence that Iran has made a "final decision" to build nuclear weapons, but this is beside the point.[308] Iran is doing everything necessary to shrink its nuclear weapons breakout timeline and build nuclear weapons quickly. By the time Iran makes a "final decision," the game will be over.

Iran claims that this is a peaceful program to produce nuclear energy, but this is untrue. There are many things Iran is doing that make no sense for a truly peaceful program. Most fundamentally, there is no reason for Iran to enrich uranium at all for a peaceful program. A peaceful program requires the operation of nuclear reactors. Nearly all countries with peaceful nuclear power programs, like Mexico and the United Arab Emirates, do not enrich their own uranium. Rather, they have fuel shipped in by a more advanced nuclear power, like France or Russia. The recipient uses the fuel to operate the reactors and then returns the spent fuel. The international community has offered fuel-cycle services to Iran for decades. If Iran really wanted a peaceful nuclear program, then this was the obvious solution. But Iran repeatedly rejected these offers.

In another telltale sign that this is not just a peaceful program, the United Nations nuclear watchdog, the International Atomic Energy Agency (IAEA), caught Iran doing critical nuclear weapons design work.[309] Why design nuclear weapons if Tehran has no interest in building nuclear weapons?

Iran possesses the most sophisticated ballistic missile program in the Middle East. Its missiles can reach US forces, bases, and allies in the region and all the way to Southern Europe. In the past, Iran was working on an intercontinental ballistic missile. The US government assesses that Iran has halted work on an ICBM, but it could always resume the program in the future.[310] Using a bit of foresight analysis, it is not hard to imagine Iran following the path of North Korea and eventually having a substantial nuclear arsenal capable of conducting a nuclear attack on the US homeland.

Iran is also the world's largest state sponsor of terror. It created the Hezbollah terror group to threaten Israel and conduct attacks globally. It also finances, trains, and arms the Hamas terrorist organization that was responsible for the barbaric attack that killed 1,200 Israeli civilians on October 7, 2023. To put this attack in perspective, this loss of life for Israel corresponds to the death of over 40,000 Americans. This land, air, and sea attack by Hamas must have taken a year to plan, and it is reasonable to assume that their paymaster in Tehran approved it. The strategic aim of this attack was to sabotage the developing normalization of relations between Israel, Saudi Arabia, and other Arab countries. Moreover, the shadowy Iranian Quds forces operate terror and proxy groups and conduct attacks throughout the world. Iran currently has credible death threats against several former Trump administration officials, including former secretary of state Mike Pompeo.[311] In 2011, Iran planned to bomb Café Milano, a popular restaurant in Washington, DC (and one of our favorites), but thankfully the plot was foiled.[312]

Through its terror and proxy networks, Iran has extended its malign influence throughout the Middle East. Iranian-backed Shia militias exert outsize influence in Iraq. Iran is arming and funding the Houthi rebels waging civil war against the government in Yemen. Hezbollah has been a major cause of the dysfunction and destabilization in Lebanon. Meanwhile, Iran's assistance has been critical to Assad's savage civil war against his people, and Tehran now holds great sway over Damascus. Indeed, Iran's influence in the Middle East is probably greater today than at any time since the ancient Persian empire more than two thousand years ago.

Finally, Iran routinely commits gross human rights abuses at home. As just one example, it hangs people on homosexuality charges.[313] Over the years, Iranian citizens have taken to the streets demanding greater freedoms. The regime cracks down. The protestors end up exiled, imprisoned, or dead. Then the cycle starts again.

In the most recent episode, in 2022, Iranian security goons beat to death a young woman for not wearing a proper head covering.[314] Many other young women went to the streets bareheaded in protest. The regime used violence to put down the uprising. It would be wonderful if Iran had a better government that respected the rights of its people and that was more cooperative internationally. The sad reality, however, has been that the Iranian regime is willing to kill to stay in power, and the Iranian people have not been willing to die in large enough numbers to take power.

The Failed Obama-Biden Approach

To address this challenge, there are several approaches that will not work. The Obama and Biden administrations attempted to solve this problem with toothless diplomacy, but their efforts failed. The starting point for today's flawed policy toward Iran was Obama's 2015 nuclear deal, the Joint Comprehensive Plan of Action (JCPOA).

The fundamental flaw with the deal is that it granted Iran the right to enrich uranium. As pointed out above, there is a big difference between operating reactors for a peaceful nuclear program and making nuclear fuel. Nuclear fuel-making is dual use in nature. Once a country can make fuel for a reactor, it can make fuel for weapons. For more than half a century, therefore, US policy has attempted to draw a bright line between sensitive and nonsensitive nuclear technologies.[315] Washington allows and even encourages countries to operate reactors, but it prohibits them from enriching uranium or reprocessing plutonium. This is a standard that applies equally to American enemies and friends. In the 1970s, South Korea and Taiwan started secret plutonium reprocessing programs, and Washington discovered them and forced the two countries to shut them down.

When it was revealed that Iran was enriching uranium in 2002, Washington's response was immediate and unsurprising. The George W. Bush administration said that Tehran must halt its uranium enrichment program. Washington won six UN Security Council resolutions demanding that Iran cease enriching uranium.[316] As a presidential candidate, Obama wrote in *Foreign Affairs* that he would stop Iran's enrichment program.[317]

Then it became too hard. The Obama administration badly wanted a deal, but Iran would not stop its enrichment program. So, Obama moved the goalposts and undermined decades of US nonproliferation policy. He signed a deal that granted Iran the ability to enrich uranium with limits.[318] But—and this is a crucial point—those limits expired over time. Fifteen years after the deal went into effect, in 2030, Iran could enrich as much weapons-grade uranium as it wanted, consistent with the terms of the deal. Obama himself acknowledged that once these "sunset clauses" kicked in, the time it would take Iran to break out and build nuclear weapons "shrinks almost down to zero."[319]

The Iran nuclear deal did not, therefore, solve the problem. It merely kicked the can down the road in a way that would make it harder for the United States to solve the problem in the future.

Moreover, the deal did not cover Iran's other destabilizing activities. It did not restrict Iran's ballistic missile production or support for terrorism. In fact, the deal lifted a longstanding UN arms embargo on Iran, making it easier for Iran to advance its deadly weapons programs.

There was bipartisan opposition to the Iran deal in the US Congress. Every Republican and some Democrats were against the deal. Several Republican candidates in the 2016 presidential race promised to tear up the deal on day one. Trump was a relative moderate who proposed to renegotiate the deal. When renegotiation proved impossible, Trump pulled out of the deal and imposed a "maximum pressure" campaign on Iran. This was the right approach, and we will recommend a variation of this strategy below.

Democrats wrongly criticized Trump for pulling out of the deal, and Biden campaigned in 2020 on returning to the Iran nuclear deal. By this point, however, Biden had essentially accepted Republicans' criticisms of the original deal. In an implicit condemnation of Obama's agreement, the Biden administration said that they would like to get a deal with longer-lasting restrictions on uranium enrichment and that also covered Iran's sponsorship of terror and ballistic missile programs. Biden's strategy was to quickly reenter the 2015 deal and then negotiate a "longer and stronger" deal.[320]

Tehran had different ideas. It smelled weakness. The supreme leader knew that Biden, like Obama, badly wanted a deal, so he pushed for terms that would have watered down the 2015 deal. Fortunately, Biden did not go for it, and they were unable to reach agreement.

Meanwhile, Iran continued to ramp up its nuclear program. Many analysts wrongly blame Iran's recent nuclear buildup on Trump's withdrawal from the deal, but the evidence tells a different story. The greatest increases in Iran's uranium enrichment program, such as enriching to high levels of purity, occurred under Biden's watch.[321] Tehran was afraid to test Trump, but they knew that Biden had no plan B, and there would be no consequences for a rapid nuclear expansion.

The twenty-year international effort to keep Tehran from the bomb may have already failed. Iran may be a nuclear-armed state before the end of the Biden administration. If so, we should remember that it happened on Biden's watch.

Either way, the next Republican president will need a better strategy. What should it be?

A Deterrence and Diplomacy Strategy for Iran

The United States should pursue a dual-track, deterrence and diplomacy strategy to solve the Iranian challenge. So long as Iran continues with its threatening behavior, Washington should lead an international coalition to increase the economic, political, and military pressure on Tehran. But, the United States should hold out the option of diplomacy, if Tehran is willing to come to the table to discuss the cessation of its destabilizing and hostile activities.

This is similar to the "maximum pressure" strategy pursued by Donald Trump. It also mirrors the dual-track strategies pursued by Bush and in Obama's first term. This strategy would have likely succeeded had the United States remained steadfast in its prosecution. Instead, Obama's weak deal and Biden's desire to return to it were the aberrations that undercut a successful bipartisan US approach.

The first step of any good strategy is to clearly articulate the goal. The US goal should be for Iran to: (1) completely dismantle its uranium enrichment program and forever forswear the building of nuclear weapons, (2) halt its production of long-range missiles, (3) cease its support to terrorist and violent proxy groups, and (4) improve its human rights record. All of these are important, but goal number one is a vital US national interest. Iran must be prevented from becoming a nuclear weapons power.

Some will argue that achieving these goals will be impossible and that Washington should settle for less. But the United States should not negotiate with itself. It should make these demands and if Iran disagrees, then they can work out their differences at the negotiating table. Moreover, as Secretary Pompeo argued, the United States did not create the above list. Iran created the list through its bad behavior.[322] Washington does not make the above demands of Canada, because Ottawa does not behave in this destabilizing manner. If Tehran wants to get out from under US pressure, then it simply needs to behave like a normal country. As Henry Kissinger said years ago, Tehran needs to decide if it wants to be "a nation or a cause."

To achieve these goals, Washington should return to the pressure track.[323] Most importantly, it should resume economic warfare against Iran. It should impose economic and financial sanctions with the goal of driving Iranian oil and gas exports to zero. These should include so-called "secondary sanctions." In other words, Washington should not just sanction Iran but any country or firm in the world that does business with Iran. The United States should make clear that if any other countries or firms in Europe, Asia, or elsewhere purchase Iranian oil and gas, then they will be in the crosshairs of the US Treasury Department. This will give the rest of the world a choice. They can buy cheap Iranian oil and gas. Or they can have access to the US dollar, the US banking system, and the US market. But they cannot have both. For the vast majority of economic players, this is no choice at all. They will be forced to sever economic ties with the rogues in Tehran in order to maintain their economic relationship with the United States. By pursuing a version of this strategy, the United States was able to drive Iran into a deep recession in the early days of the Obama administration and under Trump. But later Obama, and then Biden, let up the pressure. At the time of writing, Iran was exporting as much oil as before Trump withdrew from the JCPOA in 2018.[324]

Next, the deterrence campaign should increase the political pressure on Iran. So long as Iran is unwilling to talk seriously about dismantling its uranium enrichment program, it should be isolated diplomatically. US diplomats are too busy to waste their time in empty discussions with rogue regimes. Instead, US diplomats should spotlight Iran's role as the world's largest state sponsor of terrorism, complicity in Hamas' barbaric October 7 massacre, and daily human rights violations. Washington should take steps to support the Iranian people's aspirations for freedom, including by ensuring they have access to information and the internet despite the regime's efforts to oppress them.

Finally, and importantly, the deterrence element of the strategy will require a credible military option.[325] The United States should make clear that if Iran dashes to the bomb, Washington will use military force to stop it. The Iranian nuclear program is a big problem, but it is located in only four nuclear facilities: Isfahan, Fordow, Natanz, and Arak. The United States has the ability to destroy these facilities using airpower, as several past defense secretaries have attested. The Iranian nuclear program could be a pile of rubble by tomorrow morning. Some of these facilities are deeply buried and hardened, but the United States has a weapon, the thirty-thousand-pound Massive Ordnance Penetrator (MOP), tailor-made to destroy such facilities. If Iran thinks that it can continue to inch its way toward the bomb, then it will do so. If, on the other hand, it thinks progress on its nuclear program will lead to a military conflict with the United States, it will stop short. Iran does not want its nuclear facilities to be bombed by the Pentagon. Tehran will be boxed in. This will provide time and space for the sanctions and political pressure to work.

A credible military option is necessary for successful diplomacy. As Reagan's secretary of state George Shultz said: "Negotiations are a euphemism for capitulation if the shadow of power is not cast across the bargaining table."[326]

If, despite the resumption of a credible military option, Tehran dashes to a bomb anyway, then Washington should destroy Iran's nuclear program. It has the ability to do so, and such strikes would set Iran's program back for years if not forever. There are risks with such an action, such as Iranian military retaliation, but they pale in comparison to the risks of living with a nuclear-armed Iran forever, given Iran's profound hostility toward the United States. Moreover, as Trump showed through his airstrikes on Soleimani, Iran has few good options for military re-

MATTHEW KROENIG AND DAN NEGREA

taliation against the United States. Iran is afraid of a major war with the Pentagon and would opt for token retaliation.

The deterrence element of the strategy can succeed in two ways. The pressure may be so great that it collapses the Iranian regime, or it can set the table for diplomacy.

This brings us to the diplomacy leg of the strategy. Washington should use diplomacy even as it wages the pressure campaign to build the largest possible anti-Iran coalition. The pressure will be much more effective if European and Asian allies are supportive. Biden's failed strategy will make building a coalition easier. US allies can see that toothless diplomacy did not work, and we need a different approach. US diplomats should pressure the Iranian regime, engage with the Iranian people, and plan for a future regime transition to a better government in Tehran. Finally, diplomats should prepare for a return to nuclear negotiations if and when the mullahs are serious about a deal. The terms of the desired deal are simple. If Iran really wants a peaceful nuclear program, then it can have it, and the United States will help. The international community can provide Iran with nuclear reactors and fuel-cycle services. But Iran must forever forswear the sensitive nuclear activities of enriching uranium or reprocessing plutonium. It must completely shut down its sensitive nuclear facilities.

The Obama administration bragged that its nuclear deal with Iran was extremely detailed and ran dozens of pages.[327] They cited this as an indicator of thoroughness. In reality, it was a sign of its emptiness. It was so long because the Obama administration allowed Iran to keep such a large and sensitive nuclear program. It said that Iran can maintain several nuclear facilities, thousands of centrifuges, and stockpiles of enriched uranium. It then spelled out the details of the limits on these facilities, activities, and materials. The deal then detailed the complicated verification regime needed to monitor extensive Iranian nuclear activities.

A good deal in contrast requires only one side of a sheet of paper. It will state that, like other normal countries, Iran will never enrich uranium or reprocess plutonium. The Obama-Biden deal kicked the can down the road. The strategy articulated above will forever resolve the Iranian nuclear challenge.

CHAPTER NINE

North Korea

The United States and North Korea engaged in direct combat in the Korean War (1950–1953), and they have been bitterly at odds ever since. Recently, North Korea became only the third US adversary with the ability to hold the US homeland at risk with the threat of nuclear attack.[328] Along with the three dictatorships just reviewed, North Korea is also a member of the New Axis of Evil. This chapter will review the threats posed by Pyongyang and offer a dual-track, deterrence and diplomacy strategy for addressing them.

The North Korea Threat

North Korea is led by erratic dictator Kim Jong Un (KJU). His foremost goal is to maintain control of his personalistic, hereditary regime, and he has gone to great lengths to maintain power. Seeing his uncle as a potential threat to his rule, for example, he obliterated him at close range with an anti-aircraft gun.[329] He hired assassins to kill his brother with a chemical agent at an airport in Malaysia.[330] His people starve to death, but KJU and his cronies live a good life in Pyongyang. The top priority for North Korean diplomats overseas is to smuggle luxury goods back to the dictator.[331] On the weekends, he holds daytime whiskey parties in which he and his top government officials get drunk, consort with call girls, and make important government decisions.[332]

Some Western analysts hold that KJU is defense-minded, and his only goal is to remain in power, but this is incorrect. In addition to holding on to power through any means necessary, KJU also holds out the hope of reunifying the Korean Peninsula under his rule.[333] His grandfather Kim Il Sung started the Korean War in 1950 with this goal in mind. The elder Kim also dug tunnels under the Demilitarized Zone (DMZ) dividing North and South Korea, hoping to send an invasion force underground to pop up in South Korea and occupy the country. Fortunately, the South Koreans heard the digging and foiled the plot. (Tourists can visit the tunnels to this day).[334] Kim dreams of one day fulfilling his grandfather's vision and being the leader of a unified Korea. He believes that nuclear weapons will help him achieve both of the above goals.

North Korea is the only country to sign the Nuclear Non-Proliferation Treaty (NPT), cheat on the treaty, and succeed in building nuclear weapons.[335] North Korea conducted its first nuclear weapons test in 2006.[336] Its nuclear arsenal currently contains dozens of warheads and continues to grow. KJU is now also working on thermonuclear and tactical nuclear warheads.[337]

To deliver these warheads, North Korea possesses a large and diverse missile force. Its missiles can reach US forces, bases, and allies throughout the Indo-Pacific region. In addition, North Korea now possess ICBMs and can conduct a nuclear attack on the continental United States. KJU is also working on more sophisticated missiles, including solid-fuel, mobile, and submarine-launched variants.[338]

Why should Washington care about a nuclear-armed North Korea? Some argue that the United States successfully deterred the Soviet Union from using nuclear weapons during the First Cold War, and, therefore, it can deter the less powerful North Korea in the same way.[339] Let us hope they are right, but there are reasons to be concerned. First, proliferation might not stop with North Korea. North Korea may support other countries in building nuclear weapons. This is not idle speculation. Pyongyang has already helped Syria build a nuclear weapons program (fortunately, Israel destroyed it in a bombing raid).[340] It also helped several other countries, including Pakistan, build long-range missile programs.[341] Other nations, including US allies in the region, may decide

130

to build their own nuclear weapons to counter the Democratic People's Republic of Korea (DPRK).[342] This harms US nonproliferation goals and undermines the international nonproliferation regime.

Second, North Korea may become more aggressive. With nuclear weapons serving as a shield to deter outside attack, KJU may believe that he has free reign to provoke and attack South Korea. Indeed, since acquiring nuclear weapons, North Korea has already shelled a South Korean island and sunk a South Korean warship, killing forty-six Republic of Korea (ROK) sailors.[343]

Third, there is a risk of nuclear war. KJU does not have a death wish. But if he starts a high-stakes crisis or war with the United States, things could spin out of control. KJU might decide that by using nuclear weapons, he could save his regime from being overrun and force the United States to back down. In short, a North Korean nuclear weapon could result in nuclear war against the United States.

In the past, American analysts debated whether North Korea's nuclear program was a means to obtain a nuclear weapon or just a bargaining chip to be used in negotiations. Maybe Pyongyang just wanted to frighten the international community and then trade the program away for international aid, food, and fuel. That debate is now over. It is obvious to everyone that KJU desires nuclear weapons and sees them as essential to his foremost security objectives.

The North Korean threat goes beyond the nuclear and missile program. It is suspected that Pyongyang also possesses chemical and biological weapons.[344] It has a formidable conventional military with the second-largest standing army in the world.[345] North Korea also has large numbers of conventional artillery and missiles massed on the border that could do serious damage to Seoul and nearby US bases.[346]

Beyond the military threat, North Korea engages in other threatening and illegal activities. The economy is dysfunctional due to decades of communist rule and mismanagement, so Pyongyang earns hard currency through counterfeiting US dollars, cybercrimes, smuggling, and other illegal activities.[347]

In addition, North Korea has among the world's worst human rights records.[348] As noted above, KJU kills anyone who dares stand in his way. Prisoners are kept in work camps under slave-like conditions.[349]

A notable North Korean human rights abuse that hit home for many Americans was the case of Otto Warmbier. Otto was a student at the University of Virginia on a semester abroad in China. He hired a Chinese tourist agency to take him across the border into North Korea. When Otto removed a propaganda poster to bring home as a souvenir, North Korea arrested and jailed him for theft. The United States negotiated for his return, and he was eventually released. But he had been so badly tortured by the North Koreans that he died shortly after returning home.[350]

In short, North Korea presents a number of serious threats to American interests and values. How can the United States address this problem?

Past Approaches

There are a number of approaches that will not work. Indeed, over the past several decades there has been plenty of bipartisan policy failure to go around on North Korea. Several administrations, Democrat and Republican alike, have followed a similar pattern. They come into office thinking they will get tough on North Korea. They then pivot to diplomacy, believing they can solve the problem at the negotiating table. When that proves more difficult than they expected, they put the issue on the back burner. The cycle then repeats.

Bill Clinton

The North Korea nuclear challenge rose to the top of the US foreign policy agenda in the 1990s. North Korea had signed the NPT but had not yet negotiated a safeguards agreement with the International Atomic Energy Agency. At the time, the United States assessed that North Korea did not yet have nuclear weapons but that it possessed enough plutonium for one or two bombs.[351] Suspecting that North Korea was planning to build nuclear weapons, the Clinton administration prepared military options. In 1994, they had all but decided to strike North Korea's sole nuclear reactor at Yongbyon, but at the last moment, former president Jimmy Carter, acting as a private citizen, flew to Pyongyang to meet with then dictator Kim Jong Il.[352] Carter believed that a diplomatic solution was possible, and the Clinton administration pivoted to the engagement track.[353]

In 1994, the United States and North Korea signed the Agreed Framework. According to the terms of the deal, North Korea promised not to build nuclear weapons in exchange for food and fuel aid and help with peaceful nuclear technology.[354] The deal was controversial in Washington. The Clinton administration hailed the agreement as a historic breakthrough. Republicans in Congress bashed the deal. They said the terms were weak and that it was foolish to trust the North Koreans.[355] We now know that North Korea was cheating on the deal from day one, importing technology from Pakistan for a secret uranium enrichment program.[356]

George W. Bush

The Bush administration came into office planning to confront North Korea. After 9/11, President Bush declared North Korea to be part of an "Axis of Evil."[357] When the Bush administration presented North Korea with allegations of cheating on the 1994 Agreed Framework, Pyongyang confessed.[358]

The Bush administration was split on what to do next. It was not a priority issue because the United States had just launched the wars in Afghanistan and Iraq.

An eventual return to diplomacy led to a new negotiated settlement in 2005. The new deal traded pledges not to build nuclear weapons in exchange for international aid. The 2005 deal was much more comprehensive than the Agreed Framework, including provisions, for example, to end the Korean War and normalize relations between North Korea and the international community.[359]

This deal also fell apart, however, soon after it was struck. In 2006, North Korea conducted its first nuclear weapons test, announcing its formal entry into the nuclear club.

The Bush administration continued to try diplomacy and reached a 2007 framework that included step-by-step measures for implementing the 2005 deal, but North Korea's nuclear and missile program continued to advance.[360]

Barack Obama

Barack Obama took power believing that North Korea had been playing the United States for a sucker. There was a pattern. Pyongyang would ostentatiously advance its nuclear program and then demand concessions. The West would provide aid, things would be quiet for a while, and then North Korea would repeat the cycle. Obama did not want to play that game, and administration aides pursued a policy of "strategic patience." The United States was no longer going to reward North Korea's bad behavior. Instead, Washington would ignore North Korea's provocations and advancing nuclear and missile program.[361] By this time, it was assessed that North Korea had enough material for five to eight nuclear weapons.[362] One Obama staffer even joked that additional North Korea nuclear tests were a good thing, because Pyongyang was exhausting its limited stockpile of plutonium.

Strategic patience did not work either. Instead, North Korea's nuclear and missile program continued to advance. After several years, the Obama administration realized it needed a different approach. It restarted diplomacy, and on February 29, 2012, they achieved the "Leap Day Deal." The terms were similar to past agreements, and, like past agreements, this one quickly unraveled as well.[363] Several weeks after the deal was struck, North Korea conducted a satellite test. Satellite tests and ICBM launches rely on the exact same technology (which is why the United States was so worried about the Soviet Union's Sputnik satellite launch in the early days of the First Cold War). Washington declared the missile/satellite test a violation, and the deal unraveled.[364]

For the remainder of the administration, North Korea was not a priority. Instead, the Obama administration focused on the Iran nuclear deal. They believed that they were too late with North Korea. North Korea already had several bombs, the thinking went, and it would be difficult to put the genie back in the bottle, but there was still time to stop Tehran.

Donald J. Trump

When the Trump administration took office, the outgoing Obama administration warned that North Korea would be the most urgent challenge they needed to face.[365] By this time, North Korea was thought to have dozens of nuclear weapons and was on the verge of mastering an ICBM, which, as discussed previously, would give it the ability to threaten nuclear war against the US homeland.[366]

The Trump administration correctly made North Korea a high priority issue and put in place a "maximum pressure" campaign.[367] Trump threatened to increase the economic, political, and military pressure on North Korea to force it to negotiate. The administration put in place the toughest-ever sanctions against North Korea.[368] It introduced secondary sanctions for the first time, which resulted in sanctions against several Chinese banks facilitating trade with North Korea.[369] They also increased the military pressure, with the administration publicly floating "bloody nose" strikes against the north and Trump issuing threats to unleash "fire and fury the likes of which the world has never seen."[370] The military and economic pressure tracks were mutually reinforcing. Fearing possible conflict on the Korean Peninsula, other major powers, including Russia and China, were persuaded to go along with tougher multilateral sanctions against the DPRK.[371]

KJU buckled under the intense pressure and agreed to negotiations. Trump's maximum pressure campaign, therefore, succeeded in this important first step. Moreover, in a break from past practice, Trump agreed to meet personally with KJU in summits in Singapore and Hanoi.[372] Many pundits criticized Trump for this unorthodox approach.[373] In the past, mid-level diplomats were sent to work on nuclear negotiations with their North Korean counterparts. But Trump had promised to meet with KJU during the election campaign (he said he would sit down and hash out a deal over a hamburger), so he was following through on a campaign promise.[374] Moreover, past practices clearly were not working, so it was worth trying a new, bolder approach.

The 2018 summit in Singapore appeared to produce a breakthrough agreement in which North Korea promised to completely disarm. But the follow-up summit in 2019 in Hanoi was a disappointment. It was clear that KJU did not really mean to disarm, and Trump was right to walk out of the negotiations.[375]

The North Korea problem was once again placed on the back burner.

Joseph Biden

On the back burner is where the North Korea issue has stayed for the past several years. If Biden has a North Korea strategy, he has kept it to himself. Instead, Biden has focused on other issues, while North Korea's nuclear and missile program continues to advance largely unimpeded.

What is a better approach?

A Deterrence and Diplomacy Strategy for North Korea

To address the North Korea challenge, the United States should pursue a deterrence and diplomacy strategy. The goal of the strategy should be the complete, verifiable, and irreversible disarmament of North Korea and, ultimately, the reunification of the Korean Peninsula under the democratic government in Seoul. The strategy should pick up Trump's partially successful "maximum pressure" campaign.

Some argue that this goal is unrealistic and that Washington should learn to live with a nuclear North Korea, just as it managed to live with a nuclear-armed Soviet Union. But, it would be unacceptable to leave the security of the American people to the whims of the erratic dictator in Pyongyang. Moreover, several consecutive presidents, going back to Clinton, have maintained that a nuclear North Korea is unacceptable.[376] Washington would undermine its credibility by accepting the unacceptable.

In addition, as mentioned previously, North Korea is the first country to sign the NPT, cheat on the agreement, and continue to build nuclear weapons.[377] If Washington recognizes North Korea as a legitimate nuclear state, other countries would be tempted to follow North Korea's path, launching an illegal nuclear weapons program in the hope that one day they, too, would be welcomed into the club. This would also weaken the broader nuclear nonproliferation regime. For all of these reasons, disarmament should remain the goal.

Like under President Trump, the United States and its allies should once again increase the economic, diplomatic, and military pressure on North Korea. The US Treasury should dial up sanctions on the Kim regime. Some argue that North Korea is already the most sanctioned country in the world, and there is no room to increase sanctions.[378] This is incorrect. The United States can and should increase secondary sanctions on the Chinese firms and banks benefiting from cross-border trade with the DPRK. In the past, the United States was reluctant to sanction Chinese entities for fear of undermining the bilateral relationship, but now that Washington is ready to confront China, additional economic penalties on China through secondary sanctions is a feature, not a bug, for this approach.

In addition, the United States can further increase the economic pressure on North Korea by working with South Korea to interdict illegal shipping. Russia and other countries violate DPRK sanctions by conducting illegal ship-to-ship transfers of coal and other resources.[379] The US and ROK navies have exercised interdicting ships conducting illegal trade, and they should put into practice what they have learned.[380] Furthermore, the United States can work with its allies and partners to roll up North Korea's illegal smuggling and counterfeiting operations globally.

Unlike with past pressure campaigns, the United States cannot let up at the first sign that Pyongyang is willing to engage. Instead, Washington and its allies should be persistent in tightening the economic noose until its goals have been achieved.

Such a sustained economic pressure campaign could conceivably lead to the collapse of the Kim regime. Alternatively, fearing regime collapse, KJU may eventually be willing to come to the table to negotiate nuclear disarmament in earnest. Currently, KJU appears to believe that possessing nuclear arms is the key to his regime survival. A deterrence and diplomacy strategy would aim to persuade him that, on the contrary, clinging to nuclear weapons will place his regime at risk and that he is safer without nuclear weapons than with them.

Trump showed that a maximum pressure campaign can bring KJU to the table. When he returns, the diplomatic portion of the US strategy is simple. We should have a copy of past comprehensive deals, such as the 2005 deal, ready. Those are the terms. If KJU is willing to sign on, this issue can be resolved immediately. Half measures, such as dismantling some, but not all, of his WMD infrastructure, are unacceptable. US sanctions should not be partially lifted as a sign of goodwill. Rather, the pressure should remain and grow until KJU disarms.

Meanwhile, while the goal of the strategy is disarmament, the United States needs to deter, and if necessary, defend against the North Korean threat that exists here and now. The United States should strengthen homeland and regional missile defenses to stay ahead of the North Korean threat. It should continue to modernize its nuclear arsenal and make it abundantly clear that if KJU ever uses a nuclear weapon, it will be the last thing that he ever does.

Current US policy maintains that a North Korean attack will result in the end of the Kim regime.[381] The United States and its ROK ally should ensure that they have the military power necessary to follow through on that threat.

If North Korea prepares to use nuclear weapons, the US president would want options to stop the attack before it can kill millions. The Pentagon should improve "left of launch" cyber options to defuse a North Korean nuclear launch. It should also bolster its intelligence, surveillance, and reconnaissance (ISR) and strike capabilities to identify and destroy North Korean missiles on the launchpad before they can be used.

As noted above, North Korea is a member of the New Axis of Evil. Pyongyang and Beijing are formal treaty allies. Given their relationship and geographical proximity, it is likely that any war with China over Taiwan will spread to engulf the Korean Peninsula. Vice versa, a North Korean conflict could spread to become a direct US-China war. The Pentagon and allied defense ministries, therefore, should plan for simultaneous conflicts with China and North Korea.

WE WIN, THEY LOSE

The purpose of this planning, of course, is not to fight a war but to achieve US objectives short of armed conflict. As we explained in Chapter Three, the mantra is peace through strength.

North Korea is a challenging problem. There are no good options. The strategy laid out above, however, is the least bad option. By remaining steadfast in the pursuit of the deterrence and diplomacy strategy, Washington and its allies can, at a minimum, deter and contain the North Korea threat. At best, they may be able to achieve their long-sought objective of disarming and reunifying the Korean peninsula.

PART IV

TRANSNATIONAL ISSUES

CHAPTER TEN

Allies and Institutions

The past several chapters considered the greatest threats to US national security. But foreign policy is not only about the negative agenda—responding to threats. It is also about the positive agenda: What is the United States trying to build in the world to advance American interests? After World War II, the United States and its mostly democratic allies and partners built a dense set of international institutions and arrangements that some refer to as the "rules-based international system."[382]

The Soviet Union had very few willing allies during the First Cold War and mostly relied on occupied, captive nations. In contrast, the United States had many allies and partners, most of them democratic, that established and convened in various institutions to defend and promote their common interest in preserving their sovereignty and way of life. The triumph of America and the Free World in the First Cold War was, to a significant extent, due to the strength of this Free World system.

According to the dominant narrative in the mainstream media, Donald Trump and Republicans are increasingly isolationist and skeptical of these preexisting arrangements, whereas Joseph Biden and Democrats want to repair relationships with allies and strengthen the rules-based system.[383]

In fact, American conservatives are pragmatic when it comes to allies and institutions. America built this system, and it has worked for it for a long time.[384] At the same time, and contrary to the views of many

143

progressives, multilateral arrangements are not deities to be worshiped but tools of statecraft. Sometimes they are right for the job, in which case they should be utilized. Other times, they are not appropriate for the task at hand, and they need to be discarded or updated for a new era. In the New Cold War, America needs to strengthen traditional ties to allies and partners (NATO, Japan, South Korea, Australia, and so forth), attract new ones (Vietnam, for example), recommit to previous international institutions that work, create new ones, and tear up or adapt those that have outlived their usefulness.

This chapter will articulate an American conservative approach to allies and institutions.

The Origins of the Rules-Based International System

After the end of World War II, the United States and its allies assembled to build a new world order.[385] The security and economic arrangements that had existed previously had not been sufficient to prevent two major wars in the first half of the twentieth century. Clearly a better system was needed. New institutions and arrangements were created including: the United Nations, the North Atlantic Treaty Organization, the World Trade Organization, the World Bank, the International Monetary Fund, the Nuclear Non-Proliferation Treaty, and many others. These bodies were meant to facilitate international cooperation and stabilize the global security and economic system. After the end of the First Cold War, this system was deepened and expanded to, for example, bring in captive nations that had been locked by Communist Russia behind the Iron Curtain in Eastern Europe.

For the most part, this system advanced the interests of the American people and the Free World. For example, NATO was key to deterring the USSR's military threat against Europe and the United States. The United Nations and the Organization of American States were helpful during the Cuban Missile Crisis. The WTO unlocked untold business opportunities for the American people around the world. As we noted in Chapter Five, the world and the American people are safer and richer today than prior to World War II.

What should we call this system? There is no name that perfectly captures it. In reality, it is the US-led order, but calling it that risks turning off close US allies that also helped build, and that benefit from, the system. Some call it a "liberal" international order because it is premised on classical liberal principles of state sovereignty and free markets, but since "liberal" also means left-wing in the United States, this label risks wrongly alienating conservatives. Rules-based system may be the least bad option.

Some do not like this term because they argue that the rules are not always followed, not even by the United States. Others do not like it because it implies that there are rules made outside the United States that might be enforced by unelected bureaucrats against the interests of the American people.[386] There is truth in both these objections.

Still, despite these objections, what is most notable about the post-World War II order is the dense set of international institutions, alliances, and agreements (in short, "rules") that have no historical precedent. It makes sense that the United States and its Free World allies wanted to order the world in this way. As rule-of-law countries domestically, they feel comfortable with an international system that is also governed by something resembling the rule of law. There is, of course, an important caveat. The United States should demand that these international organizations, staffed by unelected bureaucrats, respect state sovereignty and do not usurp the will of free people in member countries.

Still, the presence of a rules-based system benefits the United States in many ways. A set of rules creates predictability. It also presents a standard for acceptable behavior, which makes it easier for the United States and the Free World to hold adversaries accountable when they break international laws and norms. The United States and its allies wrote the rules and, for most part, benefit from them. On the other hand, America's adversaries would prefer a system in which dictators can make arbitrary decisions within their spheres of influence. Or, as Putin framed it, "new rules, or no rules."[387]

America wants to safeguard the freedom, security, and prosperity of the American people without infringing on the sovereign rights of other nations. Other countries of the Free World have similar aspirations, and international institutions can be helpful in achieving this common goal. To be sure, it is mostly American power that helps Washington secure its interests abroad, but international institutions can soften global perceptions of American power and make it more palatable to the rest of the world. From a realist's perspective, institutions are the velvet glove concealing America's iron fist.

Let us take a concrete example. In the absence of the NPT, how would the United States handle the Iranian nuclear challenge? It would need to make a naked appeal to interests. It would need to argue that a nuclear-armed Iran presents a threat to the world, and therefore, other countries should unite to stop it. This is a compelling point, and Washington makes it, but it is often not enough on its own. With the NPT in place, Washington can go even further. It can also make an appeal to right and wrong and legality and illegality. The NPT enabled Washington to argue that Iran was not living up to its commitments in the NPT. It had violated its safeguards agreement. The IAEA found evidence of Iranian noncompliance and so on. For many countries, including US allies, this is a persuasive set of arguments.

Moreover, the existence of international bodies also provides a precooked set of responses. In the absence of the NPT, the United States would have had to invent ad hoc measures to prevent Iran from building nuclear weapons and for every other international problem that arises. With the NPT, the United States was able to refer Iran's case to the IAEA Board of Governors, which then referred the case to the UNSC, which then levied several rounds of multilateral sanctions against Iran. Absent the NPT, it is extremely unlikely the United States would have been able to convince Russia, China, and the rest of the world to condemn Iran and sanction it. But with the NPT in place, that is exactly what happened.

There are also, of course, downsides to a rules-based system. Democratic administrations sometimes strike multilateral agreements that do not enjoy Republican support and that are not in America's interest, like the Paris climate agreement or the JCPOA. Other countries can develop proposals for new institutions, like an International Criminal Court, that unduly constrain American power. Global conditions can change so that deals that make sense in one time period, like the INF Treaty, outlive their usefulness. The existence of institutionalized mechanisms can lead some to believe that holding a bunch of meetings is evidence of progress when, in fact, the underlying problem is not being addressed. Moreover, in recent years, China and other adversaries have become adroit in capturing these international bodies and turning them into tools of their authoritarian purposes.

The best approach, therefore, is to address international institutions in a pragmatic and case-by-case manner. The United States should seek to build and work within institutions that advance American interests. When it encounters institutions that do not advance American interests, or, even worse, actively harm them, then Washington should work around the institutions, reform them, or withdraw. And when appropriate, it should create new international institutions that are helpful in the New Cold War.

Reagan and Trump's Approach to Allies and Institutions

Reagan and Trump both pursued just such a pragmatic approach to the rules-based system, signing agreements that advanced American interests while exiting those that did not.

Among Reagan's greatest accomplishments was signing the Intermediate-Range Nuclear Forces (INF) Treaty. During the First Cold War, the Soviet Union deployed intermediate-range nuclear-armed missiles aimed at American allies and bases in Europe. In response, Reagan pursued a dual-track strategy of deterrence and diplomacy. He warned the Soviet Union to remove the missiles and threatened that, if it did not, the United States would deploy its own INF missiles in Europe pointed at Moscow. When Moscow refused, Reagan, in partnership with European allies, went ahead and began deploying Pershing missiles in Europe that could hit Moscow within minutes after being launched. The Soviet Union buckled under the pressure and agreed to the INF Treaty, which eliminated all intermediate-range missiles in Europe. The deal brought the United States and its European allies more than thirty years of relief from that category of missile threat.

Critics argue that Trump disdained multilateral institutions and delighted in tearing up existing agreements. This is false. Trump entered into several new agreements, and he exited from agreements only when he had good reason. The list of new agreements signed by Trump is long and includes: the US-Mexico-Canada free trade agreement, the Korea-US free trade agreement, a trade deal with China, and the initial denuclearization agreement with North Korea. Trump also created new coalitions. He revitalized the Quad that brings together the United States, Japan, Australia, and India to counter China. Perhaps most notably, Trump's diplomats conceived and mediated the Abraham Accords between Israel and several of its Arab neighbors, one of the greatest successes of US diplomacy in recent decades.

In fact, the criticism that Trump was hostile to international agreements was always hard to understand. The man who wrote *The Art of the Deal* clearly loved striking new deals![388]

Trump sharply criticized NATO countries for not living up to their promises to contribute 2 percent of their GDP to their own and common defense. He was right to do so. While he was in office and especially after Putin's second invasion of Ukraine, many NATO countries increased their defense spending to this level. He even agreed to an expansion of the alliance; during Trump's presidency, two new countries, Montenegro and North Macedonia, joined NATO.

It is true that Trump pulled out of several arrangements but for good reason. The JCPOA enshrined Iran's right to enrich uranium and provided it with a path to the bomb. The Paris climate agreement was ineffective, unenforceable, and inequitable. Russia was cheating on the INF and Open Skies treaties, deploying new INF missiles in violation of the treaty and using Open Skies flights to spy on US critical infrastructure to better plan attacks on the United States. These agreements did not advance America's interests, and Trump was correct to pull out of them.

The proper approach to the "rules-based system," therefore, is to consider possible agreements with pragmatism on a case-by-case basis. What does this mean for future Republican presidents?

A Strategy for Allies and Institutions for Today and Tomorrow

It can be useful to think of the "rules-based system" as divided into two major parts. First is the UN system that includes every country in the world and that gives the victors of WWII, including Russia and China, a prominent role. Second are the set of institutions that the United States established among like-minded countries in the Free World as part of its strategy of countering the Soviet Union during the First Cold War. This includes NATO, bilateral alliances in Asia, and multilateral financial institutions, among others.

There are serious problems with the UN system. Russia and China have too much power in UN institutions, including veto power in the Security Council. They are turning these institutions against their intended purpose. Russia chaired a meeting of the United Nations Security Council, for example, at the very same moment it was launching the biggest war in Europe since WWII. China prevents the WHO from conducting an effective investigation into COVID-19. The UN Human Rights Council is at times made up of a literal rogues' gallery of nations. And the list goes on.

The strategy for the UN system should be for the United States and its allies to engage in competitive multilateralism. Washington should not cede power and influence in these bodies to Russia and China but ask its diplomats to compete with them. US and allied diplomats should publicly highlight PRC and Russian bad behavior in these fora. This will make clear that these institutions' founding purpose has been perverted by autocrats that want to disrupt and displace the system. The United States should place skilled US and allied diplomats in leadership positions to wrest control of these bodies from the New Axis of Evil and once again use them to advance, as well as possible, the interests of the Free World.

The Free World institutions are functioning better, but they need to be revitalized and adapted for a new era. It is not 1945 or 1991 anymore, and Washington is not stuck with past agreements. It can breathe new life into old alliances and forge new ones. As was pointed out many times before, Washington needs to continue to insist that allies in Europe and Asia do much more to contribute to their defense and that of the Free World. NATO, the Quad, bilateral alliances in Asia, and partnerships in the Middle East should all be strengthened in this way.

During the First Cold War, America's alliances were divided by region, but we now live in a globalized world. The United States and its allies and partners in Europe and Asia are facing many of the same challenges. Moreover, they are increasingly working together on shared solutions, such as sanctions against Russia, export controls against China, and frameworks to facilitate common responses by democracies against economic aggression by China. Rather than work out these arrangements in a piecemeal manner in different fora, it should forge new bodies, led by the United States, that can bring together the Free World to counter the New Axis of Evil.

This is already starting to happen. During the Trump years, G7 meetings began regularly including South Korea, Australia, and India, bringing together the world's ten most powerful democracies. US allies in Asia have attended recent NATO summits, and NATO is considering the opening of its first office in Asia in Tokyo. The AUKUS arrangement between the United States, the UK, and Australia was a good Biden administration idea marred by bad diplomacy. It should be continued and expanded.

To deal with China's technology threat, some have proposed a new, global Democratic Technology Alliance.[389] This framework deserves further consideration. As the Free World secures supply chains by removing manufacturing from China, it can reshore and allyshore supply chains in friendly countries. This process could be formalized in a new Free World trade framework. This can also be a tool to win over states in the Global South, as these hedging states stand to benefit economically from the displaced trade from China, but only if they more closely align with the Free World.

Most broadly, the United States could think about forming a single, global body that could bring like-minded allies and partners together globally. Trump's secretary of state, Mike Pompeo, mused about creating an "alliance of democracies."[390] Washington would, however, want to be sure to include friendly autocracies, so perhaps a Free World Alliance would be the better approach.

Finally, the next Republican president will need to pull out of bad agreements. At the top of the list is the New START arms control treaty with Russia. Moscow has announced that it is suspending compliance with the treaty, yet the Biden administration foolishly follows the terms of the treaty, constraining American nuclear weapons, even as Russia and China engage in massive buildups. By the time the next GOP president assumes office, there may be other bad deals that will need to be torn up.

The world is at an inflection point. The post-Cold War world is over, and we are entering a new era, a New Cold War. This is the world's fourth opportunity in a century to build global order.[391] After the end of WWI, Woodrow Wilson and liberals failed miserably. The League of Nations led directly to World War II. After World War II, the United States and its allies got it mostly right. The post-WWII system allowed the United States to wage the First Cold War and emerge triumphant. The post-Cold War system had mixed success. It was able to expand the zone of peace, prosperity, and freedom in Europe by expanding NATO and the EU. But the United States got bogged down in nation-building campaigns in the Middle East and failed to anticipate the threats from China and Russia. It is early days in this New Cold War, and the United States and its Free World allies have another opportunity to create a global order to serve the interests of their peoples. This time, they need to get it right.

CHAPTER ELEVEN

Energy and Climate

All people want economic well-being and a clean environment for themselves and their loved ones. But some progressives have elevated climate change to the status of a secular religion. President Biden argues that climate change is an existential threat and a top national security concern. His administration advocates extreme measures that undermine American interests in the name of combatting climate change. This is unwise because the science of climate change is unsettled and because, even according to economists in Biden's White House, the effects of climate change on US interests are modest. Moreover, China is the biggest greenhouse gas emitter, but, under the Biden administration, the United States is taking costly unilateral measures while mostly giving the PRC a free pass.

Climate change is not one of the most important foreign policy challenges facing the United States, and it probably does not deserve a chapter in this book. But progressives have made it a major issue, so it is important for conservatives to lay out a more balanced approach. This chapter outlines a conservative strategy for securing both America's energy needs and its environmental future.

The Relationship between Energy and Climate

Running a modern economy requires energy. We use energy to fuel cars, planes, trains, cargo trucks, ships, and factories, heat and cool our homes, charge our phones, run our appliances, and much else. Burning fossil fuels, namely coal, oil, and gas, remains the cheapest and most efficient way to generate energy. Indeed, it was the discovery of new techniques for exploiting these energy sources that led to the Industrial Revolution and the greatest and most rapid expansion of human prosperity in history.

But, there is a downside. Burning fossil fuels contributes to climate change, which is already an issue. Average global temperatures have been steadily increasing since the Industrial Revolution in the late 1800s.[392]

Global temperatures have naturally fluctuated over the millennia. After all, the world has witnessed ice ages in the past. But it is nearly certain that human activity is contributing to this latest cycle of warming because burning fossil fuels releases carbon dioxide (CO_2) and these higher levels of CO_2 in the atmosphere contribute to rising temperatures.[393] A warming climate does not mean that we will not experience very cold days in the winter. It is about average effects. Cold days are not quite as cold as they used to be, and hot days are hotter.

Rising global temperatures can cause many problems.[394] Ice caps and glaciers melt. Sea levels rise. Low-lying areas experience more floods. Already hot areas become hotter, contributing to crop failure, drought, and famine. Desperately hungry and thirsty people in poor countries look to move, contributing to migration pressures. Hotter temperatures mean the atmosphere can hold more moisture, increasing the incidence of violent storms. There will be economic costs to deal with climate-caused natural disasters. Species adapted to certain environments go extinct as their environments change. These developments strain the resources of poorer countries, contributing to state failure and civil conflict. And so on. At the extreme, if left unabated for centuries, climate change might make Earth uninhabitable.

Still, the science is less settled than progressives would have us believe. One of Obama's top science advisers, Steve Koonin, wrote a compelling book on this subject titled *Unsettled*.[395] Among other arguments, he points out that climate scientists use computer models to estimate the effects of increased greenhouse gas emissions on the climate, but doing so is speculative because the models are crude, whereas the climate system is complex. It is very difficult to model accurately the various feedback loops between the oceans, water vapor, clouds, and other factors that affect the climate, and scientists often get it wrong. For example, they cannot explain why the Earth's average surface temperature has increased more slowly in recent years even as global emissions have increased rapidly. In addition, the climate models accurately predict melting arctic ice caps, but they cannot explain why Antarctic ice caps are actually growing and are now at record highs. It is too simplistic to argue that there is a liner relationship between increased emissions, rising temperatures, and climate disaster.

Moreover, the effects of climate change, while real, are modest. Biden's White House has quantified them. An April 2022 white paper published by the Council of Economic Advisers and the Office of Management and Budget describes the climate change assumptions embedded in the president's budget.[396] The white paper summarizes the top peer-reviewed studies that quantify the effect of climate change on US GDP. It reports that due to the costs of climate change, US GDP in 2047 is projected to be 66 percent higher than today, rather than 71 percent higher, in a projection that excludes the negative effects of climate change. That is hardly a catastrophe! A March 2023 edition of the same white paper reaches similar conclusions.[397]

Furthermore, climate change will be gradual, giving humanity time to mitigate and adapt. As we will discuss below, humanity will transition to cleaner energies over time. And, as ocean levels slowly rise over the years, for example, people living in low-lying areas can take precautionary measures or move.

As Oren Cass stated in testimony before the US House Budget Committee in 2018:

> *If those changes occur gradually (as they are expected to), if they emerge in a world far wealthier and more technologically advanced than today's (as we expect it to be), and if policymakers ensure that people have the information and incentives to plan well (something over which we have control), then climate change will*

impose real costs but ones that we should have confi-
dence in our ability to manage.[398]

Moreover, some parts of the world will benefit from climate change.[399] Colder regions will become warmer, which reduces energy and health costs and opens up new opportunities for agriculture, tourism, and so on. For example, according to Moody's, Canada's GDP by mid-century will be higher with climate change than without it.[400]

In the past, many conservatives disputed whether climate change was happening at all, but those debates are largely over. As Matt Gaetz, Republican congressman of Florida, said, "I didn't get elected to Congress to argue with a thermometer."[401]

The real debate today lies over what to do about climate change. There are two major ways to mitigate the human contribution to climate change: use less energy, or use cleaner energy. Using less energy means decreasing our standard of living. Who wants to volunteer to: take shorter or colder showers, give up driving, flying, or using appliances? Using less energy also means undercutting economic growth and security. It means less economic activity because there will be fewer factories operating, fewer long-haul trucks on the road, and so on. And less economic growth means a smaller economic base on which to fund our military and promote other US interests.

The long-term solution is in transitioning to green energy sources (those that do not emit large quantities of CO2). But rapidly switching to green energy is not a realistic option because these sources are not yet able to generate sufficient energy to sustain our current standard of living—to say nothing of continued economic growth. Nuclear energy has great promise, but its widespread use around the world is limited by concerns about nuclear accidents, nuclear weapons proliferation, and disposing of radioactive waste. These practical problems have led to heavy regulation and limited use.

There is great future promise for renewable energies, such as wind and solar power, but it will take time because the technology is still immature. Today, fossil fuels account for 79 percent of total US energy consumption, while renewables register only 10 percent (excluding hydroelectricity).[402] Little is expected to change in the next several decades given global energy demand growth and existing policies. According to the US Energy Information Administration's Annual Energy Outlook 2022, in 2050, fossil fuels will still provide 75 percent of total US energy needs, while renewables will grow to just 17 percent.[403] The fact is that fossil fuels will likely remain the central pillar of America's energy strategy for decades to come. There will be a transition to green energy at some point, but not anytime soon.

Many of the "solutions" to climate change, therefore, are distorting government interventions that artificially raise the price of fossil fuels or reduce the cost of green energy in order to encourage a faster transition than would take place if left to market forces. The short-term effects of these interventions are higher prices for energy, reduced energy consumption, or both. This means depressed standards of living and reduced economic performance.

The list of artificial government interventions includes: restricting drilling for oil and gas, which reduces energy supply and drives up prices; putting a price on carbon emissions (through a carbon tax or cap and trade systems), which increases the cost of burning fossil fuels; providing subsidies or tax breaks for green technologies to reduce their cost and make them more attractive to firms and individuals; passing regulations, such as efficiency standards for cars and appliances, which cause them to use less energy but also increase their price and reduce their performance. (Parents running a busy household rightfully doubt whether it is really "efficient" to wait hours for a dishwasher to finish a cycle!)

There are also two major geopolitical challenges to addressing climate change. The first is China. China is often wrongly portrayed as a leader when it comes to tackling climate change, and progressives often talk about climate change as an area for Sino-US cooperation. As we can see in Figure 3, however, China is the world's largest greenhouse gas emitter, producing 29 percent of global emissions, compared to only 14 percent in the United States.[404] Moreover, as we can see in Figure 4, China's share is growing, while emissions in the United States and Europe are already on the decline.[405]

Figure 3:[406]

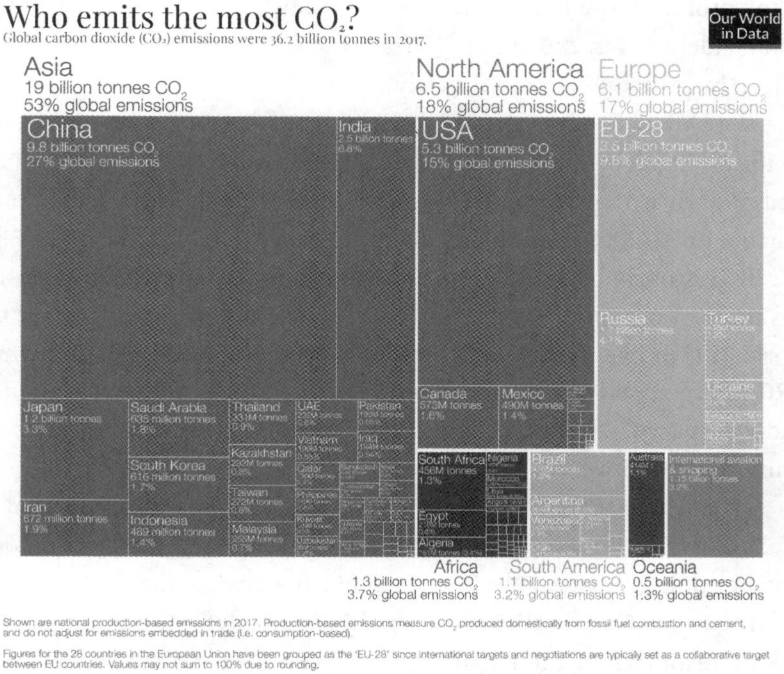

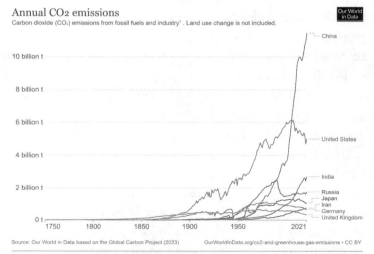

Who emits the most CO$_2$?
Global carbon dioxide (CO$_2$) emissions were 36.2 billion tonnes in 2017.

Figure 4:[407]

Annual CO2 emissions
Carbon dioxide (CO$_2$) emissions from fossil fuels and industry'. Land use change is not included.

Source: Our World in Data based on the Global Carbon Project (2023)   OurWorldInData.org/co2-and-greenhouse-gas-emissions • CC BY

1. **Fossil emissions:** Fossil emissions measure the quantity of carbon dioxide (CO$_2$) emitted from the burning of fossil fuels, and directly from industrial processes such as cement and steel production. Fossil CO$_2$ includes emissions from coal, oil, gas, flaring, cement, steel, and other industrial processes. Fossil emissions do not include land use change, deforestation, soils, or vegetation.

China is a necessary part of the solution because it is the biggest part of the problem. The United States cannot solve this problem on its own. As President Biden explained, "[I]f we [the United States] do everything perfectly, it's not going to ultimately matter."[408]

The United States is already reducing greenhouse gas emissions, but China promises to only start reducing its emissions in 2030.[409] If we promised our wives that we would start helping out more around the house starting in 2030, they would not be impressed. Moreover, like much else, the PRC is likely lying about its emissions targets. Given that it continues to open new dirty coal-fired power plants in China and around the world, it is unlikely that it will meet these pledges. Li Keqiang, a former PRC premier, said in 2021 that China's energy transition must be "sound and well-paced"—a quip by *The Economist* interpreted this as "code for using coal for longer."[410]

Given these realities, why is China often seen as a leader on climate change? It is because the CCP is massively subsidizing green technology. It is not doing this because it cares about the environment. Rather, according to the CCP itself, it is doing this in an attempt to dominate the energy resources of the twenty-first century.[411] If and when the world transitions to green energy, China wants to control the world's energy supply. Moreover, the means by which China is investing in this sector is sometimes barbaric, using slave labor in Xinjiang, for example, to make solar panels.[412]

There is a second major geopolitical obstacle to addressing climate change: the divide between rich and poor nations. Climate change is a rich person's problem. People who have their basic needs met can afford to care about a clean environment. People who are hungry or cold, however, are understandably less concerned about $CO2$ emissions. Developing countries argue that Europe and the United States got rich for centuries by using cheap and dirty fuel sources. Now that they are fat and happy, they want to kick the ladder down. The Indian government, for example, points out that it has over one billion people, many of whom want to rise out of poverty and aspire to join the global middle class.[413] Like American families, they want cars and air conditioning, and a better life for their children. To continue to increase their populations' standard of living, they will have no choice but to use cheap but dirty fuel sources, like coal.

The big strategic questions facing the United States, therefore, are: How much drastic action should the United States take to force a near-term transition to clean energy? How much unilateral action should the United States take to address climate change even if China and other nations are not doing their part? Should the United States take immediate and costly steps to reduce emissions, negatively impacting its economic performance as China continues to fuel its economy and military build-up using cheap and dirty energy sources?

Conservatives and progressives answer these questions differently.

Conservative and Progressive Views on Climate and Energy

Progressives see climate change as among the greatest challenges facing humanity.[414] They believe that the United States should take swift and strong action to reduce greenhouse gas emissions and promote clean technology.[415] They also believe that the US government should prioritize international cooperation with China and others to negotiate a binding international climate treaty.[416] Even when other countries are unwilling to contribute, they believe it is imperative for the United States to take bold steps to save the planet.[417]

This approach is consistent with a progressive mindset. Their focus is on helping all of humanity, not pursuing US national interests first. There is a naïve hope that nations can easily work together to solve shared global challenges. And there is a belief that cooperation can be best achieved through multilateral agreements.

Many believe that this progressive view of climate has become a stand-in for religion in a secularizing world.[418] There was a time when the world was pure, but through their immoral actions, humans have spoiled the planet. They, therefore, need to repent and pursue a more virtuous lifestyle in order to atone for their sin and achieve salvation.

Conservatives have a more balanced view of energy and the environment. They, too, want a clean environment. But they also understand the realities of the global energy market. They are less willing to exact immediate short-term economic costs in order to pursue some unknown future benefit of a world with reduced greenhouse gas emissions. They are also attuned to the US national interest, and they are unwilling to undertake unilateral burdens when other major powers, like China, are not doing their fair share. Importantly, they recognize that America's energy choices have a profound effect on its economic and military strength—a crucial consideration in the New Cold War. Conservatives do not see climate treaties as a necessary solution or as ends in and of themselves but evaluate them pragmatically, on their merits. They are more confident that market forces can solve the climate change challenge, through technological breakthroughs, for example, without heavy-handed government interventions.

The conservative approach to energy and climate is, therefore, consistent with the conservative approach to domestic and global affairs more broadly.

Energy and the Environment from Reagan to Biden

Conservatives have often led on environmental issues. In 1988, Ronald Reagan signed the Montreal Protocol, the most effective environmental treaty in history. The protocol phased out chlorofluorocarbons (CFCs) and other substances that had been contributing to a hole in the Earth's ozone layer. The treaty was effective in part because there were cost effective alternatives to CFCs. Eliminating them through an international agreement was a pragmatic step that greatly enhanced environmental protections.[419]

Reagan's vice president and later successor, George H. W. Bush, also led on environmental issues. He signed the 1990 US Clean Air Act into law with overwhelming bipartisan support. The legislation curbed acid rain, urban air pollution, toxic air emissions, and stratospheric ozone depletion.[420]

In 1997, Bill Clinton signed the Kyoto Protocol aimed at reducing greenhouse gas emissions, but this was a bad deal for the American people and it was never ratified by the US Senate. The protocol recognized two categories of countries, developed and developing, and only developed countries were required to take steps to reduce emissions. Developing countries received a free pass. Countries in the "developing" category included major emitters, like China and India. The US Congress passed a resolution with a 95–0 vote, stating that the United States would never ratify a treaty that both harms the economy of the United States and that does not require action from much of the rest of the world.[421]

When George W. Bush entered office, he echoed Congress's concerns about the protocol, stating, "I oppose the Kyoto Protocol because it exempts 80 percent of the world, including major population centers such as China and India, from compliance, and would cause serious harm to the US economy."[422] The Bush administration took several other pragmatic steps to improve the environment, however, including legislation to clean up brownfields, a Healthy Forests Initiative, and allocating additional resources to maintaining national parks.

The next Democratic president, Barack Obama, once again entered into an unfair and impractical multilateral climate treaty without bipartisan support. The Paris Climate Accords contained many of the same flaws as its predecessor. Like Kyoto, the agreement was unequal. There was not a universal standard to which countries committed. Rather, the agreement was made up by each country offering its own unique and unequal "nationally determined contribution" (NDC). Most notably, the United States promised immediate and costly action, whereas China vowed to act only in the distant future. Moreover, the agreement included no enforcement mechanism. If a country, like China, failed to meet its emissions targets, there would be no consequences. Paris's defenders argued that countries that fail to live up to their commitments could be "named and shamed."[423] In other words, climate activists could criticize them for not doing the right thing. That is a thin reed, and it is no surprise that many countries failed to meet their commitments under Paris.

Moreover, even if every country met their pledges, the emissions reductions would be insufficient to meet the targets set out by climate scientists. So—even if successful—Paris does not solve the problem it was intended to solve. Finally, the Obama administration knew they did not enjoy Republican support, so they never sent the agreement to Congress for approval. Instead, they advanced a legalistic argument that past congressional support for climate change was sufficient for the executive branch to enter the Paris Accord.

Given these weaknesses, it is no wonder that Trump pulled out of the agreement upon taking office in 2017. Even though the United States exited the Paris framework, it continued to reduce its greenhouse gas emissions during the Trump administration, largely due to a major technological breakthrough: the shale gas revolution. Over the past fifteen years, the United States pioneered new techniques, such as horizontal drilling and hydraulic fracturing, which have greatly increased American production of natural gas, transforming the United States into an energy superpower.[424] Since natural gas is cleaner than other fossil fuels, US emissions have fallen.

Still, climate change is an act of faith for Democrats, and Biden made reentering the Paris Accords a major pillar of his presidential campaign. He followed through on the pledge on his first day in office. In his first week, Biden also signed Executive Order (EO) 14008, putting climate change at the center of his foreign policy. He named John Kerry the climate czar, giving Kerry cabinet status and a seat on the National Security Council. Later that year, he promised to work with Congress to double to $11.4 billion per year foreign aid funds to help developing nations deal with climate change.

Moreover, Biden increased the US NDCs under Paris, promising faster and deeper cuts to US emissions. In order to meet those targets, the Biden administration waged a "war on energy."[425] Biden canceled the Keystone XL Pipeline that would have brought abundant Canadian oil into the United States. He banned new oil and gas leases on federal lands, and stopped oil and gas exploration off the Alaskan coast. He regulated extreme efficiency standards. In short, he reduced the American supply of fossil fuels before green energy technologies were ready to replace them.

As a result, American energy prices soared, contributing to record inflation and hurting the well-being of the American people.[426] To make up for the deficit, the Biden administration withdrew record amounts of fuel from the nation's Strategic Petroleum Reserve. President Biden even begged US adversaries, like Iran and Venezuela, to increase their oil production to make up for US energy shortfalls.[427] Instead of American workers and companies benefiting from energy production, Americans paid high prices to buy fuel from their adversaries. Moreover, these countries' production processes are dirtier than the United States' meaning that relying on foreign sources likely increases CO2 emissions.[428] Finally, US special envoy John Kerry and other Biden administration officials prioritized a quixotic quest to cooperate with China on climate change over the necessity to confront Beijing.[429]

This extreme approach to climate change does not reflect the interests and priorities of the American people. In a January 2022 Pew poll, respondents ranked the strength of the US economy as their top priority. Climate change came in at fourteenth.[430]

Clearly a better approach is needed.

A Strategy for Energy and Climate for Today and Tomorrow

A smart US climate and energy policy should balance American needs for both economic well-being and a clean environment. It would prioritize market forces, not distorting government interventions. It would also adopt an arms control mindset in multilateral climate negotiations with China and other countries.

To balance its climate and energy goals, the United States needs to pursue an all-of-the-above energy policy that includes: oil, gas, coal, nuclear, hydro, solar, wind, and more. Renewables are simply not ready to meaningfully replace fossil fuels in the US energy mix, and they will not be ready for several decades. Washington should end its counterproductive war on fossil fuels. It can continue to promote green energy technology, but not at the expense of our energy security and economic well-being, which is provided mostly by fossil fuels.

To promote a transition to cleaner energy, progressives believe heavy-handed government intervention is necessary. Conservatives believe the government should get out of the way and let market forces work their magic. One of the biggest obstacles to a better energy policy currently is government regulation. A prime example is the forty-year-old and heavily litigated National Environmental Policy Act. At present, infrastructure permits face average delays of more than four years (five years for nuclear plants) because of environmental impact statements alone.[431] In fact, NEPA red tape disproportionately affects clean energy and conservation-related projects. Streamlining environmental reviews and permitting will bring more natural gas, nuclear, and green energy online faster.

Nuclear energy must be an important part of the solution. The US Nuclear Regulatory Commission (NRC) should quicken the pace to approve and certify small modular reactors (SMRs). SMRs are a promising technology to meet the world's energy and climate objectives, but the current pace for approval is far too slow.[432] The United States should also step up its efforts to export clean nuclear energy technology around the world. During the First Cold War, the United States was a dominant player in the global nuclear energy market. But, in recent years, China and Russia have taken its place.[433] A strengthened US nuclear energy industry, therefore, will also become an important tool for confronting China and Russia and gaining influence in the Global South.

The United States should use its newfound position as a natural gas superpower to increase its exports of LNG. As a practical next step, this will require faster approvals for new American export terminals. Increased LNG exports will create American jobs. It will also help US allies secure their energy supplies. European nations, for example, can wean themselves off of Russian energy and rely on US energy supplies instead. Finally, because LNG is cleaner than other fossil fuels, US LNG exports will contribute to reduced greenhouse gas emissions but in a way consistent with American economic and geopolitical interests.

To transition to a green energy future, the United States should curtail heavy-handed government intervention and rely on market incentives and private innovation instead. It is obvious to everyone that there is enormous global demand for cost-efficient and clean energy sources. There are huge fortunes to be made in this field. Private entrepreneurs have plenty of incentive to pursue these technologies. Government should get out of the way and let markets do what they do best. Instead of picking winners and losers, the government's role should be limited to supporting STEM education and basic research and development.

Government should also get out of the business of providing subsidies to the fossil fuel industry. Their fortunes should rise or fall based on market forces.

Climate activists would argue that it is irresponsible to simply hope and pray that technology will come along and save us, but it has happened before. The greatest reductions in US emissions in recent years were due to the shale gas revolution, driven by the profit motive of the US private sector over the objections of environmentalists who worried about possible negative environmental effects of "fracking."[434]

There is another example of successful technological revolutions solving a looming environmental problem in our lifetimes. In the 1980s, one of the greatest environmental fears was deforestation due to humanity's growing demand for paper.[435] Modern societies and offices had enormous and growing demands for paper products for letters, memos, documents, books, and so on. Then the digital revolution came along and solved this problem. So, too, is it likely that new technology will one day render our current dependency on fossil fuels obsolete. But we are not there yet.

When it comes to international climate action, the United States should adopt an arms control mindset. Washington would never think of making drastic unilateral cuts to the size of its nuclear arsenal at a time when China is engaging in a massive nuclear buildup. Similarly, the United States should not throttle its own economic performance in the name of climate activism as China uses cheap and dirty energy sources to fuel a major economic and military expansion. In future climate treaties, the United States should insist on parity. If China is unwilling to match US action, then the agreement is not in the US national interest. This will likely make it impossible to strike any new international climate agreements in the foreseeable future, but that is OK. As conservatives understand and progressives need to learn, treaties are not desirable in and of themselves. They are only worthwhile if they advance the US national interest.

Adaptation must also be a key pillar of a US climate strategy. The reality is that some global warming is likely already baked in due to past CO2 emissions. The United States and its allies and partners, therefore, must be prepared to adapt to a changing environment. This means developing a wide range of measures including draught-resistant seeds and better irrigation systems for hot, dry areas and evacuation plans for low-lying coastal areas.

Finally, we should remind ourselves that there are ways to protect the environment other than combatting climate change. Reagan fought against CFCs with the Montreal Protocol. George H. W. Bush passed the Clean Air Act. Republican Governor of Florida Ron DeSantis restored the Everglades wetlands.[436]

Conservatives can continue to lead in similar efforts to ensure that the American people can enjoy both a clean environment and economic well-being.

CHAPTER TWELVE

Border Security and Immigration

Border security is national security. The United States needs secure borders and an effective legal immigration system. Progressives tend to discount the downsides of open borders and believe that the United States has a duty to receive migrants, regardless of their motivation for coming to the United States. Conservatives, on the other hand, generally believe that borders must be secure, illegal immigration must be stopped, and legal immigration must serve the interests of the United States. Conservatives want to continue America's tradition of providing asylum to political refugees and those fleeing wars and natural disasters, but they do not believe that immigrants pursuing only economic opportunity should be allowed to enter the United States illegally.

This chapter lays out a conservative strategy to secure US interests related to immigration and border security.

Border Security and Immigration in Theory

Border security is a defining feature of the modern state. International relations scholars maintain that, following the 1648 Treaty of Westphalia, the international system was reorganized around the principles of sovereignty and territorial integrity.[437] This means that each country has clearly defined borders and exercises unchallenged authority within those borders.

Throughout history, states have sought to protect themselves by maintaining strong borders. It is no accident that natural boundaries, like mountains, rivers, and oceans, often served as the dividing line between political entities. Where natural boundaries did not exist, countries often built walls. The Chinese empire, ancient Athens, Renaissance Lucca, and many other polities built formidable walls to defend themselves. Throughout the centuries, many wars involved sieges in which invading forces would first need to breach an enemy's fortifications before defeating the enemy waiting on the other side. The strength of one's city walls was literally the difference between life and death.

Ancient walls were rendered obsolete by modern weaponry, but fortified borders continue to play a role in the modern world. To this day, the 38th parallel dividing North and South Korea is among the world's most heavily fortified borders.

In its early days as a nation, the United States built fortifications to protect itself from its hostile neighbors including France, Britain, Spain, and Mexico.

Fortunately, today, the United States is blessed with friendly neighbors in Canada and Mexico and is protected by vast oceans. Still, there are contemporary security threats to US borders as we will discuss below, including from terrorism, drug trafficking, international crime, and others.

At the same time, over the ages, countries have benefited from having borders that were open to foreign goods, people, ideas, and money. Tolerant societies, accepting of outsiders, often thrived economically and culturally as talented people persecuted at home fled to more welcoming polities. Ancient Athens, the Roman Republic, Renaissance Venice, and the Dutch Republic in early modern Europe were among the open societies that benefited from a "brain drain" as talented and enterprising people fled oppressive societies in search of security and opportunity.[438]

The United States is a nation of immigrants. Its history is to a large extent one of oppressed people fleeing their homelands to build a life in the new world, from pilgrims seeking religious freedom to European

Jews fleeing the Holocaust and the Second World War. Others came to America mainly in pursuit of a better life or economic opportunity. This continuous influx of outside talent, ambition, entrepreneurship, and capital has helped to make the United States one of the most dynamic and wealthiest countries on the planet.

The balance that successful polities have had to strike throughout the ages, therefore, is to construct borders that keep out dangerous invaders but that are open to the kind of people that contribute to the prosperity of a nation.

There are many reasons why the United States should favor carefully designed legal immigration. The United States derives many benefits from other countries' "brain drain," as America attracts some of the best, brightest, and wealthiest people in the world.[439] During the twentieth century, some of the greatest American scientists and innovators, including Albert Einstein, were immigrants.

Second, immigrants contribute to a growing population and economic growth. Many advanced economies have low and slowing birthrates as educated women have fewer children. But declining populations mean slowing or declining economic growth rates. The United States is unique among advanced economies with projections of a steadily growing population and economy.[440] This is partly due to immigration compensating for low birth rates among US citizens.[441]

Third, immigrants perform necessary work that native-born populations often prefer to avoid, such as manual labor in cities or farming. Immigrants are often willing to work for low wages, which can keep costs down for employers and consumers.

Fourth, there is love. Americans who marry a foreigner should have the option of bringing their spouse home and making a life together in the United States.

Fifth, there is family reunification. When someone moves to the United States for any of the above reasons, should they not be able to live with family members? Clearly, they should be able to bring their spouses and young children with them. What about elderly parents? Brothers and sisters? Cousins? There are reasonable differences about where to draw the line, but there is some need for family unification in US immigration policy.

Finally, there is asylum. International and US law make provision for political refugees, those suffering human rights abuses in their home country, to apply for asylum in a different country where they can be safe.

There are also, of course, downsides to immigration. Immigrant laborers can take jobs from, or drive down wages for, native-born Americans. Some immigrant groups may be unwilling or unable to assimilate into American culture, potentially changing American society for the worse.

Moreover, and perhaps most importantly, there are limits. The United States is among the most attractive countries on the planet. There are millions, perhaps billions, of people who would like to live in America. The United States is large and welcoming, but it simply cannot accommodate every human being who would like to move here. For this reason, the United States has legal policies and procedures for immigrants to apply for asylum, residency, and citizenship.

Congress has passed laws regulating immigration. However, many people choose to enter the United States illegally. During the Biden administration, more than two million people per year broke American law and crossed the US southern border without permission.[442]

Many of these people want to become functioning members of American society. They find work (from unscrupulous employers who are also willing to break the law by hiring people without proper documentation). They purchase homes. They start families.

But illegal entry is an unlawful act. These immigrants are seizing the golden ticket of American residence illegally. Every year, tens of millions of people apply to immigrate to the United States legally.[443] They are playing by the rules, but they are waiting behind those who cross the southern border without permission.

Moreover, illegal immigrants live in the shadows. They are subject to exploitation because they do not have the protections that come with legal residence and citizenship. The US government does not know who they are and what they are doing. It cannot tax them or register them for military service and so on. Illegal aliens also strain the social safety net, often receiving benefits and utilizing public goods meant for US citizens.

Further, illegal immigration creates a marketplace for illegality in general at the US southern border. Transnational criminal organizations profit by smuggling people into the United States. Human trafficking contributes to illegality and violence as the vulnerable people being trafficked are subjected to extortion, rape, and other harm. Rival gangs compete violently for the business of smuggling people and illicit goods.

There is also an obvious national security risk. America's enemies can plot to conduct terrorist attacks in the United States by exploiting America's open southern border. As noted earlier, in 2011, Iran plotted with what it thought was a Mexican drug cartel to conduct a terror attack against a popular Washington, DC, restaurant.[444] In 2022 alone, the Customs and Border Patrol encountered almost one hundred people on the terrorist watch list at the southern border.[445] Apprehensions of Chinese nationals (many of them men of military age) crossing into the United States illegally are up more than 800 percent over the same period last fiscal year.[446] Authorities fear that some of these illegal Chinese immigrants are spies or saboteurs working for the CCP. And the porous southern border is a conduit for illegal drugs like fentanyl that last year killed one hundred thousand Americans.[447]

These facts lead to several big public policy questions: How should the United States deal with border security and illegal immigration? What should be America's policy regarding legal immigration? What should the United States do with the millions of undocumented workers that are already in the country?

Conservative and Progressive Approaches to Border Security and Immigration

Conservatives and progressives tend to view the answers to the above questions differently, and these differences are rooted in their political worldviews. As was noted in Chapter One, progressives tend to place helping others and fairness above all else. Their heart goes out to the poor people around the world struggling to get into the United States.

They would like to help underprivileged people everywhere. They argue that illegal immigrants are people just like us who just want a better life for themselves and their children. They have yard signs that read, "No human can be illegal." Progressives, therefore, tend to be soft on border security, illegal immigration, and undocumented workers. They are more likely to support allowing illegal immigrants to enter the country and stay. It is also the case that since immigrants from Latin America have tended to vote for the Democratic Party (although that may be changing), they have stood to benefit politically by adding potential new Democratic voters.

Conservatives see these issues differently. Yes, they also want to help suffering people, but that is not the only consideration. They also respect authority and law and order. They understand there are legal processes for immigration and do not believe that people who break the law should be rewarded. They believe that a culture of illegality and criminal activity on America's southern border, now spreading to its northern border, is undesirable and can negatively affect the rest of the United States.

Most importantly, conservatives believe that the job of the US government is first and foremost to advance the interests of the American people, not to help people everywhere. They, therefore, want an immigration system designed primarily to benefit the United States and its citizens. Moreover, they understand incentives. Lax border security and policies that reward illegal immigration today merely encourage others to try to cross the border illegally in the future, making the problem worse. Conservatives, therefore, are in favor of strong border security to prevent illegal immigration. They are reluctant to reward illegal immigrants with citizenship or other benefits. Finally, they support designing and enforcing a legal immigration system that advances American interests.

Over the years, Republicans and Democrats in Congress have tried to find a compromise: trading stronger border security in exchange for a path to citizenship for illegal aliens already in the United States.

How have these differences and the search for a compromise played out in US government policy from Reagan to Biden?

US Border Security and Immigration Policy in History

In the first half of the twentieth century, large numbers of Mexican immigrants entered the United States (some legally but many illegally) in search of work. In response, in 1954, the US government launched "Operation Wetback," in which it deported millions of illegal immigrants back to Mexico.[448]

Still, the illegal immigration continued. By the early 1970s, it was estimated that the illegal immigrant population in the United States was more than one million people with four out of every five coming from Mexico.[449] The situation was deemed out of control, and, in 1978, the US Congress set up a special commission to make recommendations.[450] It advocated enhanced border security, punishments for Americans employing illegal immigrants, and amnesty for illegal immigrants already in the country.

Ronald Reagan attempted to address the problem. In 1986, he signed into law the Immigration Reform and Control Act.[451] The compromise legislation reflected the recommendations of the 1978 congressional commission and enjoyed bipartisan support. It promised Republicans enhanced border security and tougher criminal penalties for employers who knowingly hire illegal immigrants in exchange for a path to citizenship for undocumented immigrants who had entered the country prior to 1982. The legislation granted amnesty to three million undocumented immigrants who came out of the shadows and registered with the authorities.[452] For a variety of reasons, the measures to crack down on employers and enhance border security were weakened in the implementation phase, and the law did not have the anticipated effect of reducing illegal immigration. Most Republicans, therefore, now see this law as a failure and "amnesty" as a political bad word.

Subsequent administrations failed in their attempts at comprehensive reform and instead took partial measures to strengthen border security or provide protections for minors brought to the United States by other adults.

By 2016, many in the Republican Party were fed up with the failure to effectively address illegal immigration. Donald Trump made building a border wall with Mexico a signature of his campaign, and, upon entering office, he followed through on his promise to address illegal immigration.

President Trump increased physical barriers along the two thousand-mile US-Mexico border. He constructed 438 miles of a "border wall system"—rebuilding dilapidated wall segments and installing new ones—more than any president in US history.[453]

Importantly, he instituted the "Remain in Mexico" policy.[454] Previously, asylum seekers from Central America could enter and reside in the United States while awaiting the adjudication of their case. In practice, many of these people would skip their hearing and stay in the United States as illegal aliens. To correct this problem, Trump negotiated a deal with the Mexican government to allow asylum seekers to remain in Mexico until their case could be reviewed.[455] The policy resulted in fifty-seven thousand asylum seekers being returned to Mexico.[456]

In 2020, as COVID-19 began to spread, President Trump used Title 42 to further limit illegal immigration. Title 42 comes from a 1944 federal law designed to prevent the spread of communicable diseases. Since it was reinstituted by Trump, 1.7 million migrants were expelled at the southern border.[457]

Trump also placed limits on legal immigration, reducing the number of approved asylum claims and increasing the standards for family reunification.

In short, Trump reduced both the number of legal and illegal immigrants entering the United States.[458]

The Biden Approach

In his first year in office, Biden took nearly three hundred executive actions pertaining to immigration, almost ninety of which undid Trump administration policies to strengthen border security.[459] He rescinded Trump's 2019 declaration of a national emergency on the southern border.[460] Instead, he stated that his priority would be to address humanitarian challenges at the border. He directed the Department of Homeland Security to refrain from apprehending or removing most illegal aliens in the United States, including those with previous criminal convictions. Perhaps most importantly, he stopped construction of the wall on the southern border.

The perception of an open southern border and the possibility of amnesty fueled a sharp increase in illegal immigration during the Biden administration. By February 2021—just weeks into Biden's presidency— thousands of migrants banded together in caravans to make their way to the southern border.[461] Those interviewed said they hoped the Biden administration would be more welcoming of illegal immigrants and that they "didn't even want to try" to enter the United States under Trump.[462] By August 2021, it was reported that "the nonstop surge of illegal immigrants across the United States-Mexico border was on path to becoming the worst ever."[463]

The waves of illegal migrants contributed to illegality at the southern border. Cartels used the profits from human smuggling and an open border to dramatically increase their traffic of narcotics into the United States. According to Customs and Border Patrol, seizures of fentanyl in San Diego were up more than 300 percent, from just 1,599 pounds in 2019 to 6,767 in 2021.[464] In February 2022 alone, more than six hundred pounds of fentanyl and twelve thousand pounds of methamphetamine were seized at the border—enough fentanyl to kill 150 million Americans.[465]

Moreover, Biden's policies negatively affected the most vulnerable, facilitating an uptick in trafficking of minors and encouraging unaccompanied children to undertake a dangerous trek over many miles to the border. The Biden administration's use of the Trafficking Victims Protection Reauthorization Act streamlines the process for unaccompanied children illegally entering the United States.[466] In doing so, the provision incentivizes parents and smugglers to traffic children into the United States. According to an HHS whistleblower, "The lowered standards led to more of these children falling into the hands of cartels, pedophiles, and pimps. Many were claimed by 'family members' they had never met and then subjected to horrendous conditions."[467]

Finally, Biden's efforts to reform immigration law have been a failure. Biden proposed the US Citizenship Act of 2021, which would provide a pathway for undocumented immigrants to "earn" citizenship and limit presidential power to ban immigration.[468] The bill was introduced in the 2021 and 2023 sessions but did not make its way through Congress.[469]

In 2022, 2.76 million people illegally crossed the southern border, setting a new record.[470] The population of illegal immigrants in the United States now stands at more than eleven million or more than 3 percent of the total US population.[471]

Clearly, a better approach is needed.

A Strategy for Border Security and Immigration for Today and Tomorrow

A smart, conservative approach to border security and immigration policy would focus on strengthening border security while expanding pathways for legal immigration for high-skilled workers who can help the United States in its struggle with China.

Let us begin with border security. The goal should be to drive illegal immigration from roughly ten thousand illegal border crossings per day to zero. This can be accomplished by finishing Trump's wall across the entirety of the southern border. New technology including unmanned aerial drones, sensors, lighting, cameras, facial recognition technology, and AI algorithms can be used to detect illicit crossings. Increased numbers of border patrol agents can interdict them.

Defense must be strengthened by deterrence. The next Republican administration should adopt stricter policies related to illegal aliens in the United States. Illegal aliens who commit crimes should be deported. Unscrupulous employers who hire illegal aliens should face stiffer penalties. These and similar polices would send a signal that a path to citizenship for illegal immigrants is not in the cards.

The United States must work with governments in Central and South America to reduce migration flows. They can collaborate to strengthen border security in their countries, counter criminal networks and human traffickers, and introduce policies that curtail illegal border crossings, like "Remain in Mexico." The United States should also encourage governments in Latin America, the main source of illegal migration, to adopt policies that increase economic opportunity in their countries. Domestic and foreign businesses would then offer opportunities for good jobs locally, and people would not need to leave their communities in search of a better life.

With a strengthened southern border and the illegal immigration problem largely addressed, the United States will be freed up to optimize its legal immigration policy. The focus should be to recruit the best and the brightest from around the world to come to work in the United States in order to strengthen America in its confrontation with China.

The current US immigration system is flawed. Nearly all green cards are awarded due to considerations other than employment, with a strong lean toward family reunification.[472] From 2006 to 2015, nearly two-thirds of all green cards issued went to immigrants who had a family member already in the United States.[473] Another 19 percent were issued to refugees, asylum seekers, diversity lottery winners, and other humanitarian categories.[474] A mere 14 percent of green cards were issued on the basis of employment.[475]

In this regard, US policy is out of line with that of other advanced economies. In Canada and Australia, for example, more than 60 percent of legal immigration visas were awarded based on employment.[476] Other countries with a merit-based immigration system include the United Kingdom, New Zealand, Japan, and China.

Family reunification should remain a consideration in US immigration policy, but it should be curtailed. Spouses and minor children of immigrants should be welcomed. But, the parents, cousins, aunts, uncles, and adult children of people already here should not be routinely offered a green card.

The United States should also continue to welcome refugees and asylum seekers. But this should be limited to people genuinely at risk of human rights abuses if they remain in their own country. And, importantly, they should also be required to apply for asylum in the first safe country they enter. Too often in the past, migrants seeking a better life for themselves and their families have abused the system by traveling from all over the world, across several safe countries, including Mexico, only to apply for asylum in the United States. This does not make sense or advance the interests of American people. The practice should be stopped immediately.

The diversity lottery system should be eliminated altogether as was recommended by the bipartisan "Gang of Eight" members of Congress in their 2013 immigration reform efforts.[477] There is no reason why the United States benefits from having a certain number of immigrants each year from Poland, Peru, Uzbekistan, or any other country.

With these immigration spaces freed up, the United States can then award green cards to the world's best and the brightest: STEM students, top scientists and engineers, investors, high-net-worth individuals, and others who will directly contribute to the wealth and power of the United States. The United States benefited from other countries' brain drain during the First Cold War, and it can do so again in the New Cold War.

China is actively looking to attract just this kind of immigrant with its "Thousand Talents" campaign.[478] But, the United States has a natural advantage in this competition. China is xenophobic, crowded, polluted, and authoritarian. Most people, especially people of talent and means, prefer to live in the United States.

This was Trump's aspiration. He said that he wanted a "big, fat, beautiful open door" in his border wall for legal immigration.[479] He described our current system as largely based on "random chance" and proposed a merit-based system instead. "We cherish the open door that we want to create for our country. But a big proportion of those immigrants must come in through merit and skill."[480] He said, "The biggest change we make is to increase the proportion of highly skilled immigration from 12 percent to 57 percent, and we'd like to even see if we can go higher."[481]

By following the above policies, the United States can restore the rule of law, reduce the harm caused by cartels and smugglers, and protect the jobs and wages of American citizens. But it would accomplish much more: an effective legal immigration policy will increase America's scientific, economic, and military leadership and help America prevail in the New Cold War with China, for the benefit of the American people and the broader Free World.

CONCLUSION

Planning for Victory

By 1987, Reagan's strategy was working. Gorbachev had been brought to power on a platform of reforming the Soviet system and reducing Cold War tensions. Moscow was negotiating in earnest to end the nuclear arms race, finalizing talks on the INF Treaty. Reagan's advisors encouraged him to ease up on the pressure so as not to risk undoing the progress that had already been made. But Reagan disagreed.

He was determined to press forward until victory was achieved. In June, he traveled to Berlin to give a speech at the Berlin Wall, the symbolic dividing line between the Free World and the Soviet empire. Reagan's foreign policy advisors reviewed early drafts of his speech, and they were not pleased. They urged him to tone it down. At a minimum, they pleaded, he had to remove that one—especially provocative—line. Reagan decided to keep it.

He then stepped up to the podium and delivered one of history's most famous political speeches.

He explained to his audience, "This is the only wall that has ever been built to keep people in, not keep people out." He continued, saying, "As long as this gate is closed, as long as this scar of a wall is permitted to stand, it is not the German question alone that remains open, but the question of freedom for all mankind."[482]

At the speech's climax, Reagan directly challenged Gorbachev. He said, "If you seek peace, if you seek prosperity for the Soviet Union and eastern Europe, if you seek liberalization: Come here to this gate! Mr. Gorbachev, open this gate! Mr. Gorbachev, tear down this wall!"

The audience roared with approval. And the provocative line about the wall earned a place in history.

Just over two years later, in November 1989, Reagan's vision became reality. The Berlin Wall fell. The First Cold War was over. We won. They lost.

Reagan developed an effective strategy for winning the First Cold War, and Reaganite principles defined GOP foreign policy for the next several decades.

When Trump took office in 2017, however, he understood that many past policies were not working. He recognized that, despite Washington's good intentions, China was forcing America to enter into a New Cold War. Trump's strategy for confronting China updated Reaganite principles and redefined Republican foreign policy for the next generation.

It will now be up to future presidents to prosecute the New Cold War, and this book aims to help them in this important task.

This book provides a conservative foreign policy strategy for the United States to win the New Cold War. It outlines a Trump-Reagan foreign policy fusion that can steer the GOP and the United States as it navigates this new and dangerous epoch.

Part I set the stage. In Chapter One, we explained that the United States is in a New Cold War started by China and Russia. It is a war it did not seek, that it cannot avoid, and that it must win. We outlined the purpose of foreign policy and the vital interests of the United States. We were also clear in defining victory: *Arriving at a point where the Chinese government no longer has the will or the capacity to threaten vital US interests.* We also described the difference between a conservative and progressive approach to foreign policy and argued that a conservative mindset is better suited for the New Cold War.

Chapter Two reviewed Biden's foreign policy record. We concluded that Biden underperformed. Moreover, we argued that his mistakes were not idiosyncratic but the direct and expected maladies that result from forcing a progressive foreign policy onto a real world that operates according to different principles.

In the second part of the book, we turned to the Trump-Reagan fusion that can unite the Republican Party on foreign policy. Chapter Three laid out the doctrine of "peace through strength." When it comes to defense policy, Republicans believe that the United States should be so strong that neither the PRC nor any other adversary dare threaten it. But they also believe that Washington should use that power sparingly and avoid dumb and protracted wars.

Chapter Four argued that Republicans should embrace free and fair trade in the international economic arena. Contrary to the popular notion that Trump radically altered the GOP's traditional free-market principles, this chapter showed that both Reagan and Trump embraced free trade. But they were also both willing to use countermeasures to level the playing field with countries like the PRC that systematically violate the rules of international trade.

We made the case for American exceptionalism in Chapter Five. While progressives often "Blame America First," Republicans believe that the United States is the greatest country in the history of the world. The New Cold War is, in part, an ideological competition, and only the United States has the power and the values required to lead the Free World in its confrontation against the New Axis of Evil. The United States must claim the moral high ground in this contest.

Part III of the book turned to the greatest national security threats facing the nation and outlined a conservative "deterrence and diplomacy" strategy for addressing them. It is notable that these threats all come from revisionist and expansionist autocracies and that these dictators are working closely together in a New Axis of Evil. Chapter Six outlined a comprehensive strategy for winning the New Cold War against the PRC. In Chapter Seven, we turned our attention to how to take on China's closest ally, Russia. We examined the nuclear proliferation and terror threat posed by Iran in Chapter Eight. Chapter Nine examined the growing North Korea challenge. In each case, we recommend confronting these dictators with increasing pressure so long as they continue to threaten the United States. But we also urge holding out the promise of diplomacy if they are willing to come to the table and cease their hostile activities.

The final segment of the book, Part IV, looked at other important transnational issues. Chapter Ten considered allies and institutions. It argued that Republicans view international agreements as a tool like any other. They should be utilized when they advance American interests. But when they do not, they should be discarded or reformed. This may seem commonsensical, but progressives often wrongly view multilateral institutions as if they were sacred creations that are owed respect even when they fail to deliver.

In Chapter Eleven, we recommend a conservative approach to managing energy and the environment. Conservatives understand that it is counterproductive to fight a war on energy or to place naïve hope in cooperation with China in a quixotic quest to stop climate change. Instead, this chapter argued for an all-of-the-above approach to energy production while unleashing private sector innovation to produce the new green technologies of the future.

In Chapter Twelve, we turned to border security and immigration. We argued that border security is national security. Republicans understand that we need a secure southern border. US immigration strategy should not be to welcome lawbreakers who illegally cross borders but to recruit the best and the brightest from around the world—in part to help America win the twenty-first century technology contest with China.

In short, this book articulated a comprehensive, conservative approach to foreign policy that will enable the United States and its Free World allies to succeed in their contest with China and its other adversaries in the New Axis of Evil.

Now that you are armed with the information in this book, what should you do next? Please help us to spread the word. You can recommend this book to others. Do you know: A conservative who would like to learn more about their party's foreign policy? A GOP official or staffer who needs a handy guide on Republican positions on the major issues? A progressive who claims the GOP does not have a coherent foreign policy agenda? A student or scholar of foreign affairs or international relations? A journalist or foreign official who is curious to know what a GOP victory in the next election will mean for the future of American foreign policy? This book is for them.

You can also help us shape the public debate and inform the American people. If you have a platform, please provide it for discussions on American foreign policy and the New Cold War. If you have an audience that might be interested in the themes of this book, for example, please invite us to speak to your group. If you are a journalist, please interview us or other Republican experts on the foreign policy issues of the day. #RepublicansAlsoKnowStuff.

The Chinese Communist Party will also likely be interested in this book. We would not be surprised if they violate the copyright, translate it into Mandarin, and make it available to their officials. If you are a CCP official reading a bootleg copy of this book, we need you to understand that the CCP's current strategy only leads to failure for the PRC. It may take decades and much effort, but America and the Free World will prevail. You have the opportunity, therefore, to save everyone a lot of trouble. Please abandon your confrontational approach now. Instead, introduce political freedoms within China and pursue more peaceful and cooperative relations with the rest of the world. That is the surest path to future Chinese success. Your children and grandchildren will thank you.

Finally, if you are a US or allied government official, we invite you to execute the strategy outlined in this book. By working together and following our recommendations, we can defeat the CCP and the New Axis of Evil, and ensure the continued peace, prosperity, and freedom for the United States and the rest of the Free World.

Now, put down the book and let us go to work. It is time to win the New Cold War!

BIBLIOGRAPHY

Acemoglu, Daron and James A. Robinson. *Why Nations Fail: The Origins of Power, Prosperity, and Poverty.* New York: Currency, 2013.

Acheson, Dean. *Present at the Creation: My Years in the State Department.* New York: W. W. Norton, 1969.

Acton, James M. "Don't Panic about China's New Nuclear Capabilities." *The Washington Post,* July 27, 2021. https://www.washingtonpost.com/politics/2021/06/30/dont-panic-about-chinas-new-nuclear-capabilities/.

"After the Deal: A New Iran Strategy." The Heritage Foundation, May 21, 2018. https://www.heritage.org/defense/event/after-the-deal-new-iran-strategy.

Ainsley, Julia. "Migrant Border Crossings in Fiscal Year 2022 Topped 2.76 Million, Breaking Previous Record." NBC News, October 22, 2022. https://www.nbcnews.com/politics/immigration/migrant-border-crossings-fiscal-year-2022-topped-276-million-breaking-rcna53517.

Alaa Abdeldaiem. "LeBron James Says Daryl Morey Was 'Misinformed' about Situation in China." *Sports Illustrated,* October 14, 2019. https://www.si.com/nba/2019/10/15/lebron-james-daryl-morey-misinformed-china-tweet.

Allen, Jonathan. "Trump Kicks Off His 2024 Campaign: 'We Are at the Brink of World War III.'" NBC News, January 28, 2023. https://www.nbcnews.com/politics/donald-trump/trump-are-brink-world-war-iii-rcna68008.

Allen, Richard V. "The Man Who Won the Cold War." Hoover Institution, January 30, 2000. https://www.hoover.org/research/man-who-won-cold-war.

Amiri, Farnoush, and Kevin Freking. "McCarthy: No 'Blank Check' for Ukraine If GOP Wins Majority." Associated Press, October 18, 2022. https://apnews.com/article/russia-ukraine-donald-trump-humanitarian-assistance-congress-c47a255738cd13576aa4d238ec076f4a.

Anderson, Stuart. "A Review of Trump Immigration Policy." *Forbes,* August 26, 2020. https://www.forbes.com/sites/stuartanderson/2020/08/26/fact-check-and-review-of-trump-immigration-policy/.

"Article VI: Anti-Dumping and Countervailing Duties." Opened for signature October 30, 1947. General Agreement on Tariffs and Trade: 10-12. https://www.wto.org/english/docs_e/legal_e/gatt47_e.pdf.

184

Auyezov, Olzhas. "Russia Sends Troops to Put Down Kazakhstan Uprising as Fresh Violence Erupts." Reuters, January 6, 2022. https://www.reuters.com/world/asia-pacific/troops-protesters-clash-almaty-main-square-kazakhstan-shots-heard-2022-01-06/.

Baker, Peter, and David E. Sanger. "In Turn to Deterrence, Biden Vows 'End' of North Korean Regime If It Attacks." *The New York Times*, April 26, 2023. https://www.nytimes.com/2023/04/26/us/politics/biden-south-korea-state-visit.html.

Banks, Jim. "A promise kept: Biden's war on American energy." Congressman Jim Banks, March 25, 2022. https://banks.house.gov/uploadedfiles/a_promise_kept.pdf.

Barkoff, Sophia. "CIA Director: Iran's Nuclear Program Advancing at 'Worrisome Pace.'" CBS News, February 26, 2023. https://www.cbsnews.com/news/william-burns-cia-director-iran-nuclear-program-face-the-nation-interview/.

Batalova, Jeanne, and Michael Fix. *New Brain Gain: Rising Human Capital among Recent Immigrants to the United States.* Migration Policy Institute, May 2017. https://www.immigrationresearch.org/system/files/RisingHumanCapital_FS-FINAL.pdf.

Becker, Andrew. "Immigration Timeline." *Frontline*, accessed June 16, 2023. https://www.pbs.org/frontlineworld/stories/mexico704/history/timeline.html.

Beckwith, Ryan Teague. "Read Donald Trump's 'America First' Foreign Policy Speech." *Time*, April 27, 2016. https://time.com/4309786/read-donald-trumps-america-first-foreign-policy-speech/.

Bedard, Paul. "Illegal Border Crossings Set to Be 'Worst in US History.'" Yahoo! News, August 18, 2021. https://www.yahoo.com/now/illegal-border-crossings-set-worst-171900391.html.

Best, Paul. "Iran Could Produce 'One Bomb's Worth of Fissile Material' in about 12 Days, Pentagon Official Tells Congress." Fox News, February 28, 2023. https://www.foxnews.com/politics/iran-could-produce-one-bombs-worth-fissile-material-12-days-pentagon-official-tells-congress.

"The Biden Administration Has Approved $4.8 Trillion of New Borrowing." Committee for a Responsible Federal Budget, September 13, 2022. https://www.crfb.org/blogs/biden-administration-has-approved-48-trillion-new-borrowing.

"Biden Has Taken Nearly 300 Executive Actions on Immigration in His First Year, Outpacing Trump." Migration Policy Institute, January 19, 2022. https://www.migrationpolicy.org/news/biden-executive-actions-immigration-first-year.

Biden, Joseph R. "Remarks by President Biden at the 2021 Virtual Munich Security Conference." Speech, Washington, D.C., February 19, 2021.

White House. https://www.whitehouse.gov/briefing-room/speeches-remarks/2021/02/19/remarks-by-president-biden-at-the-2021-virtual-munich-security-conference/.

Biden, Joseph R. "Remarks by President Biden in Address to a Joint Session of Congress." Speech, Washington, D.C., April 29, 2021. White House. https://www.whitehouse.gov/briefing-room/speeches-remarks/2021/04/29/remarks-by-president-biden-in-address-to-a-joint-session-of-congress/.

Biden, Joseph R. "Remarks by President Biden on America's Place in the World." Speech, Washington, D.C., February 4, 2021. White House. https://www.whitehouse.gov/briefing-room/speeches-remarks/2021/02/04/remarks-by-president-biden-on-americas-place-in-the-world/.

Biden, Joseph R. "Remarks by President Biden on a Successful Counterterrorism Operation in Afghanistan." Speech, Washington, D.C., August 1, 2022. White House. https://www.whitehouse.gov/briefing-room/speeches-remarks/2022/08/01/remarks-by-president-biden-on-a-successful-counter-terrorism-operation-in-afghanistan/.

Biden, Joseph R. "Remarks by President Biden on Standing Up for Democracy." Speech, Washington, D.C., November 2, 2022. White House. https://www.whitehouse.gov/briefing-room/speeches-remarks/2022/11/03/remarks-by-president-biden-on-standing-up-for-democracy/.

Biden, Joseph R. "Remarks by President Biden on the American Jobs Plan." Speech, Pittsburgh, Pennsylvania, March 31, 2021. White House. https://www.whitehouse.gov/briefing-room/speeches-remarks/2021/03/31/remarks-by-president-biden-on-the-american-jobs-plan/.

Biden, Joseph R. "Remarks by President Biden on the End of the War in Afghanistan." Speech, Washington, D.C., August 31, 2021. White House. https://www.whitehouse.gov/briefing-room/speeches-remarks/2021/08/31/remarks-by-president-biden-on-the-end-of-the-war-in-afghanistan/.

Biden, Joseph R. "Why America Must Lead Again: Rescuing U.S. Foreign Policy after Trump." *Foreign Affairs*, January 23, 2020. https://www.foreignaffairs.com/articles/united-states/2020-01-23/why-america-must-lead-again.

Bill of Rights Institute. "Tear Down This Wall: Ronald Reagan, the Cold War, and Responsibility." Accessed June 14, 2023. https://billofrightsinstitute.org/activities/tear-down-this-wall-ronald-reagan-the-cold-war-and-responsibility-handout-a-narrative.

"The Bill of Rights: A Transcription." America's Founding Documents, US National Archives and Records Administration, last modified January 31, 2023. https://www.archives.gov/founding-docs/bill-of-rights-transcript.

Blackmon, David. "Biden's 'Kind of Insane' Energy Policies Have Created an Entirely Rational Investor Response." *Forbes*, September 20, 2022. https://

www.forbes.com/sites/davidblackmon/2022/09/20/bidens-kind-of-insane-energy-policies-have-created-an-entirely-rational-investor-response/?sh=3ad98b5f174d.

Blinken, Antony J. "A Foreign Policy for the American People." Speech, Washington, D.C., March 3, 2021. U.S. Department of State. https://www.state.gov/a-foreign-policy-for-the-american-people/.

Blumenthal, Dan and Linda Zhang, "China Is Stealing Our Technology and Intellectual Property. Congress Must Stop It." *National Review*, June 2, 2021. https://www.nationalreview.com/2021/06/china-is-stealing-our-technology-and-intellectual-property-congress-must-stop-it/.

Bolton, John R. "A World without Rules." *National Review*, January 20, 2022. https://www.nationalreview.com/magazine/2022/02/07/a-world-without-rules/.

Bolton, John R. "Entente Multiplies the Threat from Russia and China." *The Wall Street Journal*, February 15, 2022. https://www.wsj.com/articles/entente-multiplies-the-threat-from-russia-and-china-foreign-policy-alliance-beijing-moscow-xi-putin-11644943618.

Bowden, John. "Ocasio-Cortez: 'World will end in 12 years' if climate change not addressed." *The Hill*, January 22, 2019. https://thehill.com/policy/energy-environment/426353-ocasio-cortez-the-world-will-end-in-12-years-if-we-dont-address/.

Boyd, Gerald M. "President Imposes Tariff on Imports against Japanese." *The New York Times*, April 18, 1987. https://www.nytimes.com/1987/04/18/business/president-imposes-tariff-on-imports-against-japanese.html.

Braithwaite, Sharon. "Zelensky Refuses U.S. Offer to Evacuate, Saying 'I Need Ammunition, Not a Ride.'" *CNN*, February 26, 2022. https://www.cnn.com/2022/02/26/europe/ukraine-zelensky-evacuation-intl/index.html.

Brands, Hal. *Making the Unipolar Moment: U.S. Foreign Policy and the Rise of the Post-Cold War Order*. Ithaca: Cornell University Press, 2016.

Brands, Hal. "The Vision Thing." Miller Center, University of Virginia, January 14, 2016. https://millercenter.org/issues-policy/foreign-policy/the-vision-thing.

Brands, H. W. *Reagan: The Life*. New York: Anchor, 2016.

Brennan, David. "Russia Desperate for Iran, North Korea Help with Missiles, Drones: U.S." *Newsweek*, January 17, 2023. https://www.newsweek.com/russia-desperate-iran-north-korea-help-missiles-drones-us-ukraine-colin-kahl-wendy-sherman-1774237.

Bressler, Danny. "Has the Nuclear Nonproliferation Treaty Limited the Spread of Nuclear Weapons? Evaluating the Arguments." Nuclear Network. Center for Strategic and International Studies, March 17, 2021. https://

nuclearnetwork.csis.org/has-the-nuclear-nonproliferation-treaty-limit-ed-the-spread-of-nuclear-weapons-evaluating-the-arguments/.

Brose, Christian. *The Kill Chain: Defending America in the Future of High-Tech Warfare*. New York: Hachette, 2020.

Brownstein, Ronald. "In 2024, Republicans May Complete a Historic Foreign Policy Reversal." CNN, March 28, 2023. https://www.cnn.com/2023/03/28/politics/gop-foreign-policy-debate-2024/index.html.

Brunnstrom, David, and Trevor Hunnicutt. "Biden Says U.S. Forces Would Defend Taiwan in the Event of a Chinese Invasion." Reuters, September 19, 2022. https://www.reuters.com/world/biden-says-us-forces-would-defend-taiwan-event-chinese-invasion-2022-09-18/.

Budiman, Abby. "Key Findings about U.S. Immigrants." Pew Research Center, August 20, 2020. https://www.pewresearch.org/short-reads/2020/08/20/key-findings-about-u-s-immigrants/.

Burns, Robert, and Lolita C. Baldor. "Milley: US Coordination with Taliban on Strikes 'Possible.'" Associated Press, September 1, 2021. https://apnews.com/article/joe-biden-ap-top-news-afghanistan-evacuations-kabul-c134d2ab-f8977b87d2965d9fe3e1565f.

Bush, George W. "State of the Union Address." *The Washington Post*, Speech, Washington, D.C., January 29, 2002. https://www.washingtonpost.com/wp-srv/onpolitics/transcripts/sou012902.htm.

Caldwell, Alicia A. "Today's Immigration Debate Rooted in 'Reagan Amnesty,' Experts Say." PBS, August 23, 2016. https://www.pbs.org/newshour/nation/todays-immigration-debate-rooted-reagan-amnesty-experts-say.

Cameron, Doug. "Pentagon Pushes Defense Companies to Limit Use of Chinese Supplies." *The Wall Street Journal*, September 18, 2022. https://www.wsj.com/articles/pentagon-pushes-defense-companies-to-limit-use-of-chinese-supplies-11663498804

Campanile, Carl. "Majority of Democrats Say US is Not World's Greatest Country: Poll." *New York Post*, September 19, 2022. https://nypost.com/2022/09/19/majority-of-democrats-say-us-is-not-worlds-greatest-country-poll/amp/.

Cannon, Lou. *President Reagan: The Role of a Lifetime*. New York: PublicAffairs, 2000.

Cardenas, Shirley. "How climate change could make some areas of Earth uninhabitable by 2500." World Economic Forum, October 21, 2021. https://www.weforum.org/agenda/2021/10/climate-change-could-make-some-areas-of-earth-uninhabitable-by-2500/.

Carl, Jeremy. "Whose Borders Should America Defend?" *Newsweek*, January 28, 2022. https://www.newsweek.com/whose-borders-should-america-defend-opinion-1673596.

Carlson, Tucker. "Tucker Carlson: Climate is now our state religion." Fox News, February 10, 2023. https://www.foxnews.com/opinion/tucker-carlson-climate-now-state-religion.

Carpenter, Ted Galen. "How China Could Test the U.S. Commitment to Taiwan." *The National Interest*, November 2, 2021. https://nationalinterest.org/blog/skeptics/how-china-could-test-us-commitment-taiwan-195759.

Cassella, Megan. "Democrats press Trump to commit to Paris climate deal as part of USMCA." *Politico*, September 17, 2019. https://www.politico.com/story/2019/09/17/democrats-trump-paris-climate-deal-usmca-1739745.

Cass, Oren M. "Testimony of Oren M. Cass before the House Committee on Science, Space, and Technology May 16, 2018." Manhattan Institute, May 16, 2018. https://media4.manhattan-institute.org/sites/default/files/Cass-Testimony-May2018.pdf.

Cadell, Cate, and Ellen Nakashima. "American Technology Boosts China's Hypersonic Missile Program." *The Washington Post*, October 17, 2022. https://www.washingtonpost.com/national-security/2022/10/17/china-hypersonic-missiles-american-technology/.

Catenacci, Thomas. "GOP lawmakers blast Biden for turning to Venezuelan dictator for oil while curbing domestic production." Fox Business, November 29, 2022. https://www.foxbusiness.com/politics/gop-lawmakers-blast-biden-turning-venezuelan-dictator-oil-while-curbing-domestic-production.

Chainey, Ross. "Trump at Davos: Trade, Taxes and What America First Means for the World." World Economic Forum, January 26, 2018. https://www.weforum.org/agenda/2018/01/trump-at-davos-trade-tax-cuts-and-america-first/.

Chapa, Sergio, Anna Shiryaevskaya, and Aaron Eglitis. "Baltic Nation Seeks to Become LNG Hub in Pivot Away from Russia." *Bloomberg*, November 7, 2022. https://www.bloomberg.com/news/articles/2022-11-07/baltic-nation-seeks-to-become-lng-hub-in-pivot-away-from-russia.

Cheng, Evelyn. "China and Russia Affirm Economic Cooperation for the Next Several Years." CNBC, March 22, 2023. https://www.cnbc.com/2023/03/22/china-and-russia-affirm-multi-year-economic-cooperation.html.

Chiba, Daina, Jesse C. Johnson, and Brett Ashley Leeds. "Careful Commitments: Democratic States and Alliance Design." *Journal of Politics* 77, no. 4 (2015): 968–982. https://doi.org/10.1086/682074.

"China Joins W.T.O. Ranks." *The New York Times*, December 12, 2001. https://www.nytimes.com/2001/12/12/world/china-joins-wto-ranks.html

"China, Russia, Iran Hold Joint Naval Drills in Gulf of Oman." Associated Press, March 15, 2023. https://apnews.com/article/china-russia-iran-naval-drills-oman-gulf-9f515b3246e4cbe0d98a35e8399dc177.

"China to Send Troops to Russia for 'Vostok' Exercise." Reuters, August 17, 2022. https://www.reuters.com/world/china/chinese-military-will-send-troops-russia-joint-exercise-2022-08-17/.

"China uses Uyghur forced labour to make solar panels, says report." BBC, May 14, 2021. https://www.bbc.com/news/world-asia-china-57124636.

Chinoy, Mike. "How Pakistan's A. Q. Khan Helped North Korea Get the Bomb." *Foreign Policy*, October 11, 2021. https://foreignpolicy.com/2021/10/11/aq-khan-pakistan-north-korea-nuclear/.

CHIPS Act of 2022. Public Law 117–167. *U.S. Statutes at Large* 136 (2022): 1366–1758. https://www.congress.gov/117/plaws/publ167/PLAW-117publ167.pdf.

Chollet, Derek and James Goldgeier. *America Between the Wars: From 11/9 to 9/11*. New York: BBS PublicAffairs, 2008.

Cobb, Jelani. "What Is Happening to the Republicans?" *New Yorker*, March 8, 2021. https://www.newyorker.com/magazine/2021/03/15/what-is-happening-to-the-republicans.

Cohn, D'Vera, and Neil G. Ruiz. "More than Half of New Green Cards Go to People Already Living in the US." Pew Research Center, July 6, 2017. https://www.pewresearch.org/short-reads/2017/07/06/more-than-half-of-new-green-cards-go-to-people-already-living-in-the-u-s/.

Colby, Elbridge A., and Kevin Roberts. "The Correct Conservative Approach to Ukraine Shifts the Focus to China." *Time*, March 21, 2023. https://time.com/6264798/conservative-approach-to-ukraine-shifts-the-focus-to-china/.

Colby, Elbridge A., and Oriana Skylar Mastro. "Ukraine Is a Distraction from Taiwan." *The Wall Street Journal*, February 13, 2022. https://www.wsj.com/articles/ukraine-is-a-distraction-from-taiwan-russia-china-nato-global-powers-military-invasion-jinping-biden-putin-europe-11644781247.

Colby, Elbridge A., and Robert D. Kaplan. "The Ideology Delusion: America's Competition with China Is Not about Doctrine." *Foreign Affairs*, September 4, 2020. https://www.foreignaffairs.com/articles/united-states/2020-09-04/ideology-delusion.

Colby, Elbridge A. *The Strategy of Denial: American Defense in an Age of Great Power Conflict*. New Haven, CT: Yale University Press, 2021.

Colby, Elbridge A. "The U.S. Must Support Ukraine, but China Must Be Our Priority." *Time*, February 27, 2022. https://time.com/6152096/us-support-ukraine-china-priority/.

Coleman, Bradley Lynn, and Kyle Longley, ed. *Reagan and the World: Leadership and National Security, 1981–1989*. Lexington: University Press of Kentucky, 2017.

Collins, Askia. "Republic of Korea, U.S. Navies Conclude Carrier Strike Group Exercise." US Navy, June 4, 2022. https://www.navy.mil/Press-Office/News-Stories/Article/3053309/republic-of-korea-us-navies-conclude-carrier-strike-group-exercise/.

Colton, Emma. "Condoleezza Rice: Putin 'Seems Erratic,' 'Descending into Something' Never Personally Seen Before." Fox News, February 27, 2022. https://www.foxnews.com/politics/condoleezza-rice-putin-russia-erratic-ukraine.

"Commerce Implements New Export Controls on Advanced Computing and Semiconductor Manufacturing Items to the People's Republic of China (PRC)." Bureau of Industry and Security, US Department of Commerce, October 7, 2022. https://www.bis.doc.gov/index.php/documents/about-bis/newsroom/press-releases/3158-2022-10-07-bis-press-release-advanced-computing-and-semiconductor-manufacturing-controls-final/file.

Congressional Budget Office. *The Demographic Outlook: 2023–2053.* January 2023. https://www.cbo.gov/system/files/2023-01/58612-Demographic-Outlook.pdf.

Conte, Niccolo. "Ranked: Top 10 Countries by Military Spending." Visual Capitalist, August 18, 2022. https://www.visualcapitalist.com/ranked-top-10-countries-by-military-spending/.

Cooper, Helene. "U.S. Considers Backing an Insurgency If Russia Invades Ukraine." *The New York Times*, January 14, 2022. https://www.nytimes.com/2022/01/14/us/politics/russia-ukraine-biden-military.html.

Copp, Tara. "Biden Rules Out Sending Troops to Ukraine, at Least for Now." *Defense One*, December 8, 2021. https://www.defenseone.com/threats/2021/12/biden-rules-out-sending-troops-ukraine-least-now/187386/.

Corn, David. "Donald Trump Says He Doesn't Believe in 'American Exceptionalism.'" *Mother Jones*, June 7, 2016. https://www.motherjones.com/politics/2016/06/donald-trump-american-exceptionalism/.

Cotton, Tom. *Only the Strong: Reversing the Left's Plot to Sabotage American Power.* New York: Twelve, 2022.

Cotton, Tom. "Speech at the Ronald Reagan Presidential Library." Speech, Simi Valley, CA, March 8, 2022. https://www.cotton.senate.gov/news/speeches/cotton-delivers-speech-at-the-ronald-reagan-presidential-library.

Council of Economic Advisers and Office of Management and Budget. *Climate-Related Macroeconomic Risks and Opportunities.* White Paper. Washington, DC: Executive Office of the President, 2022. https://www.whitehouse.gov/wp-content/uploads/2022/04/CEA_OMB_Climate_Macro_WP_2022.pdf.

Council of Economic Advisers and Office of Management and Budget. *Methodologies and Considerations for Integrating the Physical and Transition Risks of Climate Change into Macroeconomic Forecasting for the President's Budget*. White Paper. Washington, DC: Executive Office of the President, 2023. https://www.whitehouse.gov/wp-content/uploads/2023/03/CEA-OMB-White-Paper.pdf.

Council on Environmental Quality. "Environmental Impact Statement Timelines (2010-2018)." Executive Office of the President, June 12, 2020. https://ceq.doe.gov/docs/nepa-practice/CEQ_EIS_Timeline_Report_2020-6-12.pdf.

Council of Economic Advisors. *The Value of US Energy Innovation and Policies Supporting the Shale Revolution*. Executive Office of the President of the United States, 2019. https://trumpwhitehouse.archives.gov/wp-content/uploads/2019/10/The-Value-of-US-Energy-Innovation-and-Policies-Supporting-the-Shale-Revolution.pdf.

Crownhart, Casey. "We were promised smaller nuclear reactors. Where are they?" *MIT Technology Review*, February 8, 2023. https://www.technologyreview.com/2023/02/08/1067992/smaller-nuclear-reactors/.

Dalton, Toby, and Ankit Panda. "U.S. Policy Should Reflect Its Own Quiet Acceptance of a Nuclear North Korea." Carnegie Endowment for International Peace, November 15, 2022. https://carnegieendowment.org/2022/11/15/u.s.-policy-should-reflect-its-own-quiet-acceptance-of-nuclear-north-korea-pub-88399.

Dann, Carrie. "Donald Trump on Nukes: Let It Be an Arms Race," NBC News, December 23, 2016. https://www.nbcnews.com/politics/politics-news/trump-nukes-let-it-be-arms-race-n699526.

Davidson, Helen. "Xinjiang: More Than Half a Million Forced to Pick Cotton, Report Suggests." *The Guardian*, December 15, 2020. https://www.theguardian.com/world/2020/dec/15/xinjiang-china-more-than-half-a-million-forced-to-pick-cotton-report-finds.

Davis, Hannah. "Fighting Human Trafficking and Battling Biden's Open Border." The Heritage Foundation, March 14, 2023. https://www.heritage.org/immigration/commentary/fighting-human-trafficking-and-battling-bidens-open-border.

"The Day North Korea Talks Collapsed, Trump Passed Kim a Note Demanding He Turn Over His Nukes." CNBC, March 30, 2019. https://www.cnbc.com/2019/03/30/with-a-piece-of-paper-trump-called-on-kim-to-hand-over-nuclear-weapons.html.

"Decline of Global Extreme Poverty Continues but Has Slowed: World Bank." World Bank, September 19, 2018. https://

www.worldbank.org/en/news/press-release/2018/09/19/ decline-of-global-extreme-poverty-continues-but-has-slowed-world-bank.

Dehghan, Saeed Kamali. "Iran Executes Three Men on Homosexuality Charges." *The Guardian*, September 7, 2011. https://www.theguardian.com/ world/2011/sep/07/iran-executes-men-homosexuality-charges.

de Hoyos, Rafael. "Angry Voters Have a Point, but Protectionism Is Not the Answer." Brookings, March 20, 2017. https:// www.brookings.edu/blog/future-development/2017/03/20/ angry-voters-have-a-point-but-protectionism-is-not-the-answer/.

Dembicki, Geoff. "DC's Trumpiest congressman says the GOP needs to get real on climate change." Vice, March 25, 2019. https://www.vice.com/en/article/ zma97w/matt-gaetz-congress-loves-donald-trump-climate-change.

Dewar, Helen, and Kevin Sullivan. "Senate Republicans call Kyoto Pact dead." *The Washington Post*, December 11, 1997. https://www.washingtonpost. com/wp-srv/inatl/longterm/climate/stories/clim121197b.htm.

Donnelly, John M. "Inflation May Shrink Biden's Big Defense Plan." *Roll Call*, March 29, 2022. https://rollcall.com/2022/03/29/ inflation-may-shrink-bidens-big-defense-plan/.

Doyle, Michael W. "Kant, Liberal Legacies, and Foreign Affairs, Part 2." *Philosophy & Public Affairs* 12, no. 4 (1983): 323–353. http://www.jstor.org/ stable/2265377.

Doyle, Michael W. "Kant, Liberal Legacies, and Foreign Affairs." *Philosophy & Public Affairs* 12, no. 3 (1983): 205–235. http://www.jstor.org/ stable/2265298.

Draper, Theodore. *A Very Thin Line: The Iran-Contra Affairs*. New York: Hill and Wang, 1991.

Dubowitz, Mark, and Matthew Kroenig. "As Biden Relaxed Pressure, Iran Took Advantage." *The Wall Street Journal*, January 16, 2022. https://www.wsj.com/ articles/iran-nuclear-deal-jcpoa-biden-trump-diplomacy-11642192678.

Dueck, Colin. *Age of Iron: On Conservative Nationalism*. New York: Oxford University Press, 2019.

Dueck, Colin. "The GOP's Foreign-Policy Tribes Prepare for Battle." *National Review*, December 9, 2020. https://www.nationalreview.com/2020/12/ the-gops-foreign-policy-tribes-prepare-for-battle/.

Dunleavy, Jerry. "Afghanistan Debacle Played Role in Putin's Ukraine Decision, General Says." *Washington Examiner*, March 31, 2022. https://www.washingtonexaminer.com/policy/defense-national-security/afghanistan-debacl e-played-role-in-putins-ukraine-decision-general-says.

Economy, Elizabeth C. *The Third Revolution: Xi Jinping and the New Chinese State*. Oxford: Oxford University Press, 2018.

Edelman, Eric, Gary Roughead, Christine Fox, Thomas Mahnken, Kathleen Hicks, Michael McCord, Jack Keane et al. *Providing for the Common Defense: The Assessment and Recommendations of the National Defense Strategy Commission*. United States Institute of Peace, November 13, 2018. https://www.usip.org/sites/default/files/2018-11/providing-for-the-common-defense.pdf.

Editorial Board. "China's International Efforts to Silence Free Speech." *The Washington Post,* August 21, 2015. https://www.washingtonpost.com/opinions/chinas-overreach/2015/08/21/4dce4278-4516-11e5-8ab4-c73967a143d3_story.html.

Egan, Matt. "US Debt: Federal Interest Payments Could Soon Exceed Military Spending." CNN Business, November 1, 2022. https://www.cnn.com/2022/11/01/economy/inflation-fed-debt-military/index.html.

Eligon, John. "South Africa Begins Naval Drills with Russia and China, Despite Criticism that It Implies Support of the War." *The New York Times*, February 17, 2023. https://www.nytimes.com/2023/02/17/world/south-africa-begins-naval-drills-with-russia-and-china-despite-criticism-that-it-implies-support-of-the-war.html.

Ellyatt, Holly. "Russia Is Still Occupying 20% of Our Country, Georgia's Prime Minister Say." CNBC, January 22, 2019. https://www.cnbc.com/2019/01/22/russia-is-still-occupying-20percent-of-our-country-georgias-leader-says.html.

Emmons, Alex, Aída Chávez, and Akela Lacy. "Joe Biden, in Departure from Obama Policy, Says He Would Make Saudi Arabia a 'Pariah.'" *The Intercept*, November 21, 2019. https://theintercept.com/2019/11/21/democratic-debate-joe-biden-saudi-arabia/.

Encyclopædia Britannica, "Nixon, Kissinger, and the Détente Experiment." Accessed May 1, 2023. https://www.britannica.com/topic/20th-century-international-relations-2085155/Nixon-Kissinger-and-the-detente-experiment.

Evans, Pete. "Canada's economy would be less hurt by climate change than other countries, Moody's says." CBC, July 4, 2019. https://www.cbc.ca/news/business/climate-change-moody-s-1.5199652.

"Executive Order on Tackling the Climate Crisis at Home and Abroad." White House, January 27, 2021. https://www.whitehouse.gov/briefing-room/presidential-actions/2021/01/27/executive-order-on-tackling-the-climate-crisis-at-home-and-abroad/.

"Face the Nation Transcript February 5, 2017: Pence, Christie." *Face the Nation*, CBS News, February 5, 2017. https://www.cbsnews.com/news/face-the-nation-transcript-february-5-2017-pence-christie/.

"Fact Check-Pride Flags Have Been Flown by U.S. Embassies in Muslim Majority Countries during Biden Presidency." *Reuters*, June 13, 2022. https://www.reuters.com/article/factcheck-pride-flags-embassy/fact-check-pride-flags-have-been-flown-by-u-s-embassies-in-muslim-majority-countries-during-biden-presidency-idUSL1N2Y01EU.

"Fact Sheet: President Biden Sends Immigration Bill to Congress as Part of His Commitment to Modernize Our Immigration System." White House, January 20, 2021. https://www.whitehouse.gov/briefing-room/statements-releases/2021/01/20/fact-sheet-president-biden-sends-immigration-bill-to-congress-as-part-of-his-commitment-to-modernize-our-immigration-system/.

Farnsworth, Clyde H., and Daniel F. Cuff, "'Voluntary' Import Restraint." *The New York Times*, September 20, 1984. https://www.nytimes.com/1984/09/20/business/voluntary-import-restraint.html.

Farnsworth, Clyde H. "Reagan Acts to Restrict Machine Tool Imports." *The New York Times*, May 21, 1986. https://www.nytimes.com/1986/05/21/business/reagan-acts-to-restrict-machine-tool-imports.html.

Farnsworth, Clyde H. "Reagan Decides to Tighten Controls on Textile Imports." *The New York Times*, December 17, 1983. https://www.nytimes.com/1983/12/17/business/reagan-decides-to-tighten-controls-on-textile-imports.html.

Farnsworth, Clyde H. "U.S. Raises Tariff for Motorcycles." *The New York Times*, April 2, 1983. https://www.nytimes.com/1983/04/02/business/us-raises-tariff-for-motorcycles.html.

Fassihi, Farnaz. "In Iran, Woman's Death after Arrest by the Morality Police Triggers Outrage." *The New York Times*, September 16, 2022. https://www.nytimes.com/2022/09/16/world/middleeast/iran-death-woman-protests.html.

Federal Reserve Economic Data. "Crude Oil Exports for Iran, Islamic Republic of." Updated May 3, 2023. https://fred.stlouisfed.org/series/IRNNXGOCMBD.

Feith, Douglas J., John Fonte, and Jon Kyl. "The War of Law: How New International Law Undermines Democratic Sovereignty." Hudson Institute, July 1, 2013. https://www.hudson.org/national-security-defense/the-war-of-law-how-new-international-law-undermines-democratic-sovereignty.

Feng, John. "Xi Jinping Says China to Become Dominant World Power within 30 Years." *Newsweek*, July 1, 2021. https://www.newsweek.com/xi-jinping-says-china-become-dominant-world-power-within-30-years-1605848.

"Fentanyl Trafficking Tests America's Foreign Policy." *The Economist*, May 11, 2023. https://www.economist.com/united-states/2023/05/11/fentanyl-trafficking-tests-americas-foreign-policy.

"The first big energy shock of the green era." *The Economist*, October 16, 2021. https://www.economist.com/leaders/2021/10/16/the-first-big-energy-shock-of-the-green-era.

Flournoy, Michèle A. "How to Prevent a War in Asia: The Erosion of American Deterrence Raises the Risk of Chinese Miscalculation." *Foreign Affairs*, June 18, 2020. https://www.foreignaffairs.com/articles/united-states/2020-06-18/how-prevent-war-asia.

Ford, Christopher Ashley. "Bureaucracy and Counterstrategy: Meeting the China Challenge." Speech, Ft. Belvoir, VA, September 11, 2019. U.S. Department of State. https://2017-2021.state.gov/bureaucracy-and-counter-strategy-meeting-the-china-challenge/index.html.

Foreign Threats to the 2020 US Federal Elections. National Intelligence Council, March 10, 2021. https://www.dni.gov/files/ODNI/documents/assessments/ICA-declass-16MAR21.pdf.

Forgey, Quint. "'The Dawn of a New Middle East': Trump Celebrates Abraham Accords with White House Signing Ceremony." *Politico*, September 15, 2020. https://www.politico.com/news/2020/09/15/trump-abraham-accords-palestinians-peace-deal-415083.

Forsby, Andreas B. "Falling Out of Favor: How China Lost the Nordic Countries." *The Diplomat*, June 24, 2022. https://thediplomat.com/2022/06/falling-out-of-favor-how-china-lost-the-nordic-countries/.

Frangoul, Anmar. "President Xi tells UN that China will be 'carbon neutral' within four decades." CNBC, September 23, 2020. https://www.cnbc.com/2020/09/23/china-claims-it-will-be-carbon-neutral-by-the-year-2060.html.

Frankovic, Kathy. "Only One-Third of Americans Have a Valid US Passport." YouGov, April 21, 2021. https://today.yougov.com/topics/travel/articles-reports/2021/04/21/only-one-third-americans-have-valid-us-passport.

French, Howard W. "North Korea, Accusing U.S., Says Nuclear Pact Has Collapsed." *The New York Times*, November 21, 2022. https://www.nytimes.com/2002/11/21/international/north-korea-accusing-us-says-nuclear-pact-has-collapsed.html.

Friedberg, Aaron L. *Getting China Wrong*. Cambridge: Polity, 2022.

Fukuyama, Francis. "The End of History?" *The National Interest*, no. 16 (1989): 3–18. https://www.jstor.org/stable/24027184.

Fuhrmann, Matthew and Jeffrey D. Berejikian. "Disaggregating Noncompliance: Abstention versus Predation in the Nuclear Nonproliferation Treaty." *The Journal of Conflict Resolution* 56, no. 3 (2012): 355–381. http://www.jstor.org/stable/23248792.

Fung, Katherine. "Fact Check: Is Biden Administration Funding Drag Shows in Ecuador?" *Newsweek*, October 20, 2022. https://www.newsweek.com/fact-check-biden-administration-funding-drag-shows-ecuador-1753649.

Fung, Katherine. "Russia, China Join Forces against Push to Punish Iran." *Newsweek*, November 24, 2022. https://www.newsweek.com/russia-china-join-forces-against-push-punish-iran-1761510.

Garamone, Jim. "Erosion of U.S. Strength in Indo-Pacific Is Dangerous to All, Commander Says." U.S. Department of Defense, March 9, 2021. https://www.defense.gov/News/News-Stories/Article/Article/2530733/erosion-of-us-strength-in-indo-pacific-is-dangerous-to-all-commander-says/.

Garamone, Jim. "Taliban Remains Dangerous, Harbors al-Qaida, Joint Chiefs Chairman Says." U.S. Department of Defense, September 29, 2021. https://www.defense.gov/News/News-Stories/Article/Article/2793387/taliban-remains-dangerous-harbors-al-qaida-joint-chiefs-chairman-says/.

Garip, Patricia, Vivian Salama, and Kejal Vyas, "U.S. Looks to Ease Venezuela Sanctions, Enabling Chevron to Pump Oil." *The Wall Street Journal*, October 5, 2022. https://www.wsj.com/articles/u-s-plans-to-ease-venezuela-sanctions-enabling-chevron-to-pump-oil-11665005719.

Gass, Nick. "Trump: I'll Meet with Kim Jong Un in the U.S." *Politico*, June 15, 2016. https://www.politico.com/story/2016/06/donald-trump-north-korea-nukes-224385.

Gavin, Francis. *Nuclear Weapons and American Grand Strategy*. Washington, DC: Brookings Institution Press, 2020.

Geller, Patty-Jane. "Pentagon Report on China's Military Highlights Nuclear Buildup that Could Overtake America." The Heritage Foundation, December 9, 2022. https://www.heritage.org/defense/commentary/pentagon-report-chinas-military-highlights-nuclear-buildup-could-overtake.

Geraghty, Jim. "Obama's Pastor after 9/11: 'America's Chickens Are Coming Home to Roost.'" *National Review*, March 13, 2008. https://www.nationalreview.com/the-campaign-spot/obamas-pastor-after-911-americas-chickens-are-coming-home-roost-jim-geraghty/.

Gillis, Justin. "The Montreal Protocol, a little treaty that could." *The New York Times*, December 9, 2013. https://www.nytimes.com/2013/12/10/science/the-montreal-protocol-a-little-treaty-that-could.html.

Gilmer, Ellen M. "Terrorists Crossing the US Border? Rising Encounters Explained." Bloomberg Law, April 12,

2023. https://news.bloomberglaw.com/immigration/terrorists-crossing-the-us-border-rising-encounters-explained.

Gilpin, Robert. "The Theory of Hegemonic War." *The Journal of Interdisciplinary History* 18, no. 4 (1988): 591–613. https://doi.org/10.2307/204816.

Gilpin, Robert. *War and Change in World Politics*. Cambridge, Cambridge University Press, 1981. https://doi.org/10.1017/CBO9780511664267.

TheGlobalEconomy.com. "Compare Countries with Annual Data from Official Sources." Accessed April 17, 2023. https://www.theglobaleconomy.com/compare-countries/.

TheGlobalEconomy.com. "Human Rights and Rule of Law Index—Country Rankings." Accessed May 23, 2023. https://www.theglobaleconomy.com/rankings/human_rights_rule_law_index/.

Goldberg, Jeffrey. "A Party, and Nation, in Crisis." *The Atlantic*, December 6, 2021. https://www.theatlantic.com/magazine/archive/2022/01/republican-party-america-democracy-in-crisis/620839/.

Goldstein, Amy. "Two Leaders Warn North Korea." *The Washington Post*, May 24, 2003. https://www.washingtonpost.com/archive/politics/2003/05/24/two-leaders-warn-north-korea/8401cf26-172a-44d9-821e-84c2bd8e5d7d/.

Gómez, Serafin. "Trump, at CPAC, Announces 'Heaviest'-Ever North Korea Sanctions." Fox News, February 23, 2018. https://www.foxnews.com/politics/trump-at-cpac-announces-heaviest-ever-north-korea-sanctions.

Gordon, Adam. "Fentanyl Seizures at Border Continue to Spike, Making San Diego a National Epicenter for Fentanyl Trafficking; U.S. Attorney's Office Prioritizes Prosecutions and Prevention Programs." United States Attorney's Office for the Southern District of California, August 11, 2022. https://www.justice.gov/usao-sdca/pr/fentanyl-seizures-border-continue-spike-making-san-diego-national-epicenter-fentanyl.

Gorokhovskaia, Yana, Adrian Shahbaz, and Amy Slipowitz. *Freedom in the World 2023: Marking 50 Years in the Struggle for Democracy*. Freedom House, March 2023. https://freedomhouse.org/report/freedom-world/2023/marking-50-years.

"Governor Ron DeSantis signs historic executive order continuing commitment to stewardship of Florida's natural resources." Florida Governor, January 10, 2023. https://www.flgov.com/2023/01/10/governor-ron-desantis-signs-historic-executive-order-continuing-commitment-to-stewardship-of-floridas-natural-resources/.

Gramer, Robbie, and Rishi Iyengar. "How North Korea's Hackers Bankroll Its Quest for the Bomb." *Foreign Policy*, April 17, 2023. https://foreignpolicy.com/2023/04/17/north-korea-nuclear-cyber-crime-hackers-weapons/.

Gramer, Robbie. "Iran Doubles Down on Arms for Russia." *Foreign Policy*, March 3, 2023. https://foreignpolicy.com/2023/03/03/russia-iran-drones-u av-ukraine-war-military-cooperation-sanctions/.

Gray, H. Peter. *Free Trade or Protection? A Pragmatic Analysis*. London: Palgrave Macmillan, 1985. https://doi.org/10.1007/978-1-349-06983-5.

Green, Michael J. "Six Reasons Why Trump Meeting with Kim Jong Un Is a Very Bad Idea." *Foreign Policy*, May 18, 2016. https://foreignpolicy.com/2016/05/18/ six-reasons-why-trump-meeting-with-kim-jong-un-is-a-very-bad-idea/.

"The Green New Deal." Bernie Saunders, accessed June 13, 2023. https://bernie-sanders.com/issues/green-new-deal/.

Green, Ted Van, and Carroll Doherty. "Majority of U.S. Public Favors Afghan-istan Troop Withdrawal; Biden Criticized for His Handling of Situation." Pew Research Center, August 31, 2021. https://www.pewresearch.org/short-reads/2021/08/31/majority-of-u-s-public-favors-afghanistan-troop-with-drawal-biden-criticized-for-his-handling-of-situation/.

Griffiths, James. "China's Ambassador Accuses Canada of Double Standards, 'White Supremacy' over Huawei." CNN, January 10, 2019. https://www. cnn.com/2019/01/09/asia/china-canada-meng-huawei-intl/index.html.

Griswold, Daniel. "Reagan Embraced Free Trade and Immigration." Cato Institute, June 24, 2004. https://www.cato.org/commentary/ reagan-embraced-free-trade-immigration.

Griswold, Daniel. *Reforming the US Immigration System to Pro-mote Growth*. George Mason University Mercatus Center, Octo-ber 31, 2017. https://www.mercatus.org/research/research-papers/ reforming-us-immigration-system-promote-growth.

"Gross Domestic Product by State: Fourth Quarter and Annual 2017." Bureau of Economic Analysis, U.S. Department of Commerce, May 4, 2018. https:// apps.bea.gov/newsreleases/regional/gdp_state/2018/pdf/qgdpstate0518. pdf.

Grygiel, Jakub and Rebeccah Heinrichs. "Biden's Abortion Politics Will Un-dermine America's World Standing." *The Wall Street Journal*, July 22, 2022. https://www.wsj.com/articles/bidens-abortion-politics-will-under-mine-americas-world-standing-roe-v-wade-dobbs-jackson-foreign-poli-cy-11658511777.

"G7 Leaders' Hiroshima Vision on Nuclear Disarma-ment." White House, May 19, 2023. https://www.white-house.gov/briefing-room/statements-releases/2023/05/19/ g7-leaders-hiroshima-vision-on-nuclear-disarmament/.

Gutiérrez, Pablo, and Ashley Kirk. "A Year of War: How Russian Forces Have Been Pushed Back in Ukraine." *The Guardian*, February 21, 2023. https://

www.theguardian.com/world/ng-interactive/2023/feb/21/a-year-of-war-how-russian-forces-have-been-pushed-back-in-ukraine.

Hadid, Diaa. "'The Taliban Took Our Last Hope': College Education Is Banned for Women in Afghanistan." NPR, December 20, 2022. https://www.npr.org/sections/goatsandsoda/2022/12/20/1144502320/the-taliban-took-our-last-hope-college-education-is-banned-for-women-in-afghanis.

Hadley, Stephen, J. et al., *Hand-Off: The Foreign Policy George W. Bush Passed to Barack Obama*. Washington, D.C.: Brookings Institution Press, 2023.

Hafezi, Parisa. "Iran to Join Asian Security Body Led by Russia, China." Reuters, September 15, 2022. https://www.reuters.com/world/middle-east/iran-signs-memorandum-joining-shanghai-cooperation-organisation-tass-2022-09-15/.

Haidt, Jonathan. *The Righteous Mind: Why Good People Are Divided by Politics and Religion*. New York: Pantheon Books, 2012.

Haley, Nikki (@NikkiHaley). "My bro. served in Desert Storm. My husband served in Afghanistan. I know the sacrifice military families endure. Believe me when I say that I want peace—& that's why I want to renew our strength. A strong America doesn't start wars. A strong America prevents wars! #RJCinVegas." Twitter, November 19, 2022. https://twitter.com/NikkiHaley/status/1594190314520051713.

Haltiwanger, John. "How Would Trump Attack North Korea? President Considering 'Bloody Nose' Strike, Reports Say." *Newsweek*, February 1, 2018. https://www.newsweek.com/how-would-trump-attack-north-korea-president-considering-bloody-nose-strike-797807.

Hartz, Louis. *The Liberal Tradition in America: An Interpretation of American Political Thought since the Revolution*. New York: Harcourt Brace and Co., 1955.

Hasell, Joe and Max Roser. "How Do We Know the History of Extreme Poverty?" OurWorldInData.org, February 5, 2019. https://ourworldindata.org/extreme-history-methods.

Hathaway, Robert M., and Jordan Tama. "The U.S. Congress and North Korea during the Clinton Years: Talk Tough, Carry a Small Stick." *Asian Survey* 44, no. 5 (2004): 717–718. https://doi.org/10.1525/as.2004.44.5.711.

Hegre, Håvard, John R. Oneal, and Bruce Russett. "Trade Does Promote Peace: New Simultaneous Estimates of the Reciprocal Effects of Trade and Conflict." *Journal of Peace Research* 47, no. 6 (2010): 763–774. https://doi.org/10.1177/0022343310385995.

Herbst, John, and Sergei Erofeev. *The Putin Exodus: The New Russian Brain Drain*. Atlantic Council, February 2019. https://www.atlanticcouncil.org/wp-content/uploads/2019/09/The-Putin-Exodus.pdf.

Herbst, John E., et al. *Global Strategy 2022: Thwarting Kremlin Aggression Today for Constructive Relations Tomorrow.* Atlantic Council Strategy Paper series, February 8, 2022. https://www.atlanticcouncil.org/content-series/atlantic-council-strategy-paper-series/thwarting-kremlin-aggression-today-for-constructive-relations-tomorrow/.

Hicks Jr., Tommy. "Biden's Border Crisis Worsens in February: Magnitude of This Calamity Cannot Be Understated." *The Washington Times,* March 21, 2022. https://www.washingtontimes.com/news/2022/mar/21/bidens-border-crisis-worsens-in-february/.

Higgins, Andrew. "China and Russia Hold First Joint Naval Drill in the Baltic Sea." *The New York Times,* July 25, 2017. https://www.nytimes.com/2017/07/25/world/europe/china-russia-baltic-navy-exercises.html.

Hobbes, Thomas. *De Cive.* 1642.

Hooper, Kelly. "Romney: 10 Years Later, Russia Remains 'Geopolitical Foe.'" *Politico,* February 27,

2022. https://www.politico.com/video/2022/02/27/romney-10-years-later-russia-remains-geopolitical-foe-493187.

"How North Korea Got Away with the Assassination of Kim Jong-nam." *The Guardian,* April 1, 2019. https://www.theguardian.com/world/2019/apr/01/how-north-korea-got-away-with-the-assassination-of-kim-jong-nam.

"How Will the US Navy Navigate an Uncertain Security Environment? A Conversation with ADM Mike Gilday." Atlantic Council, October 19, 2022. https://www.atlanticcouncil.org/event/how-will-the-us-navy-navigate-an-uncertain-security-environment/.

Hulsman, John C., and A. Wess Mitchell. *The Godfather Doctrine: A Foreign Policy Parable.* Princeton: Princeton University Press, 2009.

Hunt, Jennifer. "Should Immigrants Be Admitted to the United States Based on Merit?" EconoFact, June 28, 2017. https://econofact.org/should-immigrants-be-admitted-to-the-united-states-based-on-merit.

Hurst, Luke. "Kim Jong-un Assembles New 'Pleasure Squad' of Young Women/" *Newsweek,* April 2, 2015. https://www.newsweek.com/kim-jong-un-assembles-new-pleasure-squad-young-women-319030.

"Immigration Bill Summary." *Politico,* June 28, 2013. https://www.politico.com/story/2013/06/immigration-bill-summary-093557.

"In a Politically Polarized Era, Sharp Divides in Both Partisan Coalitions." Pew Research Center, December 17, 2019. https://www.pewresearch.org/politics/2019/12/17/in-a-politically-polarized-era-sharp-divides-in-both-partisan-coalitions/.

Inboden, William. *The Peacemaker: Ronald Reagan, the Cold War, and the World on the Brink.* New York: Dutton, 2022.

Interim National Security Strategic Guidance. White House, March 2021. https://www.whitehouse.gov/wp-content/uploads/2021/03/NSC-1v2.pdf.

International Monetary Fund. "GDP, Current Prices." World Economic Outlook. Accessed April 18, 2023. https://www.imf.org/external/datamapper/NGDPD@WEO/OEMDC/ADVEC/WEOWORLD.

"Iran, China and Russia Hold Naval Drills in North Indian Ocean." Reuters, January 21, 2022. https://www.reuters.com/world/india/iran-china-russia-hold-naval-drills-north-indian-ocean-2022-01-21/.

The *Iran Nuclear Deal: What You Need to Know about the JCPOA*. White House, 2015. https://obamawhitehouse.archives.gov/sites/default/files/docs/jcpoa_what_you_need_to_know.pdf.

"Iran, Russia, China Hold Joint Naval Drill amid Growing Ties." Radio Free Europe/Radio Liberty, January 21, 2022. https://www.rferl.org/a/iran-russia-china-exercises/31663080.html.

"Iran Worked on Nuclear Bomb Design: IAEA." Reuters, November 8, 2011. https://www.reuters.com/article/us-nujclear-iran-iaea/iran-worked-on-nuclear-bomb-design-iaea-idUSTRE7A75JF20111108.

Irwin, Douglas A. *Peddling Protectionism: Smoot-Hawley and the Great Depression*. Princeton, Princeton University Press, 2011. https://doi.org/10.2307/j.ctt1pd2k7j.

Iwamoto, Kentaro and Take, Sayumi. "Biden Says He Would Use Force to Defend Taiwan." *Nikkei*, May 23, 2022. https://asia.nikkei.com/Politics/International-relations/Biden-s-Asia-policy/Biden-says-he-would-use-force-to-defend-Taiwan.

Jaffe, Greg and Dan Lamothe. "Russia's Failures in Ukraine Imbue Pentagon with Newfound Confidence." *The Washington Post*, March 26, 2022. https://www.washingtonpost.com/national-security/2022/03/26/russia-ukraine-pentagon-american-power/.

Jain, Ash, and Matthew Kroenig. *Present at the Re-Creation: A Global Strategy for Revitalizing, Adapting, and Defending a Rules-Based International System*. Atlantic Council, October 30, 2019. https://www.atlanticcouncil.org/wp-content/uploads/2019/10/Present-at-the-Recreation.pdf.

Jain, Ash, and Matthew Kroenig. *Toward a Democratic Technology Alliance: An Innovation Edge that Favors Freedom*. Atlantic Council, June 2022. https://www.atlanticcouncil.org/wp-content/uploads/2022/06/Toward-a-Democratic-Technology-Alliance-An-Innovation-Edge-that-Favors-Freedom.pdf.

Jennings, Ralph. "Why Russia Backs China in Disputes with Third Countries." Voice of America, August 19, 2021. https://www.voanews.com/a/europe_why-russia-backs-china-disputes-third-countries/6209752.html.

Jie, Yang, and Aaron Tilley. "Apple Makes Plans to Move Production Out of China." *The Wall Street Journal*, December 3, 2022. https://www.wsj.com/articles/apple-china-factory-protests-foxconn-manufacturing-production-supply-chain-11670023099.

Jinping, Xi. *The Governance of China: Volume 4*. Beijing: Foreign Languages Press, 2022.

Jinping, Xi. *The Governance of China: Volume 1*. Beijing: Foreign Languages Press, 2014.

Jinping, Xi. *The Governance of China: Volume 3*. Beijing: Foreign Languages Press, 2020.

Jinping, Xi. *The Governance of China: Volume 2*. Beijing: Foreign Languages Press, 2017.

Kagan, Robert. *Dangerous Nation: America's Place in the World from Its Earliest Days to the Dawn of the Twentieth Century*. New York: Alfred A. Knopf, 2006.

Kagan, Robert. *The World America Made*. New York: Alfred A. Knopf, 2012.

Kahn, Joseph. "North Korea Says It Will Abandon Nuclear Efforts." *The New York Times*, September 19, 2005. https://www.nytimes.com/2005/09/19/world/asia/north-korea-says-it-will-abandon-nuclear-efforts.html.

Kempe, Frederick. "The Fourth Inflection Point: Testimony of Frederick Kempe to the House Permanent Select Committee on Intelligence." Atlantic Council, February 28, 2023. https://www.atlanticcouncil.org/commentary/testimony/the-fourth-inflection-point-testimony-of-frederick-kempe-to-the-house-permanent-select-committee-on-intelligence/.

Kengor, Paul. *11 Principles of a Reagan Conservative*. New York: Beaufort Books, 2014.

Keohane, Robert. *After Hegemony*. Princeton: Princeton University Press, 1984.

Khadka, Navin Singh. "COP26: Did India betray vulnerable nations?" BBC, November 16, 2021. https://www.bbc.com/news/world-asia-india-59286790.

Kheel, Rebecca. "Top Admiral: North Korea Wants to Reunify Peninsula, Not Protect Rule." *The Hill*, February 14, 2018. https://thehill.com/policy/defense/373803-top-admiral-north-korea-wants-to-reunify-peninsula-not-protect-regime/.

Kilborn, Peter T. "U.S. Puts 15% Tariff on Lumber." *The New York Times*, October 17, 1986. https://www.nytimes.com/1986/10/17/business/us-puts-15-tariff-on-lumber.html.

Kimball, Daryl G. "Looking Back: The Nuclear Arms Control Legacy of Ronald Reagan." Arms Control Association, July 8, 2004. https://www.armscontrol.org/act/2004_07-08/Reagan.

Kim, Jack, and Lee Jae-won. "North Korea Shells South in Fiercest Attack in Decades." Reuters, November 22, 2010. https://www.reuters.com/article/us-korea-north-artillery/north-korea-shells-south-in-fiercest-attack-in-decades-idUSTRE6AM0YS20101123.

"Kim Jong-un's Daughter Shows Off Her US$1,900 Dior Kids Coat: The North Korean Dictator's 10-Year-Old Caused uproar with the Luxury Jacket, Just Like Her Dad Did with His IWC Portofino Automatic Watch." *South China Morning Post*, March 27, 2023. https://www.scmp.com/magazines/style/news-trends/article/3214977/kim-jong-uns-daughter-shows-her-us1900-dior-kids-coat-north-korean-dictators-10-year-old-caused.

Kindleberger, Charles P. *The World in Depression: 1929-1939*. Berkeley, University of California Press, 1973.

Kine, Phelim. "China Is 'Infinitely Stronger than the Soviet Union Ever Was.'" *Politico*, April 28, 2023. https://www.politico.com/newsletters/global-insider/2023/04/28/china-is-infinitely-stronger-than-the-soviet-union-ever-was-00094266.

King, Seth S. "U.S. Plans Quotas on Sugar Imports." *The New York Times*, May 5, 1982. https://www.nytimes.com/1982/05/05/business/us-plans-quotas-on-sugar-imports.html.

Kirkpatrick, Jeane. "'Blame America First'—Remarks at the 1984 Republican National Committee—Aug. 20, 1984." Speech, Dallas, TX, August 20, 1984. Archives of Women's Political Communication, Iowa State University. Accessed April 18, 2023. https://awpc.cattcenter.iastate.edu/2017/03/09/remarks-at-the-1984-rnc-aug-20-1984/.

Klehr, Harvey and John Earl Haynes. *The Soviet World of American Communism*. New Haven: Yale University Press, 1998.

"Knit Socks and Hosiery." Observatory of Economic Complexity, 2020. https://oec.world/en/profile/hs/knit-socks-and-hosiery.

Kochis, Daniel. "Nord Stream 2 Is Complete—What Now?" The Heritage Foundation, January 10, 2022. https://www.heritage.org/europe/report/nord-stream-2-complete-what-now.

Komiya, Ryutaro, and Mutsunori Irino. "Japan's Economic and Industrial Policy in the 1980's." In *Keynes and the Economic Policies of the 1980s*, edited by Mario Baldassarri. London: Palgrave Macmillan, 1992. https://doi.org/10.1007/978-1-349-12815-0_7.

Koonin, Steven E. *Unsettled: What Climate Science Tells Us, What it Doesn't, and Why It Matters*. New York: BenBella Books, 2021.

Koop, Avery. "Mapped: All the World's Military Personnel." *Visual Capitalist*, March 11, 2022. https://www.visualcapitalist.com/mapped-all-the-worlds-military-personnel/.

Kreutzer, David W., and Paige Lambermont. *The Environmental Quality Index: Environmental Quality Weighed Against Oil and Gas Production*. Institute for Energy Research, February 2023. https://www.instituteforenergyresearch.org/wp-content/uploads/2023/02/IER-EQI-2023.pdf.

Kristensen, Hans M., and Matt Korda. "North Korean Nuclear Weapons, 2022." *Bulletin of the Atomic Scientists* 78, no. 5 (2022): 273–294. https://doi.org/10.1080/00963402.2022.2109341.

Kroenig, Matthew and Dan Negrea. "Why 'Confrontation' with China Cannot Be Avoided." *The National Interest*, November 26, 2021. https://nationalinterest.org/feature/why-%E2%80%98confrontation%E2%80%99-china-cannot-be-avoided-196926.

Kroenig, Matthew, and Jeffrey Cimmino. *Global Strategy 2021: An Allied Strategy for China*. Atlantic Council Strategy Paper series, December 2020. https://www.atlanticcouncil.org/wp-content/uploads/2020/12/Global-Strategy-2021-An-Allied-Strategy-for-China.pdf.

Kroenig, Matthew. "China's Nuclear Silos and the Arms-Control Fantasy." *The Wall Street Journal*, July 7, 2021. https://www.wsj.com/articles/chinas-nuclear-silos-and-the-arms-control-fantasy-11625696243.

Kroenig, Matthew. *Deterring Chinese Strategic Attack: Grappling with the Implications of China's Strategic Forces Buildup*. Atlantic Council, November 2, 2021. https://www.atlanticcouncil.org/wp-content/uploads/2021/11/Deterring_Chinese_Strategic_Attack_Rpt_10312190.pdf.

Kroenig, Matthew. *Exporting the Bomb: Technology Transfer and the Spread of Nuclear Weapons*. New York: Cornell University Press, 2010.

Kroenig, Matthew. "Facing Reality: Getting NATO Ready for a New Cold War." *Survival* 57, no.1 (2015): 49–70. https://doi.org/10.1080/00396338.2015.1008295.

Kroenig, Matthew. "How to Deter Russian Nuclear Use in Ukraine—and Respond If Deterrence Fails." Memo to the President, Atlantic Council, September 16, 2022. https://www.atlanticcouncil.org/content-series/memo-to-the-president/memo-to-the-president-how-to-deter-russian-nuclear-use-in-ukraine-and-respond-if-deterrence-fails/.

Kroenig, Matthew. "The Power Delusion." *Foreign Policy*, November 11, 2020. https://foreignpolicy.com/2020/11/11/china-united-states-democracy-ideology-competition-rivalry-great-powers-power-delusion/.

Kroenig, Matthew. *The Return of Great Power Rivalry: Democracy Versus Autocracy from the Ancient World to the U.S. and China*. New York: Oxford University Press, 2020.

Kroenig, Matthew. "The Return to the Pressure Track: The Trump Administration and the Iran Nuclear Deal." *Diplomacy & Statecraft* 29, no. 1 (2018): 94–104. https://doi.org/10.1080/09592296.2017.1420529.

Kroenig, Matthew. *A Time to Attack: The Looming Iranian Threat*. New York: St. Martin's Press, 2014.

Kroenig, Matthew. "Time to Attack Iran: Why a Strike Is the Least Bad Option." *Foreign Affairs*, January 1, 2012. https://www.foreignaffairs.com/articles/middle-east/2012-01-01/time-attack-iran.

Kroenig, Matthew. "The United States Should Not Align with Russia against China." *Foreign Policy*, May 13, 2020, https://foreignpolicy.com/2020/05/13/united-states-should-not-align-russia-against-china-geopolitical-rivalry-authoritarian-partnership/.

Kroenig, Matthew. "Trump's Plan B for Iran." Atlantic Council, May 23, 2018. https://www.atlanticcouncil.org/blogs/new-atlanticist/trump-s-plan-b-for-iran/.

Kroenig, Matthew. "Washington Must Prepare for War with Both Russia and China." *Foreign Policy*, February 18, 2022. https://foreignpolicy.com/2022/02/18/us-russia-china-war-nato-quadrilateral-security-dialogue/.

Kroenig, Matthew. "Washington Needs a Better Plan for Competing with China." *Foreign Policy*, August 7, 2020. https://foreignpolicy.com/2020/08/07/washington-needs-a-better-plan-for-competing-with-china/.

Kuo, Lily. "Australia Called 'Gum Stuck to China's Shoe' by State Media in Coronavirus Investigation Stoush." *The Guardian*, April 28, 2020. https://www.theguardian.com/world/2020/apr/28/australia-called-gum-stuck-to-chinas-shoe-by-state-media-in-coronavirus-investigation-stoush.

Kurlantzick, Joshua. "China's Growing Attempts to Influence U.S. Politics." Council on Foreign Relations, October 31, 2022. https://www.cfr.org/article/chinas-growing-attempts-influence-us-politics.

Kuzio, Taras. "Putin's Failing Ukraine Invasion Proves Russia Is No Superpower." Atlantic Council, November 1, 2022. https://www.atlanticcouncil.org/blogs/ukrainealert/putins-failing-ukraine-invasion-proves-russia-is-no-superpower/.

La Barca, Giuseppe. *International Trade under President Reagan: US Trade Policy in the 1980s*. London: Bloomsbury Publishing 2023.

Lacatus, Corina. "Populism and President Trump's Approach to Foreign Policy: An Analysis of Tweets and Rally Speeches." *Political Studies* 41, no. 1 (2021): 31–47. https://doi.org/10.1177/0263395720935380.

Lafakis, Chris, et al. "The Economic Implications of Climate Change." Moody's Analytics, June 2019. https://www.moodysanalytics.com/-/media/article/2019/economic-implications-of-climate-change.pdf.

Landler, Mark, and Ana Swanson, "U.S. and Europe Outline Deal to Ease Trade Feud." *The New York Times*, July 25, 2018. https://www.nytimes.com/2018/07/25/us/politics/trump-europe-trade.html.

Lee, Amanda. "Explainer: What Is China's Social Credit System and Why Is It Controversial?" *South China Morning Post*, August 9, 2020. https://www.scmp.com/economy/china-economy/article/3096090/what-chinas-social-credit-system-and-why-it-controversial.

Leeds, Brett Ashley. "Alliance Reliability in Times of War: Explaining State Decisions to Violate Treaties." *International Organization* 57, no. 4 (2003): 801–827. http://www.jstor.org/stable/3594847.

Leeds, Brett Ashley. "Domestic Political Institutions, Credible Commitments, and International Cooperation." *American Journal of Political Science* 43, no. 4 (1999): 979–1002. https://doi.org/10.2307/2991814.

Lee, Elizabeth. "Biden Immigration Changes Raise Hopes, Concerns on US-Mexico Border." Voice of America, March 5, 2021. https://www.voanews.com/a/usa_immigration_biden-immigration-changes-raise-hopes-concerns-us-mexico-border/6202931.html.

Lehto, Essi, and Mike Stone. "Finland Orders 64 Lockheed F-35 Fighter Jets for $9.4 Bln." Reuters, December 10, 2021. https://www.reuters.com/business/aerospace-defense/lockheed-f-35-jet-wins-finnish-fighter-competition-source-2021-12-10/.

Leopold, Evelyn. "Russia, China, Object to Tough Sanctions on Iran." *Reuters*, March 8, 2007. https://www.reuters.com/article/us-iran-un-resolution/russia-china-object-to-tough-sanctions-on-iran-idUSN0847566420070309.

Lerer, Lisa. "How the G.O.P. Lost Its Clear Voice on Foreign Policy." *The New York Times*, April 15, 2021. https://www.nytimes.com/2021/04/15/us/politics/republicans-afghanistan.html.

Lettow, Paul. *Ronald Reagan and his Quest to Abolish Nuclear Weapons*. New York: Random House, 2005.

Library of Congress. "1986: Immigration Reform and Control Act of 1986." Accessed June 5, 2023. https://guides.loc.gov/latinx-civil-rights/irca.

Liebermann, Oren and Natasha Bertrand. "ISIS-K Suicide Bomber Who Carried Out Deadly Kabul Airport Attack Had Been Released from Prison Days Earlier." CNN. Updated October 6, 2021. https://www.cnn.com/2021/10/06/politics/kabul-airport-attacker-prison/index.html.

Li, Shirley. "How Hollywood Sold Out to China." *The Atlantic*, September 10, 2021. https://www.theatlantic.com/culture/archive/2021/09/how-hollywood-sold-out-to-china/620021/.

Lockie, Alex. "Trump Promises an 'Event the Likes of Which Nobody's Ever Seen' If North Korea Attacks Guam." *Insider*, August 10, 2017. https://www.businessinsider.com/trump-north-koreas-guam-nuclear-event-posture-2017-8.

Loris, Nicolas. "Paris climate agreement: Instead of regulations and mandates, embrace markets." Heritage Foundation, February 25, 2021. https://www.heritage.org/energy-economics/report/paris-climate-agreement-instead-regulations-and-mandates-embrace-markets.

Losh, Jack. "Russian Troops in Nagorno-Karabakh 'Clearly a Win for Moscow.'" *Foreign Policy*, November 25, 2020. https://foreignpolicy.com/2020/11/25/russian-troops-nagorno-karabakh-peacekeepers-win-moscow-armenia-azerbaijan/.

Lundestad, Geir. "'Empire by Invitation' in the American Century." *Diplomatic History* 23, no. 2 (1999): 189–217. http://www.jstor.org/stable/24913738.

Lundestad, Geir. "Empire by Invitation? The United States and Western Europe, 1945–1952." *Journal of Peace Research* 23, no. 3 (1986): 263–77. http://www.jstor.org/stable/423824.

Mansfield, Edward D., Helen V. Milner, and B. Peter Rosendorff. "Why Democracies Cooperate More: Electoral Control and International Trade Agreements." *International Organization* 56, no. 3 (2002): 477–513. http://www.jstor.org/stable/3078586.

Macias, Amanda. "Biden's Effort to Tout Progress in Saudi Relationship Overshadowed by Khashoggi Killing." CNBC, July 15, 2022. https://www.cnbc.com/2022/07/15/watch-biden-speaks-after-meeting-mbs-in-saudi-arabia.html.

Macias, Amanda. "Pentagon Admits Killing 10 Civilians, Including up to 7 Children, in Kabul Drone Strike Last Month." CNBC, September 17, 2021. https://www.cnbc.com/2021/09/17/us-airstrike-in-kabul-last-month-killed-10-civilians-including-seven-children-pentagon-says.html.

Macias, Amanda. "Trump Signs $783 Billion Defense Bill. Here's What the Pentagon Is Poised to Get." CNBC, December 20, 2019. https://www.cnbc.com/2019/12/21/trump-signs-738-billion-defense-bill.html.

Mackenzie, Jean. "Nuclear Weapons: Why South Koreans Want the Bomb." BBC, April 22, 2023. https://www.bbc.com/news/world-asia-65333139.

MacMillan, Margaret. *Paris 1919: Six Months that Changed the World*. New York: Random House Trade Paperbacks, 2003.

Made in China 2025: Global Ambitions Built on Local Protections. US Chamber of Commerce, 2017. https://www.uschamber.com/assets/documents/final_made_in_china_2025_report_full.pdf.

Marques, Clara Ferreira. "China is redrawing the world's energy map." *Bloomberg*, August 10, 2021. https://www.bloomberg.com/news/articles/2021-08-10/china-is-redrawing-the-world-s-energy-map.

Mason, Jeff, Humeyra Pamuk, and Dmitry Antonov. "Biden Warns Putin with Sanctions as West Steps Up Ukraine Defenses." *Reuters*, January 26, 2022. https://www.reuters.com/world/europe/us-seeks-protect-europes-energy-supplies-if-russia-invades-ukraine-2022-01-25/.

Martin, Philip L. "Select Commission Suggests Changes in Immigration Policy—A Review Essay." *Monthly Labor Review* 105 no. 2 (February 1982): 31–37. https://www.jstor.org/stable/41841751.

Masters, Jonathan. "Ukraine: Conflict at the Crossroads of Europe and Russia." Council on Foreign
Relations, February 14, 2023. https://www.cfr.org/backgrounder/ukraine-conflict-crossroads-europe-and-russia.

Mastro, Oriana Skylar. "How China Is Bending the Rules in the South China Sea." *The Interpreter*, Lowry Institute, February 17, 2021. https://www.lowyinstitute.org/the-interpreter/how-china-bending-rules-south-china-sea.

Meredith, Sam and Natasha Turak. "Trump Slams Germany at NATO Summit: It's 'Totally Controlled by Russia.'" CNBC, July 11, 2018. https://www.cnbc.com/2018/07/11/trump-slams-germany-at-nato-summit-says-its-a-captive-of-russia.html.

Lyngaas, Sean. "Russia and China Are Promoting US Voting Misinformation ahead of Midterms, FBI Warns." CNN, October 3, 2022. https://www.cnn.com/2022/10/03/politics/2022-election-security-fbi/index.html.

Macrotrends. "U.S. Trade to GDP Ratio 1970–2023." Accessed January 20, 2023. https://www.macrotrends.net/countries/USA/united-states/trade-gdp-ratio.

McConnell, Mitch. "ICYMI: McConnell Remarks at Munich Security Conference." Mitch McConnell: Senate Republican Leader, February 17, 2023. https://www.republicanleader.senate.gov/newsroom/press-releases/icymi-mcconnell-remarks-at-munich-security-conference-.

McFall, Caitlin. "Iran Reissues Threat to 'Kill Trump, Pompeo' for Soleimani Death When Announcing Long-Range Cruise Missile." Fox News, February 28, 2023. https://www.foxnews.com/world/iran-reissues-threat-kill-trump-pompeo-soleimani-death-announcing-long-range-cruise-missile.

McMaster, H. R. *Battlegrounds: The Fight to Defend the Free World.* New York: HarperCollins, 2020.

Mearsheimer, John J. *The Tragedy of Great Power Politics*. New York: W. W. Norton, 2001.

Mearsheimer, John J. "Why the Ukraine Crisis Is the West's Fault: The Liberal Delusions that Provoked Putin." *Foreign Affairs*, August 18, 2014. https://www.foreignaffairs.com/articles/russia-fsu/2014-08-18/why-ukraine-crisis-west-s-fault.

Merchant, Nomaan. "US: Russia Spent $300M to Covertly Influence World Politics." Associated Press, September 13, 2022. https://apnews.com/article/russia-ukraine-putin-biden-politics-presidential-elec-tions-03d0ae84fb34833b78b1753d0a9602db.

Merriam-Webster. "Si vis pacem, para bellum." Accessed February 14, 2023. https://www.merriam-webster.com/dictionary/si%20vis%20pacem%2C%20para%20bellum.

"Migrant Protection Protocols." Department of Homeland Security, January 24, 2019. https://www.dhs.gov/news/2019/01/24/migrant-protection-protocols.

Military and Security Developments Involving the People's Republic of China 2022. U.S. Department of Defense, November 2022. https://media.defense.gov/2022/Nov/29/2003122279/-1/-1/1/2022-military-and-security-devel-opments-involving-the-peoples-republic-of-china.pdf.

"Military Spending by Country 2023." World Population Review, 2023. https://worldpopulationreview.com/country-rankings/military-spending-by-country.

Miller, Nicholas L., and Tristan A. Volpe. "The rise of the autocratic nuclear marketplace." *Journal of Strategic Studies* (April 2022): 1-39. https://doi.org/10.1080/01402390.2022.2052725.

Miller, Paul D. *American Power and Liberal Order: A Conservative Internation-alist Grand Strategy*. Washington, D.C.: Georgetown University Press, 2016.

Milman, Oliver. "Governments falling woefully short of Paris climate pledges, study finds." *The Guardian*, September 15, 2021. https://www.theguardian.com/science/2021/sep/15/governments-falling-short-paris-climate-pledges-study.

Milner, Helen V., and Bumba Mukherjee. "Democratization and Economic Globalization." *Annual Review of Political Science* 12 (2009): 163–181. https://doi.org/10.1146/annurev.polisci.12.110507.114722.

Milner, Helen V., and Keiko Kubota. "Why the Move to Free Trade? Democracy and Trade Policy in the Developing Countries." *International Organization* 59, no. 1 (2005): 107–143. https://doi.org/10.1017/S002081830505006X.

Mollman, Steve. "Top Economist Sees 'Totally Avoidable' Recession Ahead." *Fortune*, October 9, 2022. https://fortune.com/2022/10/09/recession-fed-mistakes-interest-rates-economist-mohamed-el-erian/.

Morgan, Piers. "DeSantis Brands Putin 'a War Criminal' Who Should Be 'Held Accountable' for Ukraine Invasion." *New York Post*, March 22, 2023. https://nypost.com/2023/03/22/desantis-brands-putin-a-war-criminal-who-should-be-held-accountable-for-ukraine-invasion/.

Morrissey, Kate. "'Remain in Mexico' One Year Later: How a Single Policy Transformed the U.S. Asylum System." *The San Diego Union-Tribune*, January 29, 2020. https://www.sandiegouniontribune.com/news/immigration/story/2020-01-29/remain-in-mexico-one-year-later-how-a-single-policy-transformed-the-u-s-asylum-system.

"Mullen: Debt Is Top National Security Threat." *CNN*, August 27, 2010. http://www.cnn.com/2010/US/08/27/debt.security.mullen/index.html.

Munroe, Tony, Andrew Osborn, and Humeyra Pamuk. "China, Russia Partner Up against West at Olympics Summit." Reuters, February 4, 2022. https://www.reuters.com/world/europe/russia-china-tell-nato-stop-expansion-moscow-backs-beijing-taiwan-2022-02-04/.

Murphy, Dan. "Japan Has Become the 'Obvious Target' for Trump's Next Trade Salvo." CNBC, September 7, 2018. https://www.cnbc.com/2018/09/07/japan-has-become-the-obvious-target-for-trumps-next-trade-salvo.html.

Murray, Christine. "Shipment of Chinese Hair Goods Seized by U.S. Officials Suspecting Forced Labor." Reuters, July 1, 2020. https://www.reuters.com/article/us-usa-trafficking-seizure-trfn/shipment-of-chinese-hair-goods-seized-by-u-s-officials-suspecting-forced-labor-idUSKBN2427IN.

Nahmias, Omri. "Blinken: We Could Have Extended the Iran Arms Embargo from Inside the Deal." *The Jerusalem Post*, August 6, 2020. https://www.jpost.com/international/blinken-we-could-have-extended-the-iran-arms-embargo-from-inside-the-deal-637746.

Nakashima, Ellen, Anna Fifield, and Joby Warrick. "North Korea Could Cross ICBM Threshold Next Year, U.S. Officials Warn in New Assessment." *The Washington Post*, July 25, 2017. https://www.washingtonpost.com/world/national-security/north-korea-could-cross-icbm-threshold-next-year-us-officials-warn-in-new-assessment/2017/07/25/4107dc4a-70af-11e7-8f39-eeb7d3a2d304_story.html.

NASA. "Carbon dioxide." Vital Signs of the Planet. Accessed June 6, 2023. https://climate.nasa.gov/vital-signs/carbon-dioxide/.

NASA. "World of change: Global temperatures." Earth Observatory. Accessed June 6, 2023. https://earthobservatory.nasa.gov/world-of-change/global-temperatures.

National Oceanic and Atmospheric Administration. "Climate change impacts." Last modified August 13, 2021. https://www.noaa.gov/education/resource-collections/climate/climate-change-impacts.

National Security Strategy of the United States of America. White House, December 2017. https://trumpwhitehouse.archives.gov/wp-content/uploads/2017/12/NSS-Final-12-18-2017-0905.pdf.

National Security Strategy. White House, October 2022. https://www.whitehouse.gov/wp-content/uploads/2022/10/Biden-Harris-Administrations-National-Security-Strategy-10.2022.pdf

Nau, Henry R. *Conservative Internationalism: Armed Diplomacy under Jefferson, Polk, Truman, and Reagan*. Princeton: Princeton University Press, 2015.

Nereim, Vivian. "China and Saudi Arabia Sign Strategic Partnership as Xi Visits Kingdom." *The New York Times*, December 8, 2022. https://www.nytimes.com/2022/12/08/world/middleeast/china-saudi-arabia-agreement.html.

Nichols, Michelle. "Russia, China Build Case at U.N. to Protect Iran." Reuters, June 9, 2020. https://www.reuters.com/article/us-usa-iran-russia-china/russia-china-build-case-at-u-n-to-protect-iran-from-u-s-sanctions-threat-idUSKBN23G2YR.

Niebuhr, Reinhold. *Christian Realism and Political Problems. New York: Charles Scribner's Sons, 1953.*

Niskanen, William A. *Reaganomics: An Insider's Account of the Policies and the People*. New York: Oxford University Press, 1988.

Ni, Vincent. "John Cena 'Very Sorry' for Saying Taiwan Is a Country." *The Guardian*, May 25, 2021. https://www.theguardian.com/world/2021/may/26/john-cena-very-sorry-for-saying-taiwan-is-a-country.

Nikitin, Mary Beth D. *North Korea's Nuclear Weapons and Missile Programs*. CRS Report No. IF10472. Washington, D.C.: Congressional Research Service, 2023. https://crsreports.congress.gov/product/pdf/IF/IF10472/28.

Nikolskaya, Polina. "Exclusive: Despite Sanctions, Russian Tanker Supplied Fuel to North Korean Ship-Crew Members." Reuters, February 26, 2019. https://www.reuters.com/article/us-northkorea-sanctions-russia-exclusive/exclusive-despite-sanctions-russian-tanker-supplied-fuel-to-north-korean-ship-crew-members-idUSKCN1QF0XX.

Niksch, Larry A. *North Korea's Nuclear Development and Diplomacy*. CRS Report No. RL33590. Washington, D.C.: Congressional Research Service, 2010. http://large.stanford.edu/courses/2011/ph241/agaian1/docs/RL33590.pdf.

The 9/11 Commission Report. National Commission on Terrorist Attacks Upon the United States, July 22, 2004. https://www.9-11commission.gov/report/911Report.pdf.

Nissenbaum, Dion, and Chun Han Wong. "China, Russia, Iran Hold Joint Military Drills in Gulf of Oman." *The Wall Street Journal*, March 15, 2023. https://www.wsj.com/articles/china-russia-iran-hold-joint-military-drills-in-gulf-of-oman-aba5f55e.

"North Korean Nuclear Negotiations: 1985–2022." Council on Foreign Relations. Accessed May 23, 2023. https://www.cfr.org/timeline/north-korean-nuclear-negotiations.

"North Korea Overview." Nuclear Threat Initiative, October 19, 2021. https://www.nti.org/analysis/articles/north-korea-overview/.

"North Korea's Military Capabilities." Council on Foreign Relations, June 28, 2022. https://www.cfr.org/backgrounder/north-korea-nuclear-weapons-missile-tests-military-capabilities.

Obama, Barack. "News Conference by President Obama, 4/04/2009." Press conference, Washington, D.C., April 4, 2009, White House. https://obamawhitehouse.archives.gov/the-press-office/news-conference-president-obama-4042009.

Obama, Barack. "Renewing American Leadership." *Foreign Affairs*, July 1, 2007. https://www.foreignaffairs.com/united-states/renewing-american-leadership.

Office of the House Historian. "Depression, War, and Civil Rights: Hispanics in the Southwest." Accessed June 16, 2023. https://history.house.gov/Exhibitions-and-Publications/HAIC/Historical-Essays/Separate-Interests/Depression-War-Civil-Rights/.

Office of the Press Secretary. "Statement by the President on North Korea's Nuclear Test." White House, September 9, 2016. https://obamawhitehouse.archives.gov/the-press-office/2016/09/09/statement-president-north-koreas-nuclear-test.

O'Grady, Mary Anastasia. "Putin Is Already in Cuba and Venezuela." *The Wall Street Journal*, January 30, 2022. https://www.wsj.com/articles/putin-is-already-in-cuba-and-venezuela-south-america-influence-western-hemisphere-ukraine-11643567547.

O'Keeffe, Kate. "U.S. Approves Nearly All Tech Exports to China, Data Shows." *The Wall Street Journal*, August 16, 2022. https://www.wsj.com/articles/u-s-approves-nearly-all-tech-exports-to-china-data-shows-11660596886.

Oneal, John R. and Bruce Russett, "Assessing the Liberal Peace with Alternative Specifications: Trade Still Reduces Conflict." *Journal of Peace Research* 36, no. 4 (1999): 423–442. http://www.jstor.org/stable/425297.

"145 Key Tourism Statistics." World Tourism Organization. Last modified December 22, 2022. https://www.unwto.org/tourism-statistics/
key-tourism-statistics.

Ordoñez, Franco. "Biden Wants a 'Stable, Predictable' Relationship with
Russia. That's Complicated." NPR, May 21, 2021. https://www.npr.
org/2021/05/21/999196021/biden-wants-a-stable-predictable-relation-
ship-with-russia-thats-complicated.

Ortiz-Ospina, Esteban, Diana Beltekian, and Max Roser. "Trade and Globalization." OurWorldInData.org, 2018. https://ourworldindata.org/
trade-and-globalization.

Osborn, Andrew, and Phil Stewart. "Russia Begins Syria Air Strikes in Its Biggest
Mideast Intervention in Decades." Reuters, September 30, 2015. https://
www.reuters.com/article/us-mideast-crisis-russia/russia-begins-syria-
air-strikes-in-its-biggest-mideast-intervention-in-decades-idUSKCN-
0RU0MG20150930.

O'Sullivan, Meghan L. *Windfall: How the New Energy Abundance Upends Global
Politics and Strengthens America's Power*. New York: Simon & Schuster,
2018.

OurWorldInData.org. "GDP Per Capita, 1940 to 2018." Accessed April
14, 2023. https://ourworldindata.org/grapher/gdp-per-capita-maddi-
son-2020?tab=chart&time=1940..2018&country=OWID_WRL~USA.

Pak, Jung H. *The Education of Kim Jung-Un*. Brookings Essay series, February
2018. https://www.brookings.edu/essay/the-education-of-kim-jong-un/.

Patrick, John. "Democratic Professors Outnumber Republicans 9 to 1 at Top Colleges." *Washington Examiner*, January 23, 2020. https://www.washingtonexaminer.com/opinion/
democratic-professors-outnumber-republicans-9-to-1-at-top-colleges.

Patteson, Callie. "John Kerry Prioritizes Climate Change, Not Uyghur
Abuses, with China." *New York Post*, September 23, 2021. https://nypost.
com/2021/09/23/john-kerry-says-climate-change-is-priority-with-china/.

Pearson, Erica. "1986 West Berlin Discoteque Bombing." Encyclopedia Britannica. https://www.britannica.com/event/
West-Berlin-discotheque-bombing-1986.

Peel, Michael. "Iran, Russia and China Prop Up Assad Economy." *Financial Times*, June 27, 2013. https://www.ft.com/
content/79eca81c-df48-11e2-a9f4-00144feab7de.

Peleschuk, Dan. "As Xi and Putin Bid Farewell in Moscow, Russia Unleashed
Missiles on Ukraine." *The Sydney Morning Herald*, March 23, 2023. https://
www.smh.com.au/world/europe/we-are-driving-changes-in-the-world-

together-xi-jinping-tells-vladimir-putin-as-he-departs-kremlin-20230323-p5cuio.html.

Pence, Michael R. "Remarks by Vice President Mike Pence to the Federalist Society." Speech, Philadelphia, PA, February 4, 2017. White House. https://trumpwhitehouse.archives.gov/briefings-statements/remarks-vice-president-mike-pence-federalist-society/.

Pence, Michael R. *So Help Me God*. New York: Simon & Schuster, 2022.

Pence, Michael R (@VP45). "Peace only comes through strength. @POTUS believes we must be strong, able to confront all who would threaten our freedom & way of life." Twitter, February 18, 2017. https://twitter.com/VP45/status/832876767610183680.

Pennington, Matthew. "Trump Strategy on NKorea: 'Maximum Pressure and Engagement.'" Associated Press, April 14, 2017. https://apnews.com/article/china-ap-top-news-north-korea-asia-pacific-pyongyang-86626d21ea2b-45c79457a873a747c452.

Perry, Mark J. "Video of the Day: Reagan's Thanksgiving Radio Address on Free Trade 31 Years Ago Today." American Enterprise Institute, November 26, 2019. https://www.aei.org/carpe-diem/video-of-the-day-reagans-thanksgiving-radio-address-on-free-trade-31-years-ago-today/.

Petesch, Carley, and Gerald Imray. "Russian Mercenaries Are Putin's 'Coercive Tool' in Africa." Associated Press, April 23, 2022. https://apnews.com/article/russia-ukraine-putin-technology-business-mali-d0d2c96e-01d299a68e00d3a0828ba895.

Phillip, Abby. "O'Reilly Told Trump that Putin Is a Killer. Trump's Reply: 'You Think Our Country Is So Innocent?'" *The Washington Post*, February 4, 2017. https://www.washingtonpost.com/news/post-politics/wp/2017/02/04/oreilly-told-trump-that-putin-is-a-killer-trumps-reply-you-think-our-countrys-so-innocent/.

Pompeo, Michael R. (@mikepompeo). "America is the most exceptional nation in the history of civilization. We ought to be proud of that." Twitter, July 2, 2021. https://twitter.com/mikepompeo/status/1411086762349318145.

Pompeo, Michael R. (@mikepompeo). "Peace is achieved through strength, something this Administration has yet to show." Twitter, September 24, 2021. https://twitter.com/mikepompeo/status/1441392698552881154.

Pompeo, Michael R. "Communist China and the Free World's Future." U.S. Department of State, July 23, 2020. https://2017-2021.state.gov/communist-china-and-the-free-worlds-future-2/index.html.

Pompeo, Michael R. *Never Give an Inch: Fighting for the America I Love*. New York: Broadside Books, 2023.

Pompeo, Michael R. "War, Ukraine, and a Global Alliance for Freedom." Speech, Washington, D.C., June 24, 2022. https://s3.amazonaws.com/media. hudson.org/Transcript-War,%20Ukraine,%20and%20a%20Global%20Alliance%20for%20Freedom%20.pdf.

"Press Briefing by Press Secretary Jen Psaki." White House, October 18, 2021. https://www.whitehouse.gov/briefing-room/press-briefings/2021/10/18/ press-briefing-by-press-secretary-jen-psaki-october-18-2021/.

"Prisons of North Korea." U.S. Department of State. August 25, 2017. https://2017-2021.state.gov/prisons-of-north-korea/index.html.

Providing for the Common Defense: The Assessment and Recommendations of the National Defense Strategy Commission. United States Institute of Peace, November 13, 2018. https://www.usip.org/publications/2018/11/ providing-common-defense.

"Public's top priority for 2022: Strengthening the nation's economy." Pew Research Center, February 16, 2022. https://www.pewresearch.org/politics/2022/02/16/ publics-top-priority-for-2022-strengthening-the-nations-economy/.

Rajah, Roland, and Alyssa Leng. "Chart of the Week: Global Trade through a US-China Lens." *The Interpreter*, Lowy Institute, December 18, 2019. https://www.lowyinstitute.org/the-interpreter/ chart-week-global-trade-through-us-china-lens.

Rasser, Martijn, et al. *Common Code: An Alliance Framework for Democratic Technology Policy.* Center for a New American Security, October 21, 2020. https://www.cnas.org/publications/reports/common-code.

"Readout of President Joe Biden's Meeting with President Xi Jinping of the People's Republic of China." White House, November 14, 2022. https://www. whitehouse.gov/briefing-room/statements-releases/2022/11/14/readout-of-president-joe-bidens-meeting-with-president-xi-jinping-of-the-peoples-republic-of-china/.

Reagan, Ronald. "Address Accepting the Presidential Nomination at the Republican National Convention." Speech, Detroit, MI, July 17, 1980. The American Presidency Project, University of California Santa Barbara. https:// www.presidency.ucsb.edu/documents/address-accepting-the-presidential-nomination-the-republican-national-convention-miami.

Reagan, Ronald. "Address to the Nation on the United States Air Strike Against Libya." Speech, Washington, D.C., April 14, 1986. Ronald Reagan Presidential Library & Museum. https://www.reaganlibrary.gov/archives/speech/ address-nation-united-states-air-strike-against-libya.

Reagan, Ronald. "Evil Empire." Speech, Orlando, FL, March 8, 1983. Voices of Democracy. https://voicesofdemocracy.umd.edu/reagan-evil-empire-speech-text/

Reagan, Ronald. "Farewell Address to the Nation." Speech, Washington, D.C., January 11, 1989. Reagan Foundation. https://www.reaganfoundation.org/media/128652/farewell.pdf.

Reagan, Ronald. "Remarks at a White House Meeting with Business and Trade Leaders." Speech, Washington, D.C., September 23, 1985. Ronald Reagan Presidential Library & Museum. https://www.reaganlibrary.gov/archives/speech/remarks-white-house-meeting-business-and-trade-leaders.

"Report: China Emissions Exceed All Developed Nations Combined." BBC, May 7, 2021. https://www.bbc.com/news/world-asia-57018837.

Rhodes, Ben. *The World As It Is: A Memoir of the Obama White House*. New York: Random House, 2018.

"Rights Group: Iran Executes 2 Gay Men over Sodomy Charges." Associated Press, February 1, 2022. https://apnews.com/article/middle-east-iran-crime-dubai-united-arab-emirates-e3d7108441665c40982329f26ff07fc9.

Ritchie, Hannah, and Max Roser. "Forests and Deforestation." OurWorldInData.org, 2021. https://ourworldindata.org/forests-and-deforestation.

Ritchie, Hannah, Lucas Rodés-Guirao, Edouard Mathieu, Marcel Gerber, Esteban Ortiz-Ospina, Joe Hasell, and Max Roser. "Future Population Growth." OurWorldInData.org. Last modified November 2019. https://ourworldindata.org/future-population-growth.

Ritchie, Hannah, Max Roser and Pablo Rosado. "CO₂ and Greenhouse Gas Emissions." OurWorldInData.org, 2020. https://ourworldindata.org/co2-and-greenhouse-gas-emissions.

Rock, Taylor. "Kim Jong Un Indulges in Expensive Booze and Meat-Covered Pizza while Country Hungers, Report Says." *Los Angeles Times*, January 3, 2018. https://www.latimes.com/food/sns-dailymeal-1865335-eat-kim-jong-un-north-korea-diet-booze-and-meat-pizza-010318-20180103-story.html.

Rodgers, Lucy, and Dominic Bailey. "Trump Wall: How Much Has He Actually Built?" BBC, October 31, 2020. https://www.bbc.com/news/world-us-canada-46824649.

Roosevelt, Theodore. "Address of Vice President Roosevelt, Minnesota State Fair." Speech, Minneapolis, MN, September 2, 1901. Theodore Roosevelt Center, 2023, https://www.theodorerooseveltcenter.org/Research/Digital-Library/Record?libID=o286433.

Roser, Max, Pablo Arriagada, Joe Hasell, Hannah Ritchie and Esteban Ortiz-Os-pina. "Economic Growth." OurWorldInData.org, 2013. https://ourworldin-data.org/economic-growth.

Roth, Andrew and Julian Borger. "US Says It Will Send Troops to Eastern Europe If Russia Invades Ukraine." *The Guardian*, December 6, 2021. https://www.theguardian.com/world/2021/dec/06/us-says-it-will-send-troops-to-eastern-europe-if-russia-invades-ukraine.

Rott, Nathan. "Extreme weather, fueled by climate change, cost the US $165 billion in 2022." NPR, January 10, 2023. https://www.npr.org/2023/01/10/1147986096/extreme-weather-fueled-by-climate-change-cost-the-u-s-165-billion-in-2022.

Rove, Karl. "The President's Apology Tour." *The Wall Street Journal*, April 23, 2009. https://www.wsj.com/articles/SB124044156269345357.

Rubin, Michael. "Whose Fault Is It the Last North Korean Nuclear Agreement Didn't Work?" American Enterprise Institute, March 19, 2018. https://www.aei.org/articles/whose-fault-is-it-the-last-north-korean-nuclear-agreement-didnt-work/.

Ruger, William and Michael C. Desch "Conservatism, Realism and Foreign Policy: Kissing Cousins If Not Soulmates." *The National Interest*, July 30, 2018. https://nationalinterest.org/blog/conservatism-realism-and-foreign-policy-kissing-cousins-if-not-soulmates-27242.

Ruggie, John Gerard. "International Regimes, Transactions, and Change: Embedded Liberalism in the Postwar Economic Order." *International Organization* 36, no. 2 (1982): 379–415. https://www.doi.org/10.1017/S0020818300018993.

Russett, Bruce et al., *Grasping the Democratic Peace: Principles for a Post-Cold War World*. Princeton: Princeton University Press, 1993. http://www.jstor.org/stable/j.ctt7rqf6.

"Russia Warns West over Threatening Its Troops in Breakaway Moldovan Region." Reuters, February 24, 2023. https://www.reuters.com/world/europe/russia-warns-west-over-threatening-its-troops-moldovan-region-2023-02-24/.

Samuels, David. "The Aspiring Novelist Who Became Obama's Foreign-Policy Guru." *The New York Times*, May 5, 2016. https://www.nytimes.com/2016/05/08/magazine/the-aspiring-novelist-who-became-obamas-foreign-policy-guru.html.

Sanders, Kerry. "Honduran Migrants on Caravan Hope Biden Will Be Different from Trump Administration." NBC News, February 2, 2021. YouTube video. https://youtu.be/F-YFi0fd3rA.

Sanger, David E. "North Koreans Say They Tested Nuclear Device." *The New York Times*, October 9, 2006. https://www.nytimes.com/2006/10/09/world/asia/09korea.html.

Sang-Hun, Choe, and David E. Sanger. "North Koreans Launch Rocket in Defiant Act." *The New York Times*, December 11, 2012. https://www.nytimes.com/2012/12/12/world/asia/north-korea-launches-rocket-defying-likely-sanctions.html.

Sang-Hun, Choe. "South Korea Publicly Blames the North for Ship's Sinking." *The New York Times*, May 19, 2010. https://www.nytimes.com/2010/05/20/world/asia/20korea.html.

Schadlow, Nadia. "Conservative U.S. Statecraft for the 21st Century." *Foreign Policy*, November 7, 2022. https://foreignpolicy.com/2022/11/07/us-republicans-conservative-foreign-policy-principles/.

Schamis, Hector. "At COP26, the New Cold War Comes to Climate Change." *The National Interest*, November 19, 2021. https://nationalinterest.org/feature/cop26-new-cold-war-comes-climate-change-196711.

Scheer, Steven. "With Eye to China, Israel Forms Panel to Vet Foreign Investments." Reuters, October 30, 2019. https://www.reuters.com/article/us-israel-investment-panel/with-eye-to-china-israel-forms-panel-to-vet-foreign-investments-idUSKBN1X926T

Schemmel, Alec. "GOP Rips Congress for Sending $14 Billion to Protect Ukrainian Border but Not Funding Wall." *The National Desk*, March 9, 2022. https://thenationaldesk.com/news/americas-news-now/gop-rips-congress-for-sending-14-million-to-protect-ukrainian-border-but-not-funding-wall-republicans-senate.

Schertzer, Robert and Woods, Eric Taylor. "Donald Trump and the New Nationalism in America." Ch. 5 in *The New Nationalism in America and Beyond: The Deep Roots of Ethnic Nationalism in the Digital Age*. New York: Oxford University Press, 2022.

Schmitt, Eric and Thom Shanker. *Counterstrike: The Untold Story of America's Secret Campaign against Al Qaeda*. New York: Henry Holt and Company, 2011.

Schmitt, Eric, Maggie Haberman, David E. Sanger, Helene Cooper, and Lara Jakes. "Trump Sought Options for Attacking Iran to Stop Its Growing Nuclear Program." *The New York Times*, November 16, 2020. https://www.nytimes.com/2020/11/16/us/politics/trump-iran-nuclear.html.

Schneider, Bill. "Republicans Are the New Isolationists; Will US Retreat from World Stage?" *The Hill*, October 2, 2022. https://thehill.com/opinion/campaign/3670801-republicans-are-the-new-isolationists-will-us-retreat-from-world-stage/.

Schneider, Greg and Renae Merle, "Reagan's Defense Buildup Bridged Military Eras." *The Washington Post*, June 9, 2004. https://www.washingtonpost.com/archive/business/2004/06/09/reagans-defense-buildup-bridged-military-eras/ec621466-b78e-4a2e-9f8a-50654e3f95fa/.

Schoenwald, Jonathan M. "A New Kind of Conservative: Ronald Reagan." Ch. 7 in Jonathan M. Schoenwald, *A Time for Choosing: The Rise of Modern American Conservatism*, 190–220. New York: Oxford University Press, 2001.

Schoenfeld, Steven. "Americans Are Investing More in China—and They Don't Even Know It." *Foreign Policy*, January 14, 2020. https://foreignpolicy.com/2020/01/14/americans-investment-china-emerging-markets-united-states-trade-war/.

Schreuer, Milan. "E.U. Pledges to Fight Back on Trump Tariffs as Trade War Looms." *The New York Times*, March 7, 2018. https://www.nytimes.com/2018/03/07/business/trump-tariffs-eu-trade.html.

Schuman, Michael. "Where US-China competition leaves climate change." *The Atlantic*, November 21, 2022. https://www.theatlantic.com/international/archive/2022/11/us-china-relations-climate-change/672170/.

Scott, Robert E., and Zane Mokhiber, "Growing China Trade Deficit Cost 3.7 Million American Jobs between 2001 and 2018." Economic Policy Institute, January 30, 2020. https://www.epi.org/publication/growing-china-trade-deficits-costs-us-jobs.

Seib, Gerald F., Jay Solomon, and Carol E. Lee. "Barack Obama Warns Donald Trump on North Korea Threat." *The Wall Street Journal*, November 22, 2016. https://www.wsj.com/articles/trump-faces-north-korean-challenge-1479855286.

Serr, Marcel. "North Korea Built a Nuclear Reactor for Syria (and Israel Destroyed It)." *The National Interest*, January 4, 2018. https://nationalinterest.org/blog/the-buzz/north-korea-built-nuclear-reactor-syria-israel-destroyed-it-23922.

Sengupta, Somini. "Climate change is making armed conflict worse. Here's how." *The New York Times*, March 18, 2022. https://www.nytimes.com/2022/03/18/climate/climate-armed-conflict-water.html.

"Several European Countries Move to Rule Out GMOs." European Green Capital, European Commission. Accessed April 14, 2023. https://ec.europa.eu/environment/europeangreencapital/countriesruleoutgmos/.

Shaw, Adam, and Bill Melugin. "Border Patrol Apprehensions of Chinese Nationals at Southern Border Up 800%: Source." Fox News, February 9, 2023. https://www.foxnews.com/politics/border-patrol-apprehensions-chinese-nationals-southern-border-800-source.

Shaw, Adam. "Number of Illegal Migrants Who Entered US since Biden Took Office Approaching Two Million." Fox News, September 9, 2022. https://

www.foxnews.com/politics/number-illegal-migrants-entered-us-since-biden-took-office-approaching-two-million.

Sherman, Amy. "Joe Biden's Full Flop on Messages about Afghanistan Withdrawal." PolitiFact, August 20, 2021. https://www.politifact.com/factchecks/2021/aug/20/joe-biden/joe-bidens-full-flop-messages-about-afghanistan-wi/.

Shivaram, Deepa. "What to Know about Title 42, the Trump-Era Policy Now Central to the Border Debate." NPR, April 24, 2022. https://www.npr.org/2022/04/24/1094070784/title-42-policy-meaning.

Shultz, George P. "Moral Principles and Strategic Interests: The Worldwide Movement to Democracy." Landon Lecture Series on Public Issues, Kansas State University, April 14, 1986. https://www.k-state.edu/landon/speakers/george-shultz/transcript.html.

Silver, Laura, Kat Devlin, and Christine Huang. "Unfavorable Views of China Reach Historic Highs in Many Countries." Pew Research Center, October 6, 2020. https://www.pewresearch.org/global/2020/10/06/unfavorable-views-of-china-reach-historic-highs-in-many-countries/.

Simmons, Ann M., and Austin Ramzy. "Russia-China Summit Showcases Challenge to the West." *The Wall Street Journal*, March 21, 2023. https://www.wsj.com/articles/china-xi-jinping-vladimir-putin-meet-in-russia-400d39e1.

Singman, Brooke. "Afghan Interpreter Beaten, Tortured by Taliban in Front of Family as His SIV Application Lags." Fox News, September 10, 2021. https://www.foxnews.com/politics/afghan-interpreter-taliban-beating-siv-application-delays-veteran.

Smith, Robert, and Zoe Chace. "Drug Dealing, Counterfeiting, Smuggling: How North Korea Makes Money." NPR, August 11, 2011. https://www.npr.org/sections/money/2011/08/11/139556457/drug-dealing-counterfeiting-smuggling-how-north-korea-makes-money.

Snyder, Alison. "China Talent Program Increased Young Scientists' Productivity, Study Says." *Axios*, January 10, 2023. https://www.axios.com/2023/01/10/china-funding-young-scientists-productivity.

"Soybean 2021 Export Highlights." U.S. Department of Agriculture, 2021. https://www.fas.usda.gov/soybean-2021-export-highlights

Specia, Megan. "Built for Invasion, North Korean Tunnels Now Flow with Tourists." *The New York Times*, November 4, 2017. https://www.nytimes.com/2017/11/04/world/asia/north-korea-south-korea-demilitarized-zone-tunnel-tourism.html.

Sprunt, Barbara. "There's a Bipartisan Backlash to How Biden Handled the Withdrawal from Afghanistan." NPR, August 17, 2021. https://www.npr.org/2021/08/16/1028081817/congressional-reaction-to-bidens-afghanistan-withdrawal-has-been-scathing.

Starling, Clementine G., Tyson Wetzel, and Christian Trotti. *Seizing the Advantage: A Vision for the Next US National Defense Strategy*. Atlantic Council, December 22, 2021. https://www.atlanticcouncil.org/wp-content/uploads/2022/08/Seizing-the-Advantage_A-Vision-for-the-Next-US-National-Defense-Strategy.pdf.

Starr, Jason. "The U.N. Resolutions." *The Iran Primer*, United States Institute of Peace, accessed May 11, 2023. https://iranprimer.usip.org/resource/un-resolutions.

"Statistical Review of World Energy 2021—Middle East." BP, 2021. https://www.bp.com/content/dam/bp/business-sites/en/global/corporate/pdfs/energy-economics/statistical-review/bp-stats-review-2021-middle-east-insights.pdf.

Stein, Jeff. "Trumps Signs USMCA, Revamping North American Trade Rules." *The Washington Post*, January 29, 2020. https://www.washingtonpost.com/business/2020/01/29/trump-usmca/.

Sterngold, James. "North Korea Invites Carter to Mediate." *The New York Times*, September 2, 1994. https://www.nytimes.com/1994/09/02/world/north-korea-invites-carter-to-mediate.html.

Stolberg, Sheryl Gay. "Otto Warmbier, American Student Released from North Korea, Dies." *The New York Times*, June 19, 2017. https://www.nytimes.com/2017/06/19/us/otto-warmbier-north-korea-dies.html.

Sullivan, Becky. "Why Belarus Is So Involved in Russia's Invasion of Ukraine." NPR, March 11, 2022. https://www.npr.org/2022/03/11/1085548867/belarus-ukraine-russia-invasion-lukashenko-putin.

Swanson, Ana. "Trump to Impose Sweeping Steel and Aluminum Tariffs." *The New York Times*, March 1, 2018. https://www.nytimes.com/2018/03/01/business/trump-tariffs.html.

Swanson, Ana. "White House to Impose Metal Tariffs on E.U., Canada and Mexico." *The New York Times*, May 31, 2018. https://www.nytimes.com/2018/05/31/us/politics/trump-aluminum-steel-tariffs.html.

Swift, John. "U.S. Invasion of Grenada." *Encyclopedia Britannica*, October 18, 2022. https://www.britannica.com/event/U-S-invasion-of-Grenada.

Tagliabue, Giovanni. "The EU Legislation on 'GMOs' between Nonsense and Protectionism: An Ongoing Schumpeterian Chain of Public Choices." *GM Crops & Food* 8, no. 1 (2017): 57–73. https://doi.org/10.1080%2F21645698.2016.1270488.

Taleblu, Behnam Ben. *Arsenal: Assessing the Islamic Republic of Iran's Ballistic Missile Program*. Foundation for Defense of Democracies, February 15, 2023. https://www.fdd.org/wp-content/uploads/2023/02/fdd-monograph-arsenal-assessing-iran-ballistic-missile-program.pdf.

Tankersley, Jim. "Trumps Signs Revised Korean Trade Deal." *The New York Times*, September 24, 2018. https://www.nytimes.com/2018/09/24/politics/south-korea-trump-trade-deal.html.

"Text of a letter from the President to Senators Hagel, Helms, Craig, and Roberts." White House, March 13, 2001. https://georgewbush-whitehouse.archives.gov/news/releases/2001/03/20010314.html.

Tharoor, Ishaan. "The Limits of Biden's American Exceptionalism," *The Washington Post*, March 15, 2021. https://www.washingtonpost.com/world/2021/03/15/biden-american-exceptionalism-limits/.

Tharp, Mike. "U.S. and Japan Agree on Ceilings for Car Shipments through 1983." *The New York Times*, May 1, 1981. https://www.nytimes.com/1981/05/01/business/us-and-japan-agree-on-ceilings-for-car-shipments-through-1983.html.

Thebault, Reis. "Iranian Agents Once Plotted to Kill the Saudi Ambassador in D.C. The Case Reads Like a Spy Thriller." *The Washington Post*, January 4, 2020. https://www.washingtonpost.com/history/2020/01/04/iran-agents-once-plotted-kill-saudi-ambassador-dc-case-reads-like-spy-thriller/.

Thomsen, Jacqueline. "Trump Calls for EU to Drop All Trade Barriers Ahead of Official's Visit." *The Hill*, July 24, 2018. https://thehill.com/homenews/administration/398706-trump-calls-for-eu-to-drop-all-trade-barriers-ahead-of-official-visit/.

"Top Trading Partners—January 2017." United States Census Bureau, 2017. https://www.census.gov/foreign-trade/statistics/highlights/toppartners.html.

"Transcript: President Obama's Full NPR Interview on Iran Nuclear Deal." NPR, April 7, 2015. https://www.npr.org/2015/04/07/397933577/transcript-president-obamas-full-npr-interview-on-iran-nuclear-deal.

Trump, Donald J., and Tony Schwartz. *Trump: The Art of the Deal*. New York: Random House, 1987.

Trump, Donald J. "Remarks by President Trump on Modernizing Our Immigration System for a Stronger America." Speech, Washington, D.C., May 16, 2019. White House. https://trumpwhitehouse.archives.gov/briefings-statements/remarks-president-trump-modernizing-immigration-system-stronger-america/.

Trump, Donald J. *The America We Deserve*. Renaissance Books, 2000.

"Trump Says Agreed with EU to Work to Lower Trade Barriers." *Reuters*, July 25, 2018. https://www.reuters.com/article/usa-trade-eu-announcement/trump-says-agreed-with-eu-to-work-to-lower-trade-barriers-idINS0N-1T700I.

"Trump: I Want a 'Big, Fat, Beautiful, Open Door' for Legal Immigrants." NBC News, September 3, 2015. https://www.nbcnews.com/video/trump-i-want-a-big-fat-beautiful-open-door-for-legal-immigrants-518858307936.

Turak, Natasha. "An Iran Nuclear Deal Revival Could Dramatically Alter Oil Prices—If It Happens." *CNBC*, August 31, 2022. https://www.cnbc.com/2022/08/31/an-iran-nuclear-deal-revival-could-dramatically-alter-oil-prices.html.

Tzu, Sun. *The Art of War*, trans. Thomas Cleary. Boulder: Shambhala, 2003.

United Nations Security Council. "Resolution 2371." S/RES/2371, August 5, 2017. https://documents-dds-ny.un.org/doc/UNDOC/GEN/N17/246/68/PDF/N1724668.pdf.

Union of Concerned Scientists. "Each country's share of CO2 emissions." Updated January 14, 2022. https://www.ucsusa.org/resources/each-countrys-share-co2-emissions.

United Nations Security Council. "Resolution 2375." S/RES/2375, September 11, 2017. https://documents-dds-ny.un.org/doc/UNDOC/GEN/N17/283/67/PDF/N1728367.pdf.

United Nations Security Council. "Resolution 2397." S/RES/2397, December 22, 2017. https://documents-dds-ny.un.org/doc/UNDOC/GEN/N17/463/60/PDF/N1746360.pdf.

United States Environmental Protection Agency. "1990 Clean Air Act Amendment Summary." Last modified November 28, 2022. https://www.epa.gov/clean-air-act-overview/1990-clean-air-act-amendment-summary.

United States Institute of Peace. "Iran's Deepening Strategic Alliance with Russia." *The Iran Primer*, April 25, 2023. http://iranprimer.usip.org/blog/2023/feb/24/iran%E2%80%99s-deepening-strategic-alliance-russia.

Update to the Report of the Commission on the Theft of American Intellectual Property. The National Bureau of Asian Research, 2017. https://www.nbr.org/wp-content/uploads/pdfs/publications/IP_Commission_Report_Update.pdf.

"U.S. Appeals Court Upholds Ruling against Chinese Banks in North Korea Sanctions Probe." Reuters, July 30, 2019. https://www.reuters.com/article/us-usa-trade-china-banks/u-s-appeals-court-upholds-ruling-against-chinese-banks-in-north-korea-sanctions-probe-idUSKCN1UQ03U.

U.S. Congress. House. *Final Report: Select Committee to Investigate the January 6th Attack on the United States Capitol.* 117th Cong., 2d sess., 2022, H. Rep. 117–663. https://www.govinfo.gov/content/pkg/GPO-J6-REPORT/pdf/GPO-J6-REPORT.pdf.

U.S. Congress. House. *U.S. Citizenship Act.* HR 1177. 117th Cong., 1st sess. https://www.congress.gov/117/bills/hr1177/BILLS-117hr1177ih.pdf.

U.S. Congress. House. *U.S.* Citizenship Act. HR 3194. 118th Cong., 1st sess. https://www.congress.gov/118/bills/hr3194/BILLS-118hr3194ih.pdf.

"US Delivering 'Peace through Strength': President Trump Tells UN." United Nations, September 22, 2020. https://news.un.org/en/story/2020/09/1073002.

U.S. Department of State. "Diversity Visa Program, DV 2019–2021: Number of Entries During Each Online Registration Period by Region and Country of Chargeability." Accessed June 16, 2023. https://travel.state.gov/content/dam/visas/Diversity-Visa/DVStatistics/DV-applicant-entrants-by-country-2019-2021.pdf.

U.S. Department of State. *Joint Comprehensive Plan of Action*, July 14, 2015. https://2009-2017.state.gov/documents/organization/245317.pdf.

"US energy facts explained." U.S. Energy Information Administration, June 10, 2022. https://www.eia.gov/energyexplained/us-energy-facts/.

U.S. Energy Information Administration. "Table 1. Total Energy Supply, Disposition, and Price Summary." *Annual Energy Outlook 2022*. Accessed June 13, 2023. https://www.eia.gov/outlooks/aeo/data/browser/.

"U.S. Exports of Services: Financial Services." Federal Reserve Bank of St. Louis, 2021. https://fred.stlouisfed.org/series/ITXFISM133S.

U.S. National Archives and Records Administration. "Declaration of Independence: A Transcription." America's Founding Documents. Last modified January 31, 2023. https://www.archives.gov/founding-docs/declaration-transcript.

U.S. National Archives and Records Administration. "The Constitution of the United States: A Transcription." America's Founding Documents. Last modified February 3, 2023. https://www.archives.gov/founding-docs/constitution-transcript.

"The U.S.-North Korean Agreed Framework at a Glance." Arms Control Association, February 2022. https://www.armscontrol.org/factsheets/agreedframework.

U.S. President. Executive Order. "Executive Order 13810 of September 20, 2017: Imposing Additional Sanctions with Respect to North Korea." *Federal Register* 82, no. 184 (September 25, 2017): 44705. https://www.govinfo.gov/content/pkg/FR-2017-09-25/pdf/2017-20647.pdf.

U.S. President. Proclamation. "Termination of Emergency with Respect to the Southern Border of the United States and Redirection of Funds Diverted to Border Wall Construction, Proclamation 10142 of January 20, 2021." *Federal Register* 86, no. 16 (January 27, 2021): 7225–7227. https://www.govinfo.gov/content/pkg/FR-2021-01-27/pdf/2021-01922.pdf.

U.S. Senate Committee on Foreign Relations. *Biden's Border Crisis: Examining Policies that Encourage Illegal Migration*. Minority Report, June 2022.

https://www.risch.senate.gov/public/_cache/files/5/0/5082e293-b23d-4726-a581-dc428517a843/9FB8D6A16D2415A013D48761339299C6.bidens-border-crisis.pdf.

Vaïsse, Justin. "Neoconservatism and American Foreign Policy." Brookings, August 3, 2010. https://www.brookings.edu/on-the-record/neoconservatism-and-american-foreign-policy/.

Vela, Jakob Hanke, and Arthur Neslen. "EU Mulls Faster Genetically Modified Food Approvals for Trump." *Politico*, February 26, 2020. https://www.politico.eu/article/eu-mulls-faster-genetically-modified-food-approvals-for-trump/.

Vergun, David. "Russia Reportedly Supplying Enriched Uranium to China." U.S. Department of Defense, March 8, 2023. https://www.defense.gov/News/News-Stories/Article/Article/3323381/russia-reportedly-supplying-enriched-uranium-to-china/.

"Vladimir Putin Meets with Members of the Valdai International Discussion Club. Transcript of the Final Plenary Session." Valdai Club, October 25, 2014. https://web.archive.org/web/20141025230537/http:/valdaiclub.com/valdai_club/73300.html.

Waltz, Kenneth N. *Theory of International Politics*. New York: McGraw-Hill, 1979.

Ward, Alexander. "North Korea Displays Enough ICBMs to Overwhelm U.S. Defense System against Them." *Politico*, February 8, 2023. https://www.politico.com/news/2023/02/08/north-korea-missile-capability-icbms-00081993.

Warrick, Joby, Ellen Nakashima, and Anna Fifield. "North Korea Now Making Missile-Ready Nuclear Weapons, U.S. Analysts Say." *The Washington Post*, August 8, 2017. https://www.washingtonpost.com/world/national-security/north-korea-now-making-missile-ready-nuclear-weapons-us-analysts-say/2017/08/08/e14b882a-7b6b-11e7-9d08-b79f191668ed_story.html.

Washburn, Logan and Melissa Brown. "Nikki Haley Helps Kick Off Faith and Freedom Event as Jan. 6 Hearings Continue." *The Tennessean*, June 16, 2022. https://www.tennessean.com/story/news/politics/2022/06/16/nikki-haley-speaks-conference-while-jan-6-hearings-continue/7649025001/.

Watts, Jonathan. "How Clinton Came Close to Bombing." *The Guardian*, December 4, 2002. https://www.theguardian.com/world/2002/dec/05/northkorea.

Ward, Myah. "White House is pressed on potential oil deals with Saudi Arabia, Venezuela and Iran."

Politico, March 7, 2022. https://www.politico.com/news/2022/03/07/white-house-oil-deals-saudi-arabia-venezuela-iran-00014803.

Wee, Sui-Lee. "Giving In to China, U.S. Airlines Drop Taiwan (in Name at Least)." *The New York Times*, July 25, 2018. https://www.nytimes.com/2018/07/25/business/taiwan-american-airlines-china.html.

Weinberger, Caspar. "Use of Military Force." Speech, Washington, D.C., November 28, 1984. C-SPAN. https://www.c-span.org/video/?124872-1/military-force.

Weinstein, Emily. "Don't Underestimate China's Military-Civil Fusion Efforts." *Foreign Policy*, February 5, 2021. https://foreignpolicy.com/2021/02/05/dont-underestimate-chinas-military-civil-fusion-efforts/.

Wendt, Alexander. *Social Theory of International Politics*. New York: Cambridge University Press, 1999.

"White Evangelicals See Trump as Fighting for Their Beliefs, though Many Have Mixed Feelings about His Personal Conduct." Pew Research Center, March 12, 2020. https://www.pewresearch.org/religion/2020/03/12/white-evangelicals-see-trump-as-fighting-for-their-beliefs-though-many-have-mixed-feelings-about-his-personal-conduct/

Williams, Daniel. "U.S. Warns N. Korea on Nuclear Weapons." *The Washington Post*, July 11, 1993. https://www.washingtonpost.com/archive/politics/1993/07/11/us-warns-n-korea-on-nuclear-weapons/d7461b91-e0c1-439b-a309-dacac721ea0b/.

Wise, Lindsay. "Senate Passes $778 Billion Defense-Policy Bill." *The Wall Street Journal*, December 15, 2021. https://www.wsj.com/articles/senate-set-to-pass-778-billion-ndaa-defense-policy-bill-11639586115.

Wong, Chun Han, and Chao Deng. "China's 'Wolf Warrior' Diplomats Are Ready to Fight." *The Wall Street Journal*, May 19, 2020. https://www.wsj.com/articles/chinas-wolf-warrior-diplomats-are-ready-to-fight-11589896722.

Woodward, Bob. *Fear: Trump in the White House*. New York: Simon & Schuster, 2018.

World Bank. "GDP Per Capita (Current US$)—Russian Federation," Accessed July 29, 2023.
https://data.worldbank.org/indicator/NY.GDP.PCAP.CD?locations=RU.

World Bank. "Land Area (sq. km)." Accessed May 8, 2023. https://data.worldbank.org/indicator/AG.LND.TOTL.K2.

"Wrap-up: President Biden's unprecedented assault on American energy increased costs on American consumers and businesses." United States House Committee on Oversight and Accountability, March 30, 2023. https://oversight.house.gov/release/wrap-up-president-bidens-unprecedented-assault-on-american-energy-increased-costs-on-american-consumers-and-businesses.

Wray, Christopher. "The Threat Posed by the Chinese Government and the Chinese Communist Party to the Economic and National Security of the United States." Speech, Washington, D.C., July 7, 2020. FBI. https://www.fbi.gov/news/speeches/the-threat-posed-by-the-chinese-government-and-the-chinese-communist-party-to-the-economic-and-national-security-of-the-united-states.

Wright, Thomas. "Will Trumpism Change Republican Foreign Policy Permanently?" *The Atlantic*, August 28, 2020. https://www.theatlantic.com/ideas/archive/2020/08/will-trumpism-change-republican-foreign-policy-permanently/615745/.

Yan, Holly. "Syria Allies: Why Russia, Iran and China Are Standing by the Regime." CNN, August 29, 2013. https://www.cnn.com/2013/08/29/world/meast/syria-iran-china-russia-supporters/index.html.

Yeo, Andrew. "Why Further Sanctions against North Korea Could Be Tough to Add." Brookings, July 8, 2022. https://www.brookings.edu/blog/order-from-chaos/2022/07/08/why-further-sanctions-against-north-korea-could-be-tough-to-add/.

Zelizer, Julian E., ed. *The Presidency of Donald J. Trump: A First Historical Assessment*. Princeton, NJ: Princeton University Press, 2022.

Ziady, Hanna. "OPEC Announces the Biggest Cut to Oil Production since the Start of the Pandemic."

CNN Business, October 5, 2022. https://www.cnn.com/2022/10/05/energy/opec-production-cuts/index.html.

Zoellick, Robert B. "Whither China: From Membership to Responsibility?" Speech, New York City, NY, September 21, 2005. U.S. Department of State. https://2001-2009.state.gov/s/d/former/zoellick/rem/53682.htm.

Zucchino, David. "Kabul's Sudden Fall to Taliban Ends U.S. Era in Afghanistan," *The New York Times*, Updated August 17, 2021. https://www.nytimes.com/2021/08/15/world/asia/afghanistan-taliban-kabul-surrender.html.

NOTES

1   Richard V. Allen, "The Man Who Won the Cold War," Hoover Institution, January 30, 2000, https://www.hoover.org/research/man-who-won-cold-war.

2   *Encyclopædia Britannica*, "Nixon, Kissinger, and the Détente Experiment," accessed May 1, 2023, https://www.britannica.com/topic/20th-century-international-relations-2085155/Nixon-Kissinger-and-the-detente-experiment.

3   Allen, "The Man Who Won."

4   *National Security Strategy of the United States of America*, White House, December 2017, 27, https://trumpwhitehouse.archives.gov/wp-content/uploads/2017/12/NSS-Final-12-18-2017-0905.pdf.

5   Phelim Kine, "China Is 'Infinitely Stronger than the Soviet Union Ever Was,'" *Politico*, April 28, 2023, https://www.politico.com/newsletters/global-insider/2023/04/28/china-is-infinitely-stronger-than-the-soviet-union-ever-was-00094266.

6   For critics of today's Republican Party, see: Jeffrey Goldberg, "A Party, and Nation, in Crisis," *The Atlantic*, December 6, 2021, https://www.theatlantic.com/magazine/archive/2022/01/republican-party-america-democracy-in-crisis/620839/; Jelani Cobb, "What Is Happening to the Republicans?" *New Yorker*, March 8, 2021, https://www.newyorker.com/magazine/2021/03/15/what-is-happening-to-the-republicans; Thomas Wright, "Will Trumpism Change Republican Foreign Policy Permanently?" *The Atlantic*, August 28, 2020, https://www.theatlantic.com/ideas/archive/2020/08/will-trumpism-change-republican-foreign-policy-permanently/615745/; Lisa Lerer, "How the G.O.P. Lost Its Clear Voice on Foreign Policy," *The New York Times*, April 15, 2021, https://www.nytimes.com/2021/04/15/us/politics/republicans-afghanistan.html; Colin Dueck, "The GOP's Foreign-Policy Tribes Prepare for Battle," *National Review*, December 9, 2020, https://www.nationalreview.com/2020/12/the-gops-foreign-policy-tribes-prepare-for-battle/.

7   On the threat from China, see *National Security Strategy of the United States of America*, White House, December 2017, 27, https://trumpwhitehouse.archives.gov/wp-content/uploads/2017/12/NSS-Fi-

nal-12-18-2017-0905.pdf; *National Security Strategy*, White House, October 2022, https://www.whitehouse.gov/wp-content/uploads/2022/10/Biden-Harris-Administrations-National-Security-Strategy-10.2022.pdf; *Military and Security Developments Involving the People's Republic of China 2022*, US Department of Defense, November 2022, https://media.defense.gov/2022/Nov/29/2003122279/-1/-1/1/2022-military-and-security-developments-involving-the-peoples-republic-of-china.pdf.

8   On Reaganism, see: Jonathan M. Schoenwald, "A New Kind of Conservative: Ronald Reagan," Ch. 7 in Jonathan M. Schoenwald, *A Time for Choosing: The Rise of Modern American Conservatism* (New York: Oxford University Press, 2001), 190–220; Paul Kengor, *11 Principles of a Reagan Conservative* (New York: Beaufort Books, 2014); William A. Niskanen, *Reaganomics: An Insider's Account of the Policies and the People* (New York: Oxford University Press, 1988); Bradley Lynn Coleman and Kyle Longley, ed., *Reagan and the World: Leadership and National Security, 1981–1989* (Lexington: University Press of Kentucky, 2017).

9   On Trumpism, see: "White Evangelicals See Trump as Fighting for Their Beliefs, though Many Have Mixed Feelings about His Personal Conduct," Pew Research Center, March 12, 2020, https://www.pewresearch.org/religion/2020/03/12/white-evangelicals-see-trump-as-fighting-for-their-beliefs-though-many-have-mixed-feelings-about-his-personal-conduct/; Robert Schertzer and Eric Taylor Woods, "Donald Trump and the New Nationalism in America," Ch. 5 in *The New Nationalism in America and Beyond: The Deep Roots of Ethnic Nationalism in the Digital Age* (New York: Oxford University Press, 2022); Corina Lacatus, "Populism and President Trump's Approach to Foreign Policy: An Analysis of Tweets and Rally Speeches," *Political Studies* 41, no. 1 (2021): 31–47, https://doi.org/10.1177/0263395720935380.

10 Antony J. Blinken, "A Foreign Policy for the American People" (speech, Washington, DC, March 3, 2021), US Department of State, https://www.state.gov/a-foreign-policy-for-the-american-people/.

11 Matthew Kroenig and Dan Negrea, "Why 'Confrontation' with China Cannot Be Avoided," *The National Interest*, November 26, 2021, https://nationalinterest.org/feature/why-%E2%80%98confrontation%E2%80%99-china-cannot-be-avoided-196926.

12 For biographies of Reagan and Trump, see H. W. Brands, *Reagan: The Life* (New York: Anchor, 2016); Lou Cannon, *President Reagan: The Role of a Lifetime*, (New York: PublicAffairs, 2000); Bob Woodward, *Fear: Trump in the White House* (New York: Simon & Schuster, 2018); Julian E. Zeliz-

er, ed., *The Presidency of Donald J. Trump: A First Historical Assessment* (Princeton, NJ: Princeton University Press, 2022); respectively.

13 William Ruger and Michael C. Desch, "Conservatism, Realism and Foreign Policy: Kissing Cousins If Not Soulmates," *The National Interest*, July 30, 2018, https://nationalinterest.org/blog/conservatism-realism-and-foreign-policy-kissing-cousins-if-not-soulmates-27242; Nadia Schadlow, "Conservative U.S. Statecraft for the 21st Century," *Foreign Policy*, November 7, 2022, https://foreignpolicy.com/2022/11/07/us-republicans-conservative-foreign-policy-principles/; Justin Vaïsse, "Neoconservatism and American Foreign Policy," Brookings, August 3, 2010, https://www.brookings.edu/on-the-record/neoconservatism-and-american-foreign-policy/; Colin Dueck, *Age of Iron: On Conservative Nationalism* (New York: Oxford University Press, 2019).

14 On the Iran-Contra Affair, see: Theodore Draper, *A Very Thin Line: The Iran-Contra Affairs* (New York: Hill and Wang, 1991). On January 6, see: US Congress, House of Representatives, *Final Report: Select Committee to Investigate the January 6th Attack on the United States Capitol*, 117th Cong., 2d sess., 2022, H. Rep. 117–663, https://www.govinfo.gov/content/pkg/GPO-J6-REPORT/pdf/GPO-J6-REPORT.pdf.

15 See, illustratively, John Patrick, "Democratic Professors Outnumber Republicans 9 to 1 at Top Colleges," *Washington Examiner*, January 23, 2020, https://www.washingtonexaminer.com/opinion/democratic-professors-outnumber-republicans-9-to-1-at-top-colleges.

16 Elbridge A. Colby, *The Strategy of Denial: American Defense in an Age of Great Power Conflict* (New Haven, CT: Yale University Press, 2021).

17 Aaron L. Friedberg, *Getting China Wrong* (Cambridge: Polity, 2022).

18 Christian Brose, *The Kill Chain: Defending America in the Future of High-Tech Warfare* (New York: Hachette, 2020).

19 Colin Dueck, *Age of Iron*; Henry R. Nau, *Conservative Internationalism: Armed Diplomacy under Jefferson, Polk, Truman, and Reagan* (Princeton: Princeton University Press, 2015).

20 Paul D. Miller, *American Power and Liberal Order: A Conservative Internationalist Grand Strategy* (Washington, DC: Georgetown University Press, 2016).

21 Tom Cotton, *Only the Strong: Reversing the Left's Plot to Sabotage American Power* (New York: Twelve, 2022); Mike Pompeo, *Never Give an Inch: Fighting for the America I Love* (New York: Broadside Books, 2023); Mike Pence, *So Help Me God* (New York: Simon & Schuster, 2022).

22   "U.S. Trade to GDP Ratio 1970–2023," Macrotrends, accessed January 20, 2023, https://www.macrotrends.net/countries/USA/united-states/trade-gdp-ratio.

23   Kathy Frankovic, "Only One-Third of Americans Have a Valid US Passport," YouGov, April 21, 2021, https://today.yougov.com/topics/travel/articles-reports/2021/04/21/only-one-third-americans-have-valid-us-passport.

24   "145 Key Tourism Statistics," World Tourism Organization, last modified December 22, 2022, https://www.unwto.org/tourism-statistics/key-tourism-statistics.

25   Abby Budiman, "Key Findings about U.S. Immigrants," Pew Research Center, August 20, 2020, https://www.pewresearch.org/short-reads/2020/08/20/key-findings-about-u-s-immigrants/.

26   Sean Lyngaas, "Russia and China Are Promoting US Voting Misinformation ahead of Midterms, FBI Warns," CNN, October 3, 2022, https://www.cnn.com/2022/10/03/politics/2022-election-security-fbi/index.html.

27   US National Archives, "Declaration of Independence"; "The Constitution of the United States: A Transcription," America's Founding Documents, US National Archives and Records Administration, last modified February 3, 2023, https://www.archives.gov/founding-docs/constitution-transcript.

28   "Top Trading Partners—January 2017," United States Census Bureau, 2017, https://www.census.gov/foreign-trade/statistics/highlights/toppartners.html.

29   Ibid.

30   "Statistical Review of World Energy 2021—Middle East," BP, 2021, https://www.bp.com/content/dam/bp/business-sites/en/global/corporate/pdfs/energy-economics/statistical-review/bp-stats-review-2021-middle-east-insights.pdf.

31   Francis Gavin, *Nuclear Weapons and American Grand Strategy* (Washington, DC: Brookings Institution Press, 2020).

32   *The 9/11 Commission Report*, National Commission on Terrorist Attacks Upon the United States, July 22, 2004, https://www.9-11commission.gov/report/911Report.pdf.

33   Eric Schmitt and Thom Shanker, *Counterstrike: The Untold Story of America's Secret Campaign against Al Qaeda* (New York: Henry Holt and Company, 2011).

34   "Knit Socks and Hosiery," Observatory of Economic Complexity, 2020, https://oec.world/en/profile/hs/knit-socks-and-hosiery.

35 "Soybean 2021 Export Highlights," US Department of Agriculture, 2021, https://www.fas.usda.gov/soybean-2021-export-highlights; "U.S. Exports of Services: Financial Services," Federal Reserve Bank of St. Louis, 2021, https://fred.stlouisfed.org/series/ITXFISM133S.

36 Harvey Klehr et al., *The Soviet World of American Communism* (New Haven: Yale University Press, 1998).

37 Joshua Kurlantzick, "China's Growing Attempts to Influence U.S. Politics," Council on Foreign Relations, October 31, 2022, https://www.cfr.org/article/chinas-growing-attempts-influence-us-politics; *Foreign Threats to the 2020 US Federal Elections*, National Intelligence Council, March 10, 2021, https://www.dni.gov/files/ODNI/documents/assessments/ICA-declass-16MAR21.pdf.

38 Matthew Kroenig, *The Return of Great Power Rivalry: Democracy Versus Autocracy from the Ancient World to the U.S. and China* (New York: Oxford University Press, 2020).

39 David Samuels, "The Aspiring Novelist Who Became Obama's Foreign-Policy Guru," *The New York Times*, May 5, 2016, https://www.nytimes.com/2016/05/08/magazine/the-aspiring-novelist-who-became-obamas-foreign-policy-guru.html.

40 Friedberg, *Getting China Wrong*.

41 Jonathan Haidt, *The Righteous Mind: Why Good People Are Divided by Politics and Religion* (New York: Pantheon Books, 2012).

42 Samuel P. Huntington, "Conservatism as an Ideology," *The American Political Science Review* Vol. 51, No. 2 (June 1957), pp. 454-473.

43 Reinhold *Niebuhr, Christian Realism and Political Problems (New York: Charles Scribner's Sons, 1953).*

44 Haidt, *The Righteous Mind*.

45 Ronald Reagan, "Evil Empire" (speech, Orlando, Florida, March 8, 1983), Voices of Democracy, https://voicesofdemocracy.umd.edu/reagan-evil-empire-speech-text/; Ronald Reagan, "Farewell Address to the Nation" (speech, Washington, DC, January 11, 1989), Reagan Foundation, https://www.reaganfoundation.org/media/128652/farewell.pdf.

46 George W. Bush, "State of the Union Address" (speech, Washington, DC, January 29, 2002), *The Washington Post*, https://www.washingtonpost.com/wp-srv/onpolitics/transcripts/sou012902.htm.

47 *National Security Strategy*, White House, October 2022.

48 Jeane Kirkpatrick, "'Blame America First'—Remarks at the 1984 Republican National Committee—Aug. 20, 1984" (speech, Dallas, Texas, August 20, 1984), Archives of Women's Political Communication, Iowa

State University, accessed April 18, 2023, https://awpc.cattcenter.iastate.edu/2017/03/09/remarks-at-the-1984-rnc-aug-20-1984/.

49   Matthew Kroenig, "China's Nuclear Silos and the Arms-Control Fantasy," *The Wall Street Journal*, July 7, 2021, https://www.wsj.com/articles/chinas-nuclear-silos-and-the-arms-control-fantasy-11625696243.

50   James M. Acton, "Don't Panic about China's New Nuclear Capabilities," *The Washington Post*, July 27, 2021, https://www.washingtonpost.com/politics/2021/06/30/dont-panic-about-chinas-new-nuclear-   capabilities/.

51   Robert Keohane, *After Hegemony* (Princeton: Princeton University Press, 1984).

52   Barack Obama, "News Conference by President Obama, 4/04/2009" (press conference, Strasbourg, France, April 4, 2009), White House, https://obamawhitehouse.archives.gov/the-press-office/news-conference-president-obama-4042009.

53   "In a Politically Polarized Era, Sharp Divides in Both Partisan Coalitions," Pew Research Center, December 17, 2019, https://www.pewresearch.org/politics/2019/12/17/in-a-politically-polarized-era-sharp-divides-in-both-partisan-coalitions/.

54   Joseph R. Biden Jr., "Why America Must Lead Again: Rescuing U.S. Foreign Policy after Trump," *Foreign Affairs*, January 23, 2020, https://www.foreignaffairs.com/articles/united-states/2020-01-23/why-america-must-lead-again.

55   *National Security Strategy*, White House, October 2022.

56   Joe Biden, "Remarks by President Biden at the 2021 Virtual Munich Security Conference" (speech, Washington, DC, February 19, 2021), White House, https://www.whitehouse.gov/briefing-room/speeches-remarks/2021/02/19/remarks-by-president-biden-at-the-2021-virtual-munich-security-conference/.

57   Joe Biden, "Remarks by President Biden on the American Jobs Plan" (speech, Pittsburgh, Pennsylvania, March 31, 2021), White House, https://www.whitehouse.gov/briefing-room/speeches-remarks/2021/03/31/remarks-by-president-biden-on-the-american-jobs-plan/.

58   Alex Emmons, Aída Chávez, and Akela Lacy, "Joe Biden, in Departure from Obama Policy, Says He Would Make Saudi Arabia a 'Pariah,'" *The Intercept*, November 21, 2019, https://theintercept.com/2019/11/21/democratic-debate-joe-biden-saudi-arabia/.

59   Amanda Macias, "Biden's Effort to Tout Progress in Saudi Relationship Overshadowed by Khashoggi Killing," CNBC, July 15, 2022, https://www.

cnbc.com/2022/07/15/watch-biden-speaks-after-meeting-mbs-in-saudi-arabia.html.

60 Hanna Ziady, "OPEC Announces the Biggest Cut to Oil Production since the Start of the Pandemic," CNN Business, October 5, 2022, https://www.cnn.com/2022/10/05/energy/opec-production-cuts/index.html.

61 Joe Biden, "Remarks by President Biden on Standing Up for Democracy" (speech, Washington, DC, November 2, 2022), White House, https://www.whitehouse.gov/briefing-room/speeches-remarks/2022/11/03/remarks-by-president-biden-on-standing-up-for-democracy/.

62 Joe Biden, "Remarks by President Biden on America's Place in the World" (speech, Washington, DC, February 4, 2021), White House, https://www.whitehouse.gov/briefing-room/speeches-remarks/2021/02/04/remarks-by-president-biden-on-americas-place-in-the-world/.

63 Sam Meredith and Natasha Turak, "Trump Slams Germany at NATO Summit: It's 'Totally Controlled by Russia,'" CNBC, July 11, 2018, https://www.cnbc.com/2018/07/11/trump-slams-germany-at-nato-summit-says-its-a-captive-of-russia.html.

64 Daniel Kochis, "Nord Stream 2 Is Complete—What Now?" The Heritage Foundation, January 10, 2022, https://www.heritage.org/europe/report/nord-stream-2-complete-what-now.

65 Franco Ordoñez, "Biden Wants a 'Stable, Predictable' Relationship with Russia. That's Complicated," *National Public Radio*, May 21, 2021, https://www.npr.org/2021/05/21/999196021/biden-wants-a-stable-predictable-relationship-with-russia-thats-complicated.

66 David Brunnstrom and Trevor Hunnicutt, "Biden Says U.S. Forces Would Defend Taiwan in the Event of a Chinese Invasion," Reuters, September 19, 2022, https://www.reuters.com/world/biden-says-us-forces-would-defend-taiwan-event-chinese-invasion-2022-09-18/; Kentaro Iwamoto and Sayumi Take, "Biden Says He Would Use Force to Defend Taiwan," *Nikkei*, May 23, 2022, https://asia.nikkei.com/Politics/International-relations/Biden-s-Asia-policy/Biden-says-he-would-use-force-to-defend-Taiwan.

67 John M. Donnelly, "Inflation May Shrink Biden's Big Defense Plan," *Roll Call*, March 29, 2022, https://rollcall.com/2022/03/29/inflation-may-shrink-bidens-big-defense-plan/.

68 Matthew Kroenig, *Deterring Chinese Strategic Attack: Grappling with the Implications of China's Strategic Forces Buildup*, Atlantic Council, November 2, 2021, https://www.atlanticcouncil.org/wp-content/uploads/2021/11/Deterring_Chinese_Strategic_Attack_Rpt_10312190.pdf.

69   *Interim National Security Strategic Guidance*, White House, March 2021, https://www.whitehouse.gov/wp-content/uploads/2021/03/NSC-1v2.pdf.

70   Christopher Ashley Ford, "Bureaucracy and Counterstrategy: Meeting the China Challenge" (speech, Ft. Belvoir, Virginia, September 11, 2019), US Department of State, https://2017-2021.state.gov/bureaucracy-and-counterstrategy-meeting-the-china-challenge/index.html.

71   "Commerce Implements New Export Controls on Advanced Computing and Semiconductor Manufacturing Items to the People's Republic of China (PRC)," Bureau of Industry and Security, US Department of Commerce, October 7, 2022, https://www.bis.doc.gov/index.php/documents/about-bis/newsroom/press-releases/3158-2022-10-07-bis-press-release-advanced-computing-and-semiconductor-manufacturing-controls-final/file.

72   Kate O'Keeffe, "U.S. Approves Nearly All Tech Exports to China, Data Shows," *The Wall Street Journal*, August 16, 2022, https://www.wsj.com/articles/u-s-approves-nearly-all-tech-exports-to-china-data-shows-11660596886.

73   *National Security Strategy*, White House, October 2022.

74   "Report: China Emissions Exceed All Developed Nations Combined," BBC, May 7, 2021, https://www.bbc.com/news/world-asia-57018837.

75   On Biden's withdrawal from Afghanistan, see Barbara Sprunt, "There's a Bipartisan Backlash to How Biden Handled the Withdrawal from Afghanistan," NPR, August 17, 2021, https://www.npr.org/2021/08/16/1028081817/congressional-reaction-to-bidens-afghanistan-withdrawal-has-been-scathing; Ted Van Green and Carroll Doherty, "Majority of U.S. Public Favors Afghanistan Troop Withdrawal; Biden Criticized for His Handling of Situation," Pew Research Center, August 31, 2021, https://www.pewresearch.org/short-reads/2021/08/31/majority-of-u-s-public-favors-afghanistan-troop-withdrawal-biden-criticized-for-his-handling-of-situation/.

76   Amy Sherman, "Joe Biden's Full Flop on Messages about Afghanistan Withdrawal," PolitiFact, August 20, 2021, https://www.politifact.com/factchecks/2021/aug/20/joe-biden/joe-bidens-full-flop-messages-about-afghanistan-wi/.

77   David Zucchino, "Kabul's Sudden Fall to Taliban Ends U.S. Era in Afghanistan," *The New York Times*, updated August 17, 2021, https://www.nytimes.com/2021/08/15/world/asia/afghanistan-taliban-kabul-surrender.html.

78   Robert Burns and Lolita C. Baldor, "Milley: US Coordination with Taliban on Strikes 'Possible,'" Associated Press, September 1, 2021, https://

apnews.com/article/joe-biden-ap-top-news-afghanistan-evacuations-kabul-c134d2abf8977b87d2965d9fe3e1565f.

79   Oren Liebermann and Natasha Bertrand, "ISIS-K Suicide Bomber Who Carried Out Deadly Kabul Airport Attack Had Been Released from Prison Days Earlier," CNN, updated October 6, 2021, https://www.cnn.com/2021/10/06/politics/kabul-airport-attacker-prison/index.html.

80   Amanda Macias, "Pentagon Admits Killing 10 Civilians, Including up to 7 Children, in Kabul Drone Strike Last Month," CNBC, September 17, 2021, https://www.cnbc.com/2021/09/17/us-airstrike-in-kabul-last-month-killed-10-civilians-including-seven-children-pentagon-says.html.

81   Brooke Singman, "Afghan Interpreter Beaten, Tortured by Taliban in Front of Family as His SIV Application Lags," Fox News, September 10, 2021, https://www.foxnews.com/politics/afghan-interpreter-taliban-beating-siv-application-delays-veteran.

82   Jim Garamone, "Taliban Remains Dangerous, Harbors al-Qaida, Joint Chiefs Chairman Says," US Department of Defense, September 29, 2021, https://www.defense.gov/News/News-Stories/Article/Article/2793387/taliban-remains-dangerous-harbors-al-qaida-joint-chiefs-chairman-says/.

83   Joe Biden, "Remarks by President Biden on the End of the War in Afghanistan" (speech, Washington, DC, August 31, 2021), White House, https://www.whitehouse.gov/briefing-room/speeches-remarks/2021/08/31/remarks-by-president-biden-on-the-end-of-the-war-in-afghanistan/.

84   Joe Biden, "Remarks by President Biden on a Successful Counterterrorism Operation in Afghanistan" (speech, Washington, DC, August 1, 2022), White House, https://www.whitehouse.gov/briefing-room/speeches-remarks/2022/08/01/remarks-by-president-biden-on-a-successful-counterterrorism-operation-in-afghanistan/.

85   Diaa Hadid, "'The Taliban Took Our Last Hope': College Education Is Banned for Women in Afghanistan," NPR, December 20, 2022, https://www.npr.org/sections/goatsandsoda/2022/12/20/1144502320/the-taliban-took-our-last-hope-college-education-is-banned-for-women-in-afghanis.

86   Jerry Dunleavy, "Afghanistan Debacle Played Role in Putin's Ukraine Decision, General Says," *Washington Examiner*, March 31, 2022, https://www.washingtonexaminer.com/policy/defense-national-security/afghanistan-debacle-played-role-in-putins-ukraine-decision-general-says.

87   Tara Copp, "Biden Rules Out Sending Troops to Ukraine, at Least for Now," Defense One, December 8,

2021, https://www.defenseone.com/threats/2021/12/
biden-rules-out-sending-troops-ukraine-least-now/187386/.

88 Jeff Mason, Humeyra Pamuk, and Dmitry Antonov, "Biden Warns Putin
with Sanctions as West Steps Up Ukraine Defenses," Reuters, January 26,
2022, https://www.reuters.com/world/europe/us-seeks-protect-europes-
energy-supplies-if-russia-invades-ukraine-2022-01-25/; Andrew Roth
and Julian Borger, "US Says It Will Send Troops to Eastern Europe If
Russia Invades Ukraine," *The Guardian*, December 6, 2021, https://www.
theguardian.com/world/2021/dec/06/us-says-it-will-send-troops-to-east-
ern-europe-if-russia-invades-ukraine; Helene Cooper, "U.S. Considers
Backing an Insurgency If Russia Invades Ukraine," *The New York Times*,
January 14, 2022, https://www.nytimes.com/2022/01/14/us/politics/rus-
sia-ukraine-biden-military.html.

89 Sharon Braithwaite, "Zelensky Refuses U.S. Offer to Evacuate, Saying 'I
Need Ammunition, Not a Ride,'" CNN, February 26, 2022, https://www.
cnn.com/2022/02/26/europe/ukraine-zelensky-evacuation-intl/index.
html.

90 Farnoush Amiri and Kevin Freking, "McCarthy: No 'Blank Check' for
Ukraine If GOP Wins Majority," Associated Press, October 18, 2022,
https://apnews.com/article/russia-ukraine-donald-trump-humanitari-
an-assistance-congress-c47a255738cd13576aa4d238ec076f4a.

91 Alec Schemmel, "GOP Rips Congress for Sending $14 Billion to Protect
Ukrainian Border but Not Funding Wall," *The National Desk*, March 9,
2022, https://thenationaldesk.com/news/americas-news-now/gop-rips-
congress-for-sending-14-million-to-protect-ukrainian-border-but-not-
funding-wall-republicans-senate.

92 Mike Pompeo, "War, Ukraine, and a Global Alliance for Freedom"
(speech, Washington, DC, June 24, 2022), https://s3.amazonaws.com/
media.hudson.org/Transcript-War,%20Ukraine,%20and%20a%20
Global%20Alliance%20for%20Freedom%20.pdf.

93 *National Security Strategy of the United States of America*, White House,
December 2017.

94 *National Security Strategy*, White House, October 2022.

95 Kelly Hooper, "Romney: 10 Years Later, Russia Remains 'Geopolitical Foe,'" *Politico*, February 27,
2022, https://www.politico.com/video/2022/02/27/
romney-10-years-later-russia-remains-geopolitical-foe-493187.

96 Ash Jain and Matthew Kroenig, *Present at the Re-Creation: A Global
Strategy for Revitalizing, Adapting, and Defending a Rules-Based International System*, Atlantic Council Strategy Paper series, October 2019,

https://www.atlanticcouncil.org/wp-content/uploads/2019/10/Present-at-the-Recreation.pdf; Clementine G. Starling, Tyson Wetzel, and Christian Trotti, *Seizing the Advantage: A Vision for the Next US National Defense Strategy*, Atlantic Council, December 22, 2021, https://www.atlanticcouncil.org/wp-content/uploads/2022/08/Seizing-the-Advantage_A-Vision-for-the-Next-US-National-Defense-Strategy.pdf.

97   On the Iranian threat, see Matthew Kroenig, *A Time to Attack: The Looming Iranian Nuclear Threat* (New York: St. Martin's Press, 2014).

98   Matthew Kroenig, "Trump's Plan B for Iran," Atlantic Council, May 23, 2018, https://www.atlanticcouncil.org/blogs/new-atlanticist/trump-s-plan-b-for-iran/.

99   Mark Dubowitz and Matthew Kroenig, "As Biden Relaxed Pressure, Iran Took Advantage," *The Wall Street Journal*, January 16, 2022, https://www.wsj.com/articles/iran-nuclear-deal-jcpoa-biden-trump-diplomacy-11642192678.

100 Eric Schmitt, Maggie Haberman, David E. Sanger, Helene Cooper, and Lara Jakes, "Trump Sought Options for Attacking Iran to Stop Its Growing Nuclear Program," *The New York Times*, November 16, 2020, https://www.nytimes.com/2020/11/16/us/politics/trump-iran-nuclear.html.

101 Quint Forgey, "'The Dawn of a New Middle East': Trump Celebrates Abraham Accords with White House Signing Ceremony," *Politico*, September 15, 2020, https://www.politico.com/news/2020/09/15/trump-abraham-accords-palestinians-peace-deal-415083.

102 Vivian Nereim, "China and Saudi Arabia Sign Strategic Partnership as Xi Visits Kingdom," *The New York Times*, December 8, 2022, https://www.nytimes.com/2022/12/08/world/middleeast/china-saudi-arabia-agreement.html.

103 Hans M. Kristensen and Matt Korda, "North Korean Nuclear Weapons, 2022," *Bulletin of the Atomic Scientists*, 78, no. 5 (2022): 273–294, https://doi.org/10.1080/00963402.2022.2109341.

104 David Blackmon, "Biden's 'Kind of Insane' Energy Policies Have Created an Entirely Rational Investor Response," *Forbes*, September 20, 2022, https://www.forbes.com/sites/davidblackmon/2022/09/20/bidens-kind-of-insane-energy-policies-have-created-an-entirely-rational-investor-response/?sh=3ad98b5f174d.

105 Patricia Garip, Vivian Salama, and Kejal Vyas, "U.S. Looks to Ease Venezuela Sanctions, Enabling Chevron to Pump Oil," *The Wall Street Journal*, October 5, 2022, https://www.wsj.com/articles/u-s-plans-to-ease-venezuela-sanctions-enabling-chevron-to-pump-oil-11665005719; Natasha Turak, "An Iran Nuclear Deal Revival Could Dramatically Alter

Oil Prices—If It Happens," CNBC, August 31, 2022, https://www.cnbc.com/2022/08/31/an-iran-nuclear-deal-revival-could-dramatically-alter-oil-prices.html.

106 *Biden's Border Crisis: Examining Policies that Encourage Illegal Migration*, US Senate Committee on Foreign Relations, Minority Report, June 2022, https://www.risch.senate.gov/public/_cache/files/5/0/5082e293-b23d-4726-a581-dc428517a843/9FB8D6A16D2415A013D48761339299C6.bidens-border-crisis.pdf.

107 "Mullen: Debt Is Top National Security Threat," CNN, August 27, 2010, http://www.cnn.com/2010/US/08/27/debt.security.mullen/index.html.

108 "The Biden Administration Has Approved $4.8 Trillion of New Borrowing," Committee for a Responsible Federal Budget, September 13, 2022, https://www.crfb.org/blogs/biden-administration-has-approved-48-trillion-new-borrowing.

109 Matt Egan, "US Debt: Federal Interest Payments Could Soon Exceed Military Spending," CNN Business, November 1, 2022, https://www.cnn.com/2022/11/01/economy/inflation-fed-debt-military/index.html.

110 Jim Garamone, "Erosion of U.S. Strength in Indo-Pacific Is Dangerous to All, Commander Says," US Department of Defense, March 9, 2021, https://www.defense.gov/News/News-Stories/Article/Article/2530733/erosion-of-us-strength-in-indo-pacific-is-dangerous-to-all-commander-says/.

111 Steve Mollman, "Top Economist Sees 'Totally Avoidable' Recession Ahead," *Fortune*, October 9, 2022, https://fortune.com/2022/10/09/recession-fed-mistakes-interest-rates-economist-mohamed-el-erian/.

112 "Si vis pacem, para bellum," Merriam-Webster, accessed February 14, 2023, https://www.merriam-webster.com/dictionary/si%20vis%20pacem%2C%20para%20bellum.

113 Kenneth N. Waltz, *Theory of International Politics* (Reading: Addison-Wesley, 1979); John Mearsheimer, *The Tragedy of Great Power Politics* (New York: W. W. Norton, 2014); Robert Keohane, *After Hegemony: Cooperation and Discord in the World Political Economy* (Princeton: Princeton University Press, 1984); Alexander Wendt, *Social Theory of International Politics* (New York: Cambridge University Press, 1999).

114 Thomas Hobbes, *De Cive* (1642).

115 John C. Hulsman and A. Wess Mitchell, *The Godfather Doctrine: A Foreign Policy Parable* (Princeton: Princeton University Press, 2009).

116 Caspar Weinberger, "Use of Military Force" (speech, Washington, DC, November 28, 1984), C-SPAN, https://www.c-span.org/video/?124872-1/military-force.

117 Theodore Roosevelt, "Address of Vice President Roosevelt, Minnesota State Fair" (speech, Minneapolis, Minnesota, September 2, 1901), Theodore Roosevelt Center, 2023, https://www.theodorerooseveltcenter.org/Research/Digital-Library/Record?libID=o286433.

118 William Inboden, *The Peacemaker: Ronald Reagan, the Cold War, and the World on the Brink* (Dutton, 2022).

119 Ronald Reagan, "Acceptance Speech at 1980 Republican Convention" (speech, Detroit, Michigan, July 17, 1980), Teaching American History, https://teachingamericanhistory.org/document/acceptance-speech-at-1980-republican-convention/.

120 Hal Brands, "The Vision Thing," Miller Center, University of Virginia, January 14, 2016, https://millercenter.org/issues-policy/foreign-policy/the-vision-thing.

121 Greg Schneider and Renae Merle, "Reagan's Defense Build-up Bridged Military Eras," *The Washington Post*, June 9, 2004, https://www.washingtonpost.com/archive/business/2004/06/09/reagans-defense-buildup-bridged-military-eras/ec621466-b78e-4a2e-9f8a-50654e3f95fa/.

122 Ibid.

123 Daryl G. Kimball, "Looking Back: The Nuclear Arms Control Legacy of Ronald Reagan," Arms Control Association, July 8, 2004, https://www.armscontrol.org/act/2004_07-08/Reagan.

124 Paul Lettow, *Ronald Reagan and His Quest to Abolish Nuclear Weapons* (New York: Random House, 2005).

125 Hal Brands, *Making the Unipolar Moment: U.S. Foreign Policy and the Rise of the Post-Cold War Order* (Ithaca: Cornell University Press, 2016).

126 John Swift, "U.S. Invasion of Grenada," *Encyclopedia Britannica*, October 18, 2022, https://www.britannica.com/event/U-S-invasion-of-Grenada.

127 Erica Pearson, "1986 West Berlin Discoteque Bombing," Encyclopedia Britannica, https://www.britannica.com/event/West-Berlin-discotheque-bombing-1986

128 Ronald Reagan, "Address to the Nation on the United States Air Strike Against Libya" (speech, Washington, DC, April 14, 1986), Ronald Reagan Presidential Library & Museum, https://www.reaganlibrary.gov/archives/speech/address-nation-united-states-air-strike-against-libya.

129 H. R. McMaster, *Battlegrounds: The Fight to Defend the Free World* (New York: HarperCollins, 2020).

130 "US Delivering 'Peace through Strength': President Trump Tells UN," United Nations, September 22, 2020, https://news.un.org/en/story/2020/09/1073002.

131 Amanda Macias, "Trump Signs $783 Billion Defense Bill. Here's What the Pentagon Is Poised to Get," CNBC, December 20, 2019, https://www.cnbc.com/2019/12/21/trump-signs-738-billion-defense-bill.html.

132 Carrie Dann, "Donald Trump on Nukes: Let It Be an Arms Race," NBC News, December 23, 2016, https://www.nbcnews.com/politics/politics-news/trump-nukes-let-it-be-arms-race-n699526.

133 Derek Chollet and James Goldgeier, *America Between the Wars: From 11/9 to 9/11* (New York: BBS PublicAffairs, 2008).

134 Ibid.

135 Stephen J. Hadley et al., *Hand-Off: The Foreign Policy George W. Bush Passed to Barack Obama* (Washington, DC: Brookings Institution Press, 2023).

136 Ben Rhodes, *The World As It Is: A Memoir of the Obama White House* (New York: Random House, 2018).

137 Jonathan Allen, "Trump Kicks Off His 2024 Campaign: 'We Are at the Brink of World War III,'" NBC News, January 28, 2023, https://www.nbcnews.com/politics/donald-trump/trump-are-brink-world-war-iii-rcna68008.

138 Mike Pence (@VP45), "Peace only comes through strength. @POTUS believes we must be strong, able to confront all who would threaten our freedom & way of life," Twitter, February 18, 2017, https://twitter.com/VP45/status/832876767610183680.

139 Mike Pompeo (@mikepompeo), "Peace is achieved through strength, something this Administration has yet to show," Twitter, September 24, 2021, https://twitter.com/mikepompeo/status/1441392698552881154.

140 Nikki Haley (@NikkiHaley), "My bro. served in Desert Storm. My husband served in Afghanistan. I know the sacrifice military families endure. Believe me when I say that I want peace—& that's why I want to renew our strength. A strong America doesn't start wars. A strong America prevents wars! #RJCinVegas," Twitter, November 19, 2022, https://twitter.com/NikkiHaley/status/1594190314520051713.

141 Tom Cotton, "Speech at the Ronald Reagan Presidential Library" (speech, Simi Valley, California, March 8, 2022), Senator Tom Cotton, https://www.cotton.senate.gov/news/speeches/cotton-delivers-speech-at-the-ronald-reagan-presidential-library.

142 Amanpour, "US admiral sounds alarm on China's military ambitions in Asia," CNN, March 9, 2021, https://www.cnn.com/videos/world/2021/03/10/admiral-davidson-china-taiwan-concerns-kirby-sot-vpx-amanpour.cnn.

143 Ibid.

144 "Iran, Russia, China Hold Joint Naval Drill amid Growing Ties," Radio Free Europe/Radio Liberty, January 21, 2022, https://www.rferl.org/a/iran-russia-china-exercises/31663080.html; David Brennan, "Russia Desperate for Iran, North Korea Help with Missiles, Drones: U.S.," *Newsweek*, January 17, 2023, https://www.newsweek.com/russia-desperate-iran-north-korea-help-missiles-drones-us-ukraine-colin-kahl-wendy-sherman-1774237.

145 Matthew Kroenig, "Washington Must Prepare for War with Both Russia and China," *Foreign Policy*, February 18, 2022, https://foreignpolicy.com/2022/02/18/us-russia-china-war-nato-quadrilateral-security-dialogue/.

146 Elbridge Colby and Oriana Skylar Mastro, "Ukraine Is a Distraction from Taiwan," *The Wall Street Journal*, February 13, 2022, https://www.wsj.com/articles/ukraine-is-a-distraction-from-taiwan-russia-china-nato-global-powers-military-invasion-jinping-biden-putin-europe-11644781247.

147 John Bolton, "Entente Multiplies the Threat from Russia and China," *The Wall Street Journal*, February 15, 2022, https://www.wsj.com/articles/entente-multiplies-the-threat-from-russia-and-china-foreign-policy-alliance-beijing-moscow-xi-putin-11644943618.

148 "Providing for the Common Defense: The Assessment and Recommendations of the National Defense Strategy Commission," November 13, 2018, https://www.usip.org/publications/2018/11/providing-common-defense.

149 Lindsay Wise, "Senate Passes $778 Billion Defense-Policy Bill," *The Wall Street Journal*, December 15, 2021, https://www.wsj.com/articles/senate-set-to-pass-778-billion-ndaa-defense-policy-bill-11639586115; "Military Spending by Country 2023," World Population Review, 2023, https://worldpopulationreview.com/country-rankings/military-spending-by-country.

150 H. Peter Gray, *Free Trade or Protection? A Pragmatic Analysis* (London: Palgrave Macmillan, 1985), 8, https://doi.org/10.1007/978-1-349-06983-5.

151 Charles P. Kindleberger, *The World in Depression: 1929-1939* (Berkeley, University of California Press, 1973); Robert Gilpin, *War and Change in World Politics* (Cambridge, Cambridge University Press, 1981), https://doi.org/10.1017/CBO9780511664267; and Robert Gilpin, "The Theory of Hegemonic War," *The Journal of Interdisciplinary History* 18, no. 4 (1988): 591–613, https://doi.org/10.2307/204816.

152 John R. Oneal and Bruce Russett, "Assessing the Liberal Peace with Alternative Specifications: Trade Still Reduces Conflict," *Journal of Peace Research* 36, no. 4 (1999): 423–442, http://www.jstor.org/stable/425297; and Håvard Hegre, John R. Oneal, and Bruce Russett, "Trade Does Promote Peace: New Simultaneous Estimates of the Reciprocal Effects of Trade and Conflict," *Journal of Peace Research* 47, no. 6 (2010): 763–774, https://doi.org/10.1177/0022343310385995.

153 Douglas A. Irwin, *Peddling Protectionism: Smoot-Hawley and the Great Depression* (Princeton, Princeton University Press, 2011), https://doi.org/10.2307/j.ctt1pd2k7j.

154 Rafael de Hoyos, "Angry Voters Have a Point, but Protectionism Is Not the Answer," Brookings, March 20, 2017, https://www.brookings.edu/blog/future-development/2017/03/20/angry-voters-have-a-point-but-protectionism-is-not-the-answer/.

155 Giovanni Tagliabue, "The EU Legislation on 'GMOs' between Nonsense and Protectionism: An Ongoing Schumpeterian Chain of Public Choices," *GM Crops & Food* 8, no. 1 (2017): 57–73, https://doi.org/10.1080%2F21645698.2016.1270488; Jakob Hanke Vela and Arthur Neslen, "EU Mulls Faster Genetically Modified Food Approvals for Trump," *Politico*, February 26, 2020, https://www.politico.eu/article/eu-mulls-faster-genetically-modified-food-approvals-for-trump/; "Eight Things You Should Know about GMOs," European Parliament, updated October 27, 2015, https://www.europarl.europa.eu/news/en/headlines/society/20151013S-TO97392/eight-things-you-should-know-about-gmos#:~:text=Are%20GMOs%20allowed%20in%20the,in%20the%20EU%20so%20far.

156 "Declaration of Independence: A Transcription," America's Founding Documents, US National Archives and Records Administration, last modified January 31, 2023, https://www.archives.gov/founding-docs/declaration-transcript.

157 John Gerard Ruggie, "International Regimes, Transactions, and Change: Embedded Liberalism in the Postwar Economic Order," *International Organization* 36, no. 2 (1982): 379–415, doi:10.1017/S0020818300018993.

158 Esteban Ortiz-Ospina, Diana Beltekian, and Max Roser, "Trade and Globalization," OurWorldInData.org, 2018, https://ourworldindata.org/trade-and-globalization.

159 Joe Hasell and Max Roser, "How Do We Know the History of Extreme Poverty?" OurWorldInData.org, February 5, 2019, https://ourworldindata.org/extreme-history-methods; "Decline of Global Extreme Poverty Continues but Has Slowed: World Bank," World Bank, September 19,

2018, https://www.worldbank.org/en/news/press-release/2018/09/19/de-cline-of-global-extreme-poverty-continues-but-has-slowed-world-bank.

160 Max Roser et al., "Economic Growth," OurWorldInData.org, 2013, https://ourworldindata.org/economic-growth.

161 Giuseppe La Barca, *International Trade under President Reagan: US Trade Policy in the 1980s* (London: Bloomsbury Publishing 2023).

162 Mark J. Perry, "Video of the Day: Reagan's Thanksgiving Radio Address on Free Trade 31 Years Ago Today," American Enterprise Institute, November 26, 2019, https://www.aei.org/carpe-diem/video-of-the-day-reagans-thanksgiving-radio-address-on-free-trade-31-years-ago-today/.

163 Ronald Reagan, "Remarks at a White House Meet-ing with Business and Trade Leaders" (speech, Washing-ton, DC, September 23, 1985), Ronald Reagan Presidential Library & Museum, https://www.reaganlibrary.gov/archives/speech/remarks-white-house-meeting-business-and-trade-leaders.

164 Ibid.

165 Ryutaro Komiya and Mutsunori Irino, "Japan's Economic and Industrial Policy in the 1980's," in *Keynes and the Economic Policies of the 1980s,* ed. Mario Baldassarri (London: Palgrave Macmillan, 1992), https://doi.org/10.1007/978-1-349-12815-0_7.

166 Mike Tharp, "U.S. and Japan Agree on Ceilings for Car Shipments through 1983," *The New York Times,* May 1, 1981, https://www.nytimes.com/1981/05/01/business/us-and-japan-agree-on-ceilings-for-car-ship-ments-through-1983.html; Clyde H. Farnsworth, "U.S. Raises Tariff for Motorcycles," *The New York Times,* April 2, 1983, https://www.nytimes.com/1983/04/02/business/us-raises-tariff-for-motorcycles.html; Gerald M. Boyd, "President Imposes Tariff on Imports against Japanese," *The New York Times,* April 18, 1987, https://www.nytimes.com/1987/04/18/business/president-imposes-tariff-on-imports-against-japanese.html.

167 Peter T. Kilborn, "U.S. Puts 15% Tariff on Lumber," *The New York Times,* October 17, 1986, https://www.nytimes.com/1986/10/17/business/us-puts-15-tariff-on-lumber.html; Clyde H. Farnsworth, "Reagan Decides to Tighten Controls on Textile Imports," *The New York Times,* December 17, 1983, https://www.nytimes.com/1983/12/17/business/reagan-decides-to-tighten-controls-on-textile-imports.html; Seth S. King, "U.S. Plans Quotas on Sugar Imports," *The New York Times,* May 5, 1982, https://www.nytimes.com/1982/05/05/business/us-plans-quotas-on-sugar-im-ports.html; Clyde H. Farnsworth and Daniel F. Cuff, "'Voluntary' Import Restraint," *The New York Times,* September 20, 1984, https://www.ny-times.com/1984/09/20/business/voluntary-import-restraint.html; Clyde

H. Farnsworth, "Reagan Acts to Restrict Machine Tool Imports," *The New York Times*, May 21, 1986, https://www.nytimes.com/1986/05/21/business/reagan-acts-to-restrict-machine-tool-imports.html.

168 Daniel Griswold, "Reagan Embraced Free Trade and Immigration," Cato Institute, June 24, 2004, https://www.cato.org/commentary/reagan-embraced-free-trade-immigration.

169 "GDP Per Capita, 1940 to 2018," OurWorldInData.org, accessed April 14, 2023, https://ourworldindata.org/grapher/gdp-per-capita-maddison-2020?tab=chart&time=1940..2018&country=OWID_WRL~USA.

170 Francis Fukuyama, "The End of History?," *The National Interest*, no. 16 (1989): 3–18, https://www.jstor.org/stable/24027184.

171 "China Joins W.T.O. Ranks," *The New York Times*, December 12, 2001, https://www.nytimes.com/2001/12/12/world/china-joins-wto-ranks.html.

172 Aaron L. Friedberg, *Getting China Wrong* (Cambridge: Polity, 2022).

173 Robert E. Scott and Zane Mokhiber, "Growing China Trade Deficit Cost 3.7 Million American Jobs between 2001 and 2018," Economic Policy Institute, January 30, 2020, https://www.epi.org/publication/growing-china-trade-deficits-costs-us-jobs.

174 "Compare Countries with Annual Data from Official Sources," TheGlobalEconomy.com, accessed April 17, 2023, https://www.theglobaleconomy.com/compare-countries/.

175 Elizabeth C. Economy, *The Third Revolution: Xi Jinping and the New Chinese State* (Oxford: Oxford University Press, 2018).

176 Robert B. Zoellick, "Whither China: From Membership to Responsibility?" (speech, New York City, New York, September 21, 2005), US Department of State, https://2001-2009.state.gov/s/d/former/zoellick/rem/53682.htm.

177 Donald Trump, *The America We Deserve* (Renaissance Books, 2000).

178 Ross Chainey, "Trump at Davos: Trade, Taxes and What America First Means for the World," World Economic Forum, January 26, 2018, https://www.weforum.org/agenda/2018/01/trump-at-davos-trade-tax-cuts-and-america-first/.

179 Ana Swanson, "Trump to Impose Sweeping Steel and Aluminum Tariffs," *The New York Times*, March 1, 2018, https://www.nytimes.com/2018/03/01/business/trump-tariffs.html.

180 Milan Schreuer, "E.U. Pledges to Fight Back on Trump Tariffs as Trade War Looms," *The New York Times*, March 7, 2018, https://www.nytimes.com/2018/03/07/business/trump-tariffs-eu-trade.html.

181 Ana Swanson, "White House to Impose Metal Tariffs on E.U., Canada and Mexico," *The New York Times*, May 31, 2018, https://www.nytimes.com/2018/05/31/us/politics/trump-aluminum-steel-tariffs.html; Dan Murphy, "Japan Has Become the 'Obvious Target' for Trump's Next Trade Salvo," CNBC, September 7, 2018, https://www.cnbc.com/2018/09/07/japan-has-become-the-obvious-target-for-trumps-next-trade-salvo.html.

182 Jacqueline Thomsen, "Trump Calls for EU to Drop All Trade Barriers Ahead of Official's Visit," *The Hill*, July 24, 2018, https://thehill.com/homenews/administration/398706-trump-calls-for-eu-to-drop-all-trade-barriers-ahead-of-official-visit/.

183 Mark Landler and Ana Swanson, "U.S. and Europe Outline Deal to Ease Trade Feud," *The New York Times*, July 25, 2018, https://www.nytimes.com/2018/07/25/us/politics/trump-europe-trade.html.

184 "Trump Says Agreed with EU to Work to Lower Trade Barriers," Reuters, July 25, 2018, https://www.reuters.com/article/usa-trade-eu-announcement/trump-says-agreed-with-eu-to-work-to-lower-trade-barriers-idINS0N1T700I.

185 Jim Tankersley, "Trumps Signs Revised Korean Trade Deal," *The New York Times*, September 24, 2018, https://www.nytimes.com/2018/09/24/us/politics/south-korea-trump-trade-deal.html; Jeff Stein, "Trumps Signs USMCA, Revamping North American Trade Rules," *The Washington Post*, January 29, 2020, https://www.washingtonpost.com/business/2020/01/29/trump-usmca/.

186 Matthew Kroenig and Jeffrey Cimmino, *Global Strategy 2021: An Allied Strategy for China*, Atlantic Council Strategy Paper series, December 2020, https://www.atlanticcouncil.org/wp-content/uploads/2020/12/Global-Strategy-2021-An-Allied-Strategy-for-China.pdf.

187 Cate Cadell and Ellen Nakashima, "American Technology Boosts China's Hypersonic Missile Program," *The Washington Post*, October 17, 2022, https://www.washingtonpost.com/national-security/2022/10/17/china-hypersonic-missiles-american-technology/.

188 Emily Weinstein, "Don't Underestimate China's Military-Civil Fusion Efforts," *Foreign Policy*, February 5, 2021, https://foreignpolicy.com/2021/02/05/dont-underestimate-chinas-military-civil-fusion-efforts/.

189 Steven Schoenfeld, "Americans Are Investing More in China—and They Don't Even Know It," *Foreign Policy*, January 14, 2020, https://foreignpolicy.com/2020/01/14/americans-investment-china-emerging-markets-united-states-trade-war/.

190 Dan Blumenthal and Linda Zhang, "China Is Stealing Our Technology and Intellectual Property. Congress Must Stop It," *National Review*, June 2, 2021, https://www.nationalreview.com/2021/06/china-is-stealing-our-technology-and-intellectual-property-congress-must-stop-it/.

191 Doug Cameron, "Pentagon Pushes Defense Companies to Limit Use of Chinese Supplies," *The Wall Street Journal*, September 18, 2022, https://www.wsj.com/articles/pentagon-pushes-defense-companies-to-limit-use-of-chinese-supplies-11663498804.

192 Steven Scheer, "With Eye to China, Israel Forms Panel to Vet Foreign Investments," Reuters, October 30, 2019, https://www.reuters.com/article/us-israel-investment-panel/with-eye-to-china-israel-forms-panel-to-vet-foreign-investments-idUSKBN1X926T; Andreas B. Forsby, "Falling Out of Favor: How China Lost the Nordic Countries," *The Diplomat*, June 24, 2022, https://thediplomat.com/2022/06/falling-out-of-favor-how-china-lost-the-nordic-countries/.

193 Helen Davidson, "Xinjiang: More Than Half a Million Forced to Pick Cotton, Report Suggests," *The Guardian*, December 15, 2020, https://www.theguardian.com/world/2020/dec/15/xinjiang-china-more-than-half-a-million-forced-to-pick-cotton-report-finds.

194 Christine Murray, "Shipment of Chinese Hair Goods Seized by U.S. Officials Suspecting Forced Labor," Reuters, July 1, 2020, https://www.reuters.com/article/us-usa-trafficking-seizure-trfn/shipment-of-chinese-hair-goods-seized-by-u-s-officials-suspecting-forced-labor-idUSKBN2427IN.

195 Shirley Li, "How Hollywood Sold Out to China," *The Atlantic*, September 10, 2021, https://www.theatlantic.com/culture/archive/2021/09/how-hollywood-sold-out-to-china/620021/.

196 Vincent Ni, "John Cena 'Very Sorry' for Saying Taiwan Is a Country," *The Guardian*, May 25, 2021, https://www.theguardian.com/world/2021/may/26/john-cena-very-sorry-for-saying-taiwan-is-a-country.

197 "Article VI: Anti-Dumping and Countervailing Duties," opened for signature October 30, 1947, General Agreement on Tariffs and Trade: 10–12, https://www.wto.org/english/docs_e/legal_e/gatt47_e.pdf.

198 "Trade in Goods with China," United States Census Bureau, accessed April 7, 2023, https://www.census.gov/foreign-trade/balance/c5700.html#2022.

199 *CHIPS Act of 2022*, Public Law 117–167, US Statutes at Large 136 (2022): 1366–1758, https://www.congress.gov/117/plaws/publ167/PLAW-117publ167.pdf.

200 Yang Jie and Aaron Tilley, "Apple Makes Plans to Move Production Out of China," *The Wall Street Journal*, December 3, 2022, https://www.wsj.

com/articles/apple-china-factory-protests-foxconn-manufacturing-pro-
duction-supply-chain-11670023099.

201 Roland Rajah and Alyssa Leng, "Chart of the Week: Global Trade
through a US-China Lens," *The Interpreter*, Lowy Institute, December 18, 2019, https://www.lowyinstitute.org/the-interpreter/
chart-week-global-trade-through-us-china-lens.

202 Yana Gorokhovskaia, Adrian Shahbaz, and Amy Slipowitz, *Freedom
in the World 2023: Marking 50 Years in the Struggle for Democracy*,
Freedom House, March 2023, https://freedomhouse.org/report/
freedom-world/2023/marking-50-years.

203 Carl Campanile, "Majority of Democrats Say US Is Not
World's Greatest Country: Poll," *New York Post*, September 19, 2022, https://nypost.com/2022/09/19/majority-of-
democrats-say-us-is-not-worlds-greatest-country-poll/
amp/.

204 "Declaration of Independence: A Transcription," America's Founding
Documents, US National Archives and Records Administration, last
modified January 31, 2023, https://www.archives.gov/founding-docs/
declaration-transcript.

205 Ibid.

206 Louis Hartz, *The Liberal Tradition in America: An Interpretation of American Political Thought since the Revolution* (New York: Harcourt Brace
and Co., 1955).

207 Robert Kagan, *Dangerous Nation: America's Place in the World from Its
Earliest Days to the Dawn of the Twentieth Century* (New York: Alfred A.
Knopf, 2006).

208 US National Archives, "Declaration of Independence"; "The Constitution
of the United States: A Transcription," America's Founding Documents,
US National Archives and Records Administration, last modified
February 3, 2023, https://www.archives.gov/founding-docs/constitu-
tion-transcript; "The Bill of Rights: A Transcription," America's Founding
Documents, US National Archives and Records Administration, last
modified January 31, 2023, https://www.archives.gov/founding-docs/
bill-of-rights-transcript.

209 Michael W. Doyle, "Kant, Liberal Legacies, and Foreign Affairs," *Philosophy & Public Affairs* 12, no. 3 (1983): 205–235, http://www.jstor.org/
stable/2265298; Michael W. Doyle, "Kant, Liberal Legacies, and Foreign
Affairs, Part 2," *Philosophy & Public Affairs* 12, no. 4 (1983): 323–353,
http://www.jstor.org/stable/2265377; Bruce Russett et al., *Grasping the*

Democratic Peace: Principles for a Post-Cold War World (Princeton: Princeton University Press, 1993), http://www.jstor.org/stable/j.ctt7rqf6.

210 Brett Ashley Leeds, "Domestic Political Institutions, Credible Commitments, and International Cooperation," *American Journal of Political Science* 43, no. 4 (1999): 979–1002, https://doi.org/10.2307/2991814; Brett Ashley Leeds, "Alliance Reliability in Times of War: Explaining State Decisions to Violate Treaties," *International Organization* 57, no. 4 (2003): 801–827, http://www.jstor.org/stable/3594847; Daina Chiba, Jesse C. Johnson, and Brett Ashley Leeds, "Careful Commitments: Democratic Atates and Alliance Design," *Journal of Politics* 77, no. 4 (2015): 968–982, https://doi.org/10.1086/682074.

211 Matthew Fuhrmann and Jeffrey D. Berejikian, "Disaggregating Noncompliance: Abstention versus Predation in the Nuclear Nonproliferation Treaty," *The Journal of Conflict Resolution* 56, no. 3 (2012): 355–381, http://www.jstor.org/stable/23248792.

212 Helen V. Milner and Keiko Kubota, "Why the Move to Free Trade? Democracy and Trade Policy in the Developing Countries," *International Organization* 59, no. 1 (2005): 107–143, https://doi.org/10.1017/S002081830505006X; Helen V. Milner and Bumba Mukherjee, "Democratization and Economic Globalization," *Annual Review of Political Science* 12 (2009): 163–181, https://doi.org/10.1146/annurev.polisci.12.110507.114722.

213 Matthew Kroenig, *The Return of the Great Power Rivalry: Democracy versus Autocracy from the Ancient World to the U.S. and China* (Oxford: Oxford University Press, 2020).

214 "GDP, Current Prices," World Economic Outlook (April 2023), International Monetary Fund, accessed April 18, 2023, https://www.imf.org/external/datamapper/NGDPD@WEO/OEMDC/ADVEC/WEOWORLD.

215 Niccolo Conte, "Ranked: Top 10 Countries by Military Spending," Visual Capitalist, August 18, 2022, https://www.visualcapitalist.com/ranked-top-10-countries-by-military-spending/.

216 Robert Kagan, *The World America Made* (New York: Alfred A. Knopf, 2012).

217 Geir Lundestad, "Empire by Invitation? The United States and Western Europe, 1945–1952," *Journal of Peace Research* 23, no. 3 (1986): 263–77, http://www.jstor.org/stable/423824; Geir Lundestad. "'Empire by Invitation' in the American Century," *Diplomatic History* 23, no. 2 (1999): 189–217, http://www.jstor.org/stable/24913738.

218 Ash Jain and Matthew Kroenig, *Present at the Re-Creation: A Global Strategy for Revitalizing, Adapting, and Defending a Rules-Based Inter-*

national System, Atlantic Council Strategy Paper series, October 2019, https://www.atlanticcouncil.org/wp-content/uploads/2019/10/Present-at-the-Recreation.pdf.

219 Jeane Kirkpatrick, "Blame America First" (speech, Dallas, Texas, August 20, 1984), Archives of Women's Political Communication, Iowa State University, https://awpc.cattcenter.iastate.edu/2017/03/09/remarks-at-the-1984-rnc-aug-20-1984/.

220 "Rights Group: Iran Executes 2 Gay Men over Sodomy Charges," Associated Press, February 1, 2022, https://apnews.com/article/middle-east-iran-crime-dubai-united-arab-emirates-e3d-7108441665c40982329f26ff07fc9.

221 "Prisons of North Korea," US Department of State, published August 25, 2017, https://2017-2021.state.gov/prisons-of-north-korea/index.html.

222 John J. Mearsheimer, *The Tragedy of Great Power Politics* (New York: W. W. Norton & Company, 2001).

223 Elbridge Colby and Robert D. Kaplan, "The Ideology Delusion: America's Competition with China Is Not about Doctrine," *Foreign Affairs*, September 4, 2020, https://www.foreignaffairs.com/articles/united-states/2020-09-04/ideology-delusion.

224 Elbridge A. Colby, "The U.S. Must Support Ukraine, but China Must Be Our Priority," *Time*, February 27, 2022, https://time.com/6152096/us-support-ukraine-china-priority/; Elbridge A. Colby and Kevin Roberts, "The Correct Conservative Approach to Ukraine Shifts the Focus to China," *Time*, March 21, 2023, https://time.com/6264798/conservative-approach-to-ukraine-shifts-the-focus-to-china/.

225 Margaret MacMillan, *Paris 1919: Six Months that Changed the World* (New York: Random House Trade Paperbacks, 2003).

226 Jakub Grygiel and Rebeccah Heinrichs, "Biden's Abortion Politics Will Undermine America's World Standing," *The Wall Street Journal*, July 22, 2022, https://www.wsj.com/articles/bidens-abortion-politics-will-undermine-americas-world-standing-roe-v-wade-dobbs-jackson-foreign-policy-11658511777.

227 Ronald Reagan, "Farewell Address to the Nation" (speech, Washington, DC, January 11, 1989), Ronald Reagan Presidential Library & Museum, https://www.reaganlibrary.gov/archives/speech/farewell-address-nation.

228 Jim Geraghty, "Obama's Pastor after 9/11: 'America's Chickens Are Coming Home to Roost,'" *National Review*, March 13, 2008, https://www.nationalreview.com/the-campaign-spot/obamas-pastor-after-911-americas-chickens-are-coming-home-roost-jim-geraghty/.

229 Karl Rove, "The President's Apology Tour," *The Wall Street Journal*, April 23, 2009, https://www.wsj.com/articles/SB124044156269345357.

230 Barack Obama, "News Conference by President Obama, 4/04/2009" (press conference, Strasbourg, France, April 4, 2009), White House, https://obamawhitehouse.archives.gov/the-press-office/news-conference-president-obama-4042009.

231 "Face the Nation Transcript February 5, 2017: Pence, Christie," *Face the Nation*, CBS News, February 5, 2017, https://www.cbsnews.com/news/face-the-nation-transcript-february-5-2017-pence-christie/.

232 Mike Pence, "Remarks by Vice President Mike Pence to the Federalist Society" (speech, Philadelphia, Pennsylvania, February 4, 2017), White House, https://trumpwhitehouse.archives.gov/briefings-statements/remarks-vice-president-mike-pence-federalist-society/.

233 Mike Pompeo (@mikepompeo), "America is the most exceptional nation in the history of civilization. We ought to be proud of that.," Twitter, July 2, 2021, https://twitter.com/mikepompeo/status/1411086762349318145.

234 Logan Washburn and Melissa Brown, "Nikki Haley Helps Kick Off Faith and Freedom Event as Jan. 6 Hearings Continue," *The Tennessean*, June 16, 2022, https://www.tennessean.com/story/news/politics/2022/06/16/nikki-haley-speaks-conference-while-jan-6-hearings-contin-ue/7649025001/.

235 Ryan Teague Beckwith, "Read Donald Trump's 'America First' Foreign Policy Speech," *Time*, April 27, 2016, https://time.com/4309786/read-donald-trumps-america-first-foreign-policy-speech/.

236 David Corn, "Donald Trump Says He Doesn't Believe in 'American Exceptionalism,'" *Mother Jones*, June 7, 2016, https://www.motherjones.com/politics/2016/06/donald-trump-american-exceptionalism/.

237 Ibid.

238 Abby Phillip, "O'Reilly Told Trump that Putin Is a Killer. Trump's Reply: 'You Think Our Country Is So Innocent?'," *The Washington Post*, February 4, 2017, https://www.washingtonpost.com/news/post-politics/wp/2017/02/04/oreilly-told-trump-that-putin-is-a-killer-trumps-reply-you-think-our-countrys-so-innocent/.

239 Ishaan Tharoor, "The Limits of Biden's American Exceptionalism," *The Washington Post*, March 15, 2021, https://www.washingtonpost.com/world/2021/03/15/biden-american-exceptionalism-limits/.

240 Andrea Shalal, "Biden, Harris condemn U.S. racism, sexism in blunt language," Reuters, March 27, 2021, https://www.reuters.com/article/us-usa-biden-racism/biden-harris-condemn-u-s-racism-sexism-in-blunt-language-idUSKBN2BE019.

241 "Fact Check-Pride Flags Have Been Flown by U.S. Embassies in Muslim Majority Countries during Biden Presidency," Reuters, June 13, 2022, https://www.reuters.com/article/factcheck-pride-flags-embassy/fact-check-pride-flags-have-been-flown-by-u-s-embassies-in-muslim-majority-countries-during-biden-presidency-idUSL1N2Y01EU.

242 Katherine Fung, "Fact Check: Is Biden Administration Funding Drag Shows in Ecuador?" *Newsweek*, October 20, 2022, https://www.newsweek.com/fact-check-biden-administration-funding-drag-shows-ecuador-1753649.

243 This passage draws heavily on Matthew Kroenig, "The Power Delusion," *Foreign Policy*, November 11, 2020, https://foreignpolicy.com/2020/11/11/china-united-states-democracy-ideology-competition-rivalry-great-powers-power-delusion/.

244 Eric Edelman et al., *Providing for the Common Defense: The Assessment and Recommendations of the National Defense Strategy Commission*, United States Institute of Peace, November 13, 2018, https://www.usip.org/sites/default/files/2018-11/providing-for-the-common-defense.pdf.

245 Daron Acemoglu and James A. Robinson, *Why Nations Fail: The Origins of Power, Prosperity, and Poverty* (New York: Currency, 2013).

246 Edward D. Mansfield, Helen V. Milner, and B. Peter Rosendorff, "Why Democracies Cooperate More: Electoral Control and International Trade Agreements," International Organization 56, no. 3 (2002): 477–513, http://www.jstor.org/stable/3078586.

247 Gorokhovskaia, Shahbaz, and Slipowitz, "Freedom in the World 2023."

248 Editorial Board, "China's International Efforts to Silence Free Speech," *The Washington Post*, August 21, 2015, https://www.washingtonpost.com/opinions/chinas-overreach/2015/08/21/4dce4278-4516-11e5-8ab4-c73967a143d3_story.html.

249 Kroenig, *The Return of the Great Power Rivalry*.

250 Laura Silver, Kat Devlin, and Christine Huang, "Unfavorable Views of China Reach Historic Highs in Many Countries," Pew Research Center, October 6, 2020, https://www.pewresearch.org/global/2020/10/06/unfavorable-views-of-china-reach-historic-highs-in-many-countries/.

251 Matthew Kroenig, "Washington Needs a Better Plan for Competing with China," *Foreign Policy*, August 7, 2020, https://foreignpolicy.com/2020/08/07/washington-needs-a-better-plan-for-competing-with-china/.

252 John Feng, "Xi Jinping Says China to Become Dominant World Power within 30 Years," *Newsweek*, July 1, 2021, https://www.newsweek.com/

xi-jinping-says-china-become-dominant-world-power-within-30-years-1605848.

253 International Monetary Fund, "GDP, Current Prices."

254 *Update to the Report of the Commission on the Theft of American Intellectual Property*, The National Bureau of Asian Research, 2017, https://www.nbr.org/wp-content/uploads/pdfs/publications/IP_Commission_Report_Update.pdf; "Gross Domestic Product by State: Fourth Quarter and Annual 2017," Bureau of Economic Analysis, US Department of Commerce, May 4, 2018, https://apps.bea.gov/newsreleases/regional/gdp_state/2018/pdf/qgdpstate0518.pdf.

255 *Made in China 2025: Global Ambitions Built on Local Protections*, US Chamber of Commerce, 2017, https://www.uschamber.com/assets/documents/final_made_in_china_2025_report_full.pdf.

256 Amanda Lee, "Explainer: What Is China's Social Credit System and Why Is It Controversial?," *South China Morning Post*, August 9, 2020, https://www.scmp.com/economy/china-economy/article/3096090/what-chinas-social-credit-system-and-why-it-controversial.

257 Xi Jinping, *The Governance of China*: *Volume 1* (Beijing: Foreign Languages Press, 2014); Xi Jinping, *The Governance of China*: *Volume 2* (Beijing: Foreign Languages Press, 2017); Xi Jinping, *The Governance of China*: *Volume 3* (Beijing: Foreign Languages Press, 2020); Xi Jinping, *The Governance of China*: *Volume 4* (Beijing: Foreign Languages Press, 2022).

258 Christopher Wray, "The Threat Posed by the Chinese Government and the Chinese Communist Party to the Economic and National Security of the United States," FBI, July 7, 2020, https://www.fbi.gov/news/speeches/the-threat-posed-by-the-chinese-government-and-the-chinese-communist-party-to-the-economic-and-national-security-of-the-united-states.

259 Ni, "John Cena 'Very Sorry.'"

260 Sui-Lee Wee, "Giving In to China, U.S. Airlines Drop Taiwan (in Name at Least)," *The New York Times*, July 25, 2018, https://www.nytimes.com/2018/07/25/business/taiwan-american-airlines-china.html.

261 Alaa Abdeldaiem, "LeBron James Says Daryl Morey Was 'Misinformed' about Situation in China," *Sports Illustrated*, October 14, 2019, https://www.si.com/nba/2019/10/15/lebron-james-daryl-morey-misinformed-china-tweet.

262 Lily Kuo, "Australia Called 'Gum Stuck to China's Shoe' by State Media in Coronavirus Investigation Stoush," *The Guardian*, April 28, 2020, https://www.theguardian.com/world/2020/apr/28/australia-called-gum-stuck-to-chinas-shoe-by-state-media-in-coronavirus-investigation-stoush.

263 Chun Han Wong and Chao Deng, "China's 'Wolf Warrior' Diplomats Are Ready to Fight," *The Wall Street Journal*, May 19, 2020, https://www.wsj.com/articles/chinas-wolf-warrior-diplomats-are-ready-to-fight-11589896722.

264 James Griffiths, "China's Ambassador Accuses Canada of Double Standards, 'White Supremacy' over Huawei," CNN, January 10, 2019, https://www.cnn.com/2019/01/09/asia/china-canada-meng-huawei-intl/index.html.

265 Tony Munroe, Andrew Osborn, and Humeyra Pamuk, "China, Russia Partner Up against West at Olympics Summit," Reuters, February 4, 2022, https://www.reuters.com/world/europe/russia-china-tell-nato-stop-expansion-moscow-backs-beijing-taiwan-2022-02-04/.

266 Sun Tzu, *The Art of War*, trans. Thomas Cleary (Boulder: Shambhala, 2003), 68.

267 Patty-Jane Geller, "Pentagon Report on China's Military Highlights Nuclear Buildup that Could Overtake America," The Heritage Foundation, December 9, 2022, https://www.heritage.org/defense/commentary/pentagon-report-chinas-military-highlights-nuclear-buildup-could-overtake.

268 Richard V. Allen, "The Man Who Won the Cold War," Hoover Institution, January 30, 2000, https://www.hoover.org/research/man-who-won-cold-war.

269 Kroenig, *The Return of the Great Power Rivalry*.

270 This chapter draws on Matthew Kroenig and Dan Negrea, "Why 'Confrontation' with China Cannot Be Avoided," *The National Interest*, November 26, 2021, https://nationalinterest.org/feature/why-%E2%80%98confrontation%E2%80%99-china-cannot-be-avoided-196926; "Press Briefing by Press Secretary Jen Psaki," the White House, published October 18, 2021, https://www.whitehouse.gov/briefing-room/press-briefings/2021/10/18/press-briefing-by-press-secretary-jen-psaki-october-18-2021/.

271 Elbridge A. Colby, *The Strategy of Denial: American Defense in an Era of Great Power Conflict* (New Haven: Yale University Press, 2021).

272 Michèle A. Flournoy, "How to Prevent a War in Asia: The Erosion of American Deterrence Raises the Risk of Chinese Miscalculation," *Foreign Affairs*, June 18, 2020, https://www.foreignaffairs.com/articles/united-states/2020-06-18/how-prevent-war-asia.

273 Hector Schamis, "At COP26, the New Cold War Comes to Climate Change," *The National Interest*, November 19, 2021, https://nationalinterest.org/feature/cop26-new-cold-war-comes-climate-change-196711.

274 Ted Galen Carpenter, "How China Could Test the U.S. Commitment to Taiwan," *The National Interest*, November 2, 2021, https://nationalinterest.org/blog/skeptics/how-china-could-test-us-commitment-taiwan-195759.

275 Ann M. Simmons and Austin Ramzy, "Russia-China Summit Showcases Challenge to the West," *The Wall Street Journal*, March 21, 2023, https://www.wsj.com/articles/china-xi-jinping-vladimir-putin-meet-in-russia-400d39e1.

276 Tony Munroe, Andrew Osborn, and Humeyra Pamuk, "China, Russia Partner Up against West at Olympics Summit," Reuters, February 4, 2022, https://www.reuters.com/world/europe/russia-china-tell-nato-stop-expansion-moscow-backs-beijing-taiwan-2022-02-04/.

277 Dan Peleschuk, "As Xi and Putin Bid Farewell in Moscow, Russia Unleashed Missiles on Ukraine," *The Sydney Morning Herald*, March 23, 2023, https://www.smh.com.au/world/europe/we-are-driving-changes-in-the-world-together-xi-jinping-tells-vladimir-putin-as-he-departs-kremlin-20230323-p5cuio.html.

278 Evelyn Cheng, "China and Russia Affirm Economic Cooperation for the Next Several Years," CNBC, March 22, 2023, https://www.cnbc.com/2023/03/22/china-and-russia-affirm-multi-year-economic-cooperation.html; David Vergun, "Russia Reportedly Supplying Enriched Uranium to China," US Department of Defense, March 8, 2023, https://www.defense.gov/News/News-Stories/Article/Article/3323381/russia-reportedly-supplying-enriched-uranium-to-china/.

279 Andrew Higgins, "China and Russia Hold First Joint Naval Drill in the Baltic Sea," *The New York Times*, July 25, 2017, https://www.nytimes.com/2017/07/25/world/europe/china-russia-baltic-navy-exercises.html; John Eligon, "South Africa Begins Naval Drills with Russia and China, Despite Criticism that It Implies Support of the War," *The New York Times*, February 17, 2023, https://www.nytimes.com/2023/02/17/world/south-africa-begins-naval-drills-with-russia-and-china-despite-criticism-that-it-implies-support-of-the-war.html; Dion Nissenbaum and Chun Han Wong, "China, Russia, Iran Hold Joint Military Drills in Gulf of Oman," *The Wall Street Journal*, March 15, 2023, https://www.wsj.com/articles/china-russia-iran-hold-joint-military-drills-in-gulf-of-oman-aba5f55e; "China to Send Troops to Russia for 'Vostok' Exercise," Reuters, August 17, 2022, https://www.reuters.com/world/china/chinese-military-will-send-troops-russia-joint-exercise-2022-08-17/.

280 John Herbst and Sergei Erofeev, *The Putin Exodus: The New Russian Brain Drain*, Atlantic Council, February 2019, https://www.atlanticcouncil.org/wp-content/uploads/2019/09/The-Putin-Exodus.pdf.

281 "GDP Per Capita (Current US$)—Russian Federation," World Bank, accessed July 29, 2023, https://data.worldbank.org/indicator/NY.GDP. PCAP.CD?locations=RU.

282 Holly Ellyatt, "Russia Is Still Occupying 20% of Our Country, Georgia's Prime Minister Says," CNBC, January 22, 2019, https://www.cnbc. com/2019/01/22/russia-is-still-occupying-20percent-of-our-country-georgias-leader-says.html; Jonathan Masters, "Ukraine: Conflict at the Crossroads of Europe and Russia," Council on Foreign Relations, February 14, 2023, https://www.cfr.org/backgrounder/ukraine-conflict-crossroads-europe-and-russia; "Russia Warns West over Threatening Its Troops in Breakaway Moldovan Region," Reuters, February 24, 2023, https://www.reuters.com/world/europe/russia-warns-west-over-threat-ening-its-troops-moldovan-region-2023-02-24/.

283 Becky Sullivan, "Why Belarus Is So Involved in Russia's Invasion of Ukraine," NPR, March 11, 2022, https://www.npr. org/2022/03/11/1085548867/belarus-ukraine-russia-invasion-lukashen-ko-putin; Jack Losh, "Russian Troops in Nagorno-Karabakh 'Clearly a Win for Moscow,'" Foreign Policy, November 25, 2020, https://foreign-policy.com/2020/11/25/russian-troops-nagorno-karabakh-peacekeep-ers-win-moscow-armenia-azerbaijan/.

284 Olzhas Auyezov, "Russia Sends Troops to Put Down Kazakhstan Uprising as Fresh Violence Erupts," Reuters, January 6, 2022, https://www. reuters.com/world/asia-pacific/troops-protesters-clash-almaty-main-square-kazakhstan-shots-heard-2022-01-06/.

285 Emma Colton, "Condoleezza Rice: Putin 'Seems Erratic,' 'Descending into Something' Never Personally Seen Before," Fox News, February 27, 2022, https://www.foxnews.com/politics/ condoleezza-rice-putin-russia-erratic-ukraine.

286 John J. Mearsheimer, "Why the Ukraine Crisis Is the West's Fault: The Liberal Delusions that Provoked Putin," Foreign Affairs, August 18, 2014, https://www.foreignaffairs.com/articles/russia-fsu/2014-08-18/ why-ukraine-crisis-west-s-fault.

287 Taras Kuzio, "Putin's Failing Ukraine Invasion Proves Russia Is No Superpower," Atlantic Council, November 1, 2022, https://www.atlanticcouncil. org/blogs/ukrainealert/putins-failing-ukraine-invasion-proves-russia-is-no-superpower/; Pablo Gutiérrez and Ashley Kirk, "A Year of War: How Russian Forces Have Been Pushed Back in Ukraine," The Guardian, February 21, 2023, https://www.theguardian.com/world/ng-interac-tive/2023/feb/21/a-year-of-war-how-russian-forces-have-been-pushed-

back-in-ukraine; "Land Area (sq. km)," The World Bank, accessed May 8, 2023, https://data.worldbank.org/indicator/AG.LND.TOTL.K2.

288 Matthew Kroenig, "Facing Reality: Getting NATO Ready for a New Cold War," *Survival* 57, no.1 (2015): 49–70, https://doi.org/10.1080/00396338.2 015.1008295.

289 Andrew Osborn and Phil Stewart, "Russia Begins Syria Air Strikes in Its Biggest Mideast Intervention in Decades," Reuters, September 30, 2015, https://www.reuters.com/article/us-mideast-crisis-russia/ russia-begins-syria-air-strikes-in-its-biggest-mideast-intervention-in-decades-idUSKCN0RU0MG20150930; Nomaan Merchant, "US: Russia Spent $300M to Covertly Influence World Politics," Associated Press, September 13, 2022, https://apnews.com/article/russia-ukraine-pu-tin-biden-politics-presidential-elections-03d0ae84fb34833b78b-1753d0a9602db; Mary Anastasia O'Grady, "Putin Is Already in Cuba and Venezuela," *The Wall Street Journal*, January 30, 2022, https://www.wsj. com/articles/putin-is-already-in-cuba-and-venezuela-south-america-in-fluence-western-hemisphere-ukraine-11643567547; "Iran's Deepening Strategic Alliance with Russia," *The Iran Primer*, United States Institute of Peace, April 25, 2023, http://iranprimer.usip.org/blog/2023/feb/24/ iran%E2%80%99s-deepening-strategic-alliance-russia; Carley Petesch and Gerald Imray, "Russian Mercenaries Are Putin's 'Coercive Tool' in Africa," Associated Press, April 23, 2022, https://apnews.com/article/rus-sia-ukraine-putin-technology-business-mali-d0d2c96e01d299a68e00d-3a0828ba895.

290 Piers Morgan, "DeSantis Brands Putin 'a War Criminal' Who Should Be 'Held Accountable' for Ukraine Invasion," *New York Post*, March 22, 2023, https://nypost.com/2023/03/22/desantis-brands-putin-a-war-criminal-who-should-be-held-accountable-for-ukraine-invasion/.

291 This section draws from Matthew Kroenig, "The United States Should Not Align with Russia against China," *Foreign Policy*, May 13, 2020, https://foreignpolicy.com/2020/05/13/unit-ed-states-should-not-align-russia-against-china-geopolitical-rivalry-au-thoritarian-partnership/.

292 Elbridge A. Colby and Kevin Roberts, "The Correct Con-servative Approach to Ukraine Shifts the Focus to China," *Time*, March 21, 2023, https://time.com/6264798/ conservative-approach-to-ukraine-shifts-the-focus-to-china/.

293 Jeremy Carl, "Whose Borders Should America Defend?," *Newsweek*, January 28, 2022, https://www.newsweek.com/ whose-borders-should-america-defend-opinion-1673596.

294 Bill Bostock, "Biden Suggests Russia May Not Be Heavily Punished for a 'Minor Incursion' into Ukraine, Prompting White House Scramble to Clarify," *Insider*, January 20, 2022, https://www.businessinsider.com/biden-suggests-russia-no-punishment-minor-ukraine-invasion-wh-clarify-2022-1.

295 Farnoush Amiri and Kevin Freking, "McCarthy: No 'Blank Check' for Ukraine If GOP Wins Majority," Associated Press, October 18, 2022, https://apnews.com/article/russia-ukraine-donald-trump-humanitarian-assistance-congress-c47a255738cd13576aa4d238ec076f4a.

296 Matthew Kroenig, "How to Deter Russian Nuclear Use in Ukraine—and Respond If Deterrence Fails," Memo to the President, Atlantic Council, September 16, 2022, https://www.atlanticcouncil.org/content-series/memo-to-the-president/memo-to-the-president-how-to-deter-russian-nuclear-use-in-ukraine-and-respond-if-deterrence-fails/.

297 Essi Lehto and Mike Stone, "Finland Orders 64 Lockheed F-35 Fighter Jets for $9.4 Bln," Reuters, December 10, 2021, https://www.reuters.com/business/aerospace-defense/lockheed-f-35-jet-wins-finnish-fighter-competition-source-2021-12-10/.

298 Sergio Chapa, Anna Shiryaevskaya, and Aaron Eglitis, "Baltic Nation Seeks to Become LNG Hub in Pivot Away from Russia," *Bloomberg*, November 7, 2022, https://www.bloomberg.com/news/articles/2022-11-07/baltic-nation-seeks-to-become-lng-hub-in-pivot-away-from-russia.

299 John E. Herbst et al., *Global Strategy 2022: Thwarting Kremlin Aggression Today for Constructive Relations Tomorrow*, Atlantic Council Strategy Paper series, February 8, 2022, https://www.atlanticcouncil.org/content-series/atlantic-council-strategy-paper-series/thwarting-kremlin-aggression-today-for-constructive-relations-tomorrow/.

300 This chapter draws heavily on Matthew Kroenig, *A Time to Attack: The Looming Iranian Threat* (New York: St. Martin's Press, 2014).

301 Robbie Gramer, "Iran Doubles Down on Arms for Russia," *Foreign Policy*, March 3, 2023, https://foreignpolicy.com/2023/03/03/russia-iran-drones-uav-ukraine-war-military-cooperation-sanctions/.

302 "Iran, China and Russia Hold Naval Drills in North Indian Ocean," Reuters, January 21, 2022, https://www.reuters.com/world/india/iran-china-russia-hold-naval-drills-north-indian-ocean-2022-01-21/; "China, Russia, Iran Hold Joint Naval Drills in Gulf of Oman," Associated Press, March 15, 2023, https://apnews.com/article/china-russia-iran-naval-drills-oman-gulf-9f515b3246e4cbe0d98a35e8399dc177.

303 Evelyn Leopold, "Russia, China, Object to Tough Sanctions on Iran," Reuters, March 8, 2007, https://www.reuters.com/article/

us-iran-un-resolution/russia-china-object-to-tough-sanctions-on-iran-idUSN0847566420070309; Michelle Nichols, "Russia, China Build Case at U.N. to Protect Iran," Reuters, June 9, 2020, https://www.reuters.com/article/us-usa-iran-russia-china/russia-china-build-case-at-u-n-to-protect-iran-from-u-s-sanctions-threat-idUSKBN23G2YR; Katherine Fung, "Russia, China Join Forces against Push to Punish Iran," *Newsweek*, November 24, 2022, https://www.newsweek.com/russia-china-join-forces-against-push-punish-iran-1761510.

304 Michael Peel, "Iran, Russia and China Prop Up Assad Economy," *Financial Times*, June 27, 2013, https://www.ft.com/content/79e-ca81c-df48-11e2-a9f4-00144feab7de; Holly Yan, "Syria Allies: Why Russia, Iran and China Are Standing by the Regime," CNN, August 29, 2013, https://www.cnn.com/2013/08/29/world/meast/syria-iran-china-russia-supporters/index.html.

305 Ralph Jennings, "Why Russia Backs China in Disputes with Third Countries," Voice of America, August 19, 2021, https://www.voanews.com/a/europe_why-russia-backs-china-disputes-third-countries/6209752.html; Oriana Skylar Mastro, "How China Is Bending the Rules in the South China Sea," *The Interpreter*, Lowry Institute, February 17, 2021, https://www.lowyinstitute.org/the-interpreter/how-china-bending-rules-south-china-sea.

306 Parisa Hafezi, "Iran to Join Asian Security Body Led by Russia, China," Reuters, September 15, 2022, https://www.reuters.com/world/middle-east/iran-signs-memorandum-joining-shanghai-cooperation-organisation-tass-2022-09-15/.

307 Paul Best, "Iran Could Produce 'One Bomb's Worth of Fissile Material' in about 12 Days, Pentagon Official Tells Congress," Fox News, February 28, 2023, https://www.foxnews.com/politics/iran-could-produce-one-bombs-worth-fissile-material-12-days-pentagon-official-tells-congress.

308 Sophia Barkoff, "CIA Director: Iran's Nuclear Program Advancing at 'Worrisome Pace,'" CBS News, February 26, 2023, https://www.cbsnews.com/news/william-burns-cia-director-iran-nuclear-program-face-the-nation-interview/.

309 "Iran Worked on Nuclear Bomb Design: IAEA," Reuters, November 8, 2011, https://www.reuters.com/article/us-nujclear-iran-iaea/iran-worked-on-nuclear-bomb-design-iaea-idUSTRE7A75JF20111108.

310 Behnam Ben Taleblu, *Arsenal: Assessing the Islamic Republic of Iran's Ballistic Missile Program*, Foundation for Defense of Democracies, February 15, 2023, 44, https://www.fdd.org/wp-content/uploads/2023/02/fdd-monograph-arsenal-assessing-iran-ballistic-missile-program.pdf.

311   Caitlin McFall, "Iran Reissues Threat to 'Kill Trump, Pompeo' for Solei-
      mani Death When Announcing Long-Range Cruise Missile," Fox News,
      February 28, 2023, https://www.foxnews.com/world/iran-reissues-threat-
      kill-trump-pompeo-soleimani-death-announcing-long-range-cruise-
      missile.

312   Reis Thebault, "Iranian Agents Once Plotted to Kill the Saudi Ambassa-
      dor in D.C. The Case Reads Like a Spy Thriller.," The Washington Post,
      January 4, 2020, https://www.washingtonpost.com/history/2020/01/04/
      iran-agents-once-plotted-kill-saudi-ambassador-dc-case-reads-like-spy-
      thriller/.

313   Saeed Kamali Dehghan, "Iran Executes Three Men on Homosex-
      uality Charges," The Guardian, September 7, 2011, https://www.
      theguardian.com/world/2011/sep/07/iran-executes-men-homosexu-
      ality-charges; "Rights Group: Iran Executes 2 Gay Men over Sodomy
      Charges," Associated Press, February 1, 2022, https://apnews.com/
      article/middle-east-iran-crime-dubai-united-arab-emirates-e3d-
      7108441665c40982329f26ff07fc9.

314   Farnaz Fassihi, "In Iran, Woman's Death after Arrest by the Morality
      Police Triggers Outrage," The New York Times, September 16, 2022,
      https://www.nytimes.com/2022/09/16/world/middleeast/iran-death-
      woman-protests.html.

315   Matthew Kroenig, Exporting the Bomb: Technology Transfer and the
      Spread of Nuclear Weapons (New York: Cornell University Press, 2010).

316   Jason Starr, "The U.N. Resolutions," The Iran Primer, United States
      Institute of Peace, accessed May 11, 2023, https://iranprimer.usip.org/
      resource/un-resolutions.

317   Barack Obama, "Renewing American Leadership," Foreign Af-
      fairs, July 1, 2007, https://www.foreignaffairs.com/united-states/
      renewing-american-leadership.

318   US Department of State, Joint Comprehensive Plan of Action, July 14,
      2015, 6–7, https://2009-2017.state.gov/documents/organization/245317.
      pdf.

319   "Transcript: President Obama's Full NPR Interview on Iran Nuclear
      Deal," NPR, April 7, 2015, https://www.npr.org/2015/04/07/397933577/
      transcript-president-obamas-full-npr-interview-on-iran-nuclear-deal.

320   Omri Nahmias, "Blinken: We Could Have Extended the Iran Arms Em-
      bargo from Inside the Deal," The Jerusalem Post, August 6, 2020, https://
      www.jpost.com/international/blinken-we-could-have-extended-the-iran-
      arms-embargo-from-inside-the-deal-637746.

321 Mark Dubowitz and Matthew Kroenig, "As Biden Relaxed Pressure, Iran Took Advantage," *The Wall Street Journal*, January 16, 2022, https://www.wsj.com/articles/iran-nuclear-deal-jcpoa-biden-trump-diplomacy-11642192678.

322 "After the Deal: A New Iran Strategy," The Heritage Foundation, May 21, 2018, https://www.heritage.org/defense/event/after-the-deal-new-iran-strategy.

323 Matthew Kroenig, "The Return to the Pressure Track: The Trump Administration and the Iran Nuclear Deal," *Diplomacy & Statecraft* 29, no. 1 (2018): 94–104, https://doi.org/10.1080/09592296.2017.1420529.

324 "Crude Oil Exports for Iran, Islamic Republic of," Federal Reserve Economic Data, updated May 3, 2023, https://fred.stlouisfed.org/series/IRNNXGOCMBD.

325 Matthew Kroenig, "Time to Attack Iran: Why a Strike Is the Least Bad Option," *Foreign Affairs*, January 1, 2012, https://www.foreignaffairs.com/articles/middle-east/2012-01-01/time-attack-iran.

326 George P. Shultz, "Moral Principles and Strategic Interests: The Worldwide Movement to Democracy," Landon Lecture Series on Public Issues, Kansas State University, April 14, 1986, https://www.k-state.edu/landon/speakers/george-shultz/transcript.html.

327 *The Iran Nuclear Deal: What You Need to Know about the JCPOA*, White House, 2015, 4–6, 95, https://obamawhitehouse.archives.gov/sites/default/files/docs/jcpoa_what_you_need_to_know.pdf.

328 Alexander Ward, "North Korea Displays Enough ICBMs to Overwhelm U.S. Defense System against Them," *Politico*, February 8, 2023, https://www.politico.com/news/2023/02/08/north-korea-missile-capability-icbms-00081993.

329 Jung H. Pak, *The Education of Kim Jung-Un*, Brookings Essay series, February 2018, https://www.brookings.edu/essay/the-education-of-kim-jong-un/.

330 "How North Korea Got Away with the Assassination of Kim Jong-nam," *The Guardian*, April 1, 2019, https://www.theguardian.com/world/2019/apr/01/how-north-korea-got-away-with-the-assassination-of-kim-jong-nam.

331 "Kim Jong-un's Daughter Shows Off Her US$1,900 Dior Kids Coat: The North Korean Dictator's 10-Year-Old Caused uproar with the Luxury Jacket, Just Like Her Dad Did with His IWC Portofino Automatic Watch," *South China Morning Post*, March 27, 2023, https://www.scmp.com/magazines/style/news-trends/article/3214977/kim-jong-uns-daughter-shows-her-us1900-dior-kids-coat-north-korean-dictators-10-year-old-caused.

332 Taylor Rock, "Kim Jong Un Indulges in Expensive Booze and Meat-Covered Pizza while Country Hungers, Report Says," *Los Angeles Times*, January 3, 2018, https://www.latimes.com/food/sns-dailymeal-1865335-eat-kim-jong-un-north-korea-diet-booze-and-meat-pizza-010318-20180103-story.html; Luke Hurst, "Kim Jong-un Assembles New 'Pleasure Squad' of Young Women," *Newsweek*, April 2, 2015, https://www.newsweek.com/kim-jong-un-assembles-new-pleasure-squad-young-women-319030.

333 Rebecca Kheel, "Top Admiral: North Korea Wants to Reunify Peninsula, Not Protect Rule," *The Hill*, February 14, 2018, https://thehill.com/policy/defense/373803-top-admiral-north-korea-wants-to-reunify-peninsula-not-protect-regime/.

334 Megan Specia, "Built for Invasion, North Korean Tunnels Now Flow with Tourists," *The New York Times*, November 4, 2017, https://www.nytimes.com/2017/11/04/world/asia/north-korea-south-korea-demilitarized-zone-tunnel-tourism.html.

335 Danny Bressler, "Has the Nuclear Nonproliferation Treaty Limited the Spread of Nuclear Weapons? Evaluating the Arguments," Nuclear Network, Center for Strategic and International Studies, March 17, 2021, https://nuclearnetwork.csis.org/has-the-nuclear-nonproliferation-treaty-limited-the-spread-of-nuclear-weapons-evaluating-the-arguments/.

336 David E. Sanger, "North Koreans Say They Tested Nuclear Device," *The New York Times*, October 9, 2006, https://www.nytimes.com/2006/10/09/world/asia/09korea.html.

337 Mary Beth D. Nikitin, *North Korea's Nuclear Weapons and Missile Programs*, CRS Report No. IF10472 (Washington, DC: Congressional Research Service, 2023), 1–2, https://crsreports.congress.gov/product/pdf/IF/IF10472/28.

338 Ibid.

339 Toby Dalton and Ankit Panda, "U.S. Policy Should Reflect Its Own Quiet Acceptance of a Nuclear North Korea," Carnegie Endowment for International Peace, November 15, 2022, https://carnegieendowment.org/2022/11/15/u.s.-policy-should-reflect-its-own-quiet-acceptance-of-nuclear-north-korea-pub-88399.

340 Marcel Serr, "North Korea Built a Nuclear Reactor for Syria (and Israel Destroyed It)," *The National Interest*, January 4, 2018, https://nationalinterest.org/blog/the-buzz/north-korea-built-nuclear-reactor-syria-israel-destroyed-it-23922.

341 Mike Chinoy, "How Pakistan's A. Q. Khan Helped North Korea Get the Bomb," *Foreign Policy*, October 11, 2021, https://foreignpolicy.com/2021/10/11/aq-khan-pakistan-north-korea-nuclear/.

342 Jean Mackenzie, "Nuclear Weapons: Why South Koreans Want the Bomb," BBC, April 22, 2023, https://www.bbc.com/news/world-asia-65333139.

343 Jack Kim, Lee Jae-won, "North Korea Shells South in Fiercest Attack in Decades," Reuters, November 22, 2010, https://www.reuters.com/article/us-korea-north-artillery/north-korea-shells-south-in-fiercest-attack-in-decades-idUSTRE6AM0YS20101123; Choe Sang-Hun, "South Korea Publicly Blames the North for Ship's Sinking," *The New York Times*, May 19, 2010, https://www.nytimes.com/2010/05/20/world/asia/20korea.html.

344 "North Korea Overview," Nuclear Threat Initiative, October 19, 2021, https://www.nti.org/analysis/articles/north-korea-overview/.

345 Avery Koop, "Mapped: All the World's Military Personnel," *Visual Capitalist*, March 11, 2022, https://www.visualcapitalist.com/mapped-all-the-worlds-military-personnel/.

346 "North Korea's Military Capabilities," Council on Foreign Relations, June 28, 2022, https://www.cfr.org/backgrounder/north-korea-nuclear-weapons-missile-tests-military-capabilities.

347 Robert Smith and Zoe Chace, "Drug Dealing, Counterfeiting, Smuggling: How North Korea Makes Money," NPR, August 11, 2011, https://www.npr.org/sections/money/2011/08/11/139556457/drug-dealing-counterfeiting-smuggling-how-north-korea-makes-money; Robbie Gramer and Rishi Iyengar, "How North Korea's Hackers Bankroll Its Quest for the Bomb," *Foreign Policy*, April 17, 2023, https://foreignpolicy.com/2023/04/17/north-korea-nuclear-cyber-crime-hackers-weapons/.

348 "Human Rights and Rule of Law Index—Country Rankings," TheGlobalEconomy.com, accessed May 23, 2023, https://www.theglobaleconomy.com/rankings/human_rights_rule_law_index/.

349 "Prisons of North Korea," US Department of State.

350 Sheryl Gay Stolberg, "Otto Warmbier, American Student Released from North Korea, Dies," *The New York Times*, June 19, 2017, https://www.nytimes.com/2017/06/19/us/otto-warmbier-north-korea-dies.html.

351 James Sterngold, "North Korea Invites Carter to Mediate," *The New York Times*, September 2, 1994, https://www.nytimes.com/1994/09/02/world/north-korea-invites-carter-to-mediate.html.

352 Jonathan Watts, "How Clinton Came Close to Bombing," *The Guardian*, December 4, 2002, https://www.theguardian.com/world/2002/dec/05/northkorea.

353 Sterngold, "North Korea Invites Carter."

354 "The U.S.-North Korean Agreed Framework at a Glance," Arms Control Association, February 2022, https://www.armscontrol.org/factsheets/agreedframework.

355 Robert M. Hathaway and Jordan Tama, "The U.S. Congress and North Korea during the Clinton Years: Talk Tough, Carry a Small Stick," *Asian Survey* 44, no. 5 (2004): 717–718, https://doi.org/10.1525/as.2004.44.5.711.

356 Michael Rubin, "Whose Fault Is It the Last North Korean Nuclear Agreement Didn't Work?," American Enterprise Institute, March 19, 2018, https://www.aei.org/articles/whose-fault-is-it-the-last-north-korean-nuclear-agreement-didnt-work/.

357 "North Korean Nuclear Negotiations: 1985–2022," Council on Foreign Relations, accessed May 23, 2023, https://www.cfr.org/timeline/north-korean-nuclear-negotiations.

358 Howard W. French, "North Korea, Accusing U.S., Says Nuclear Pact Has Collapsed," *The New York Times*, November 21, 2022, https://www.nytimes.com/2002/11/21/international/north-korea-accusing-us-says-nuclear-pact-has-collapsed.html.

359 Joseph Kahn, "North Korea Says It Will Abandon Nuclear Efforts," *The New York Times*, September 19, 2005, https://www.nytimes.com/2005/09/19/world/asia/north-korea-says-it-will-abandon-nuclear-efforts.html.

360 "North Korean Nuclear Negotiations," Council on Foreign Relations.

361 Ibid.

362 Larry A. Niksch, *North Korea's Nuclear Development and Diplomacy*, CRS Report No. RL33590 (Washington, DC: Congressional Research Service, 2010), 4, http://large.stanford.edu/courses/2011/ph241/agaian1/docs/RL33590.pdf.

363 "North Korean Nuclear Negotiations," Council on Foreign Relations.

364 Choe Sang-Hun and David E. Sanger, "North Koreans Launch Rocket in Defiant Act," *The New York Times*, December 11, 2012, https://www.nytimes.com/2012/12/12/world/asia/north-korea-launches-rocket-defying-likely-sanctions.html.

365 Gerald F. Seib, Jay Solomon, and Carol E. Lee, "Barack Obama Warns Donald Trump on North Korea Threat," *The Wall Street Journal*, November 22, 2016, https://www.wsj.com/articles/trump-faces-north-korean-challenge-1479855286.

366 Joby Warrick, Ellen Nakashima, and Anna Fifield, "North Korea Now Making Missile-Ready Nuclear Weapons, U.S. Analysts Say," *The

Washington Post, August 8, 2017, https://www.washingtonpost.com/world/national-security/north-korea-now-making-missile-ready-nuclear-weapons-us-analysts-say/2017/08/08/e14b882a-7b6b-11e7-9d08-b79f191668ed_story.html; Ellen Nakashima, Anna Fifield, and Joby Warrick, "North Korea Could Cross ICBM Threshold Next Year, U.S. Officials Warn in New Assessment," *The Washington Post*, July 25, 2017, https://www.washingtonpost.com/world/national-security/north-korea-could-cross-icbm-threshold-next-year-us-officials-warn-in-new-assessment/2017/07/25/4107dc4a-70af-11e7-8f39-eeb7d3a2d304_story.html.

367 Matthew Pennington, "Trump Strategy on NKorea: 'Maximum Pressure and Engagement,'" Associated Press, April 14, 2017, https://apnews.com/article/china-ap-top-news-north-korea-asia-pacific-pyongyang-86626d21ea2b45c79457a873a747c452.

368 Serafin Gómez, "Trump, at CPAC, Announces 'Heaviest'-Ever North Korea Sanctions," Fox News, February 23, 2018, https://www.foxnews.com/politics/trump-at-cpac-announces-heaviest-ever-north-korea-sanctions.

369 US President, Executive Order, "Executive Order 13810 of September 20, 2017: Imposing Additional Sanctions with Respect to North Korea," *Federal Register* 82, no. 184 (September 25, 2017): 44705, https://www.govinfo.gov/content/pkg/FR-2017-09-25/pdf/2017-20647.pdf; "U.S. Appeals Court Upholds Ruling against Chinese Banks in North Korea Sanctions Probe," Reuters, July 30, 2019, https://www.reuters.com/article/us-usa-trade-china-banks/u-s-appeals-court-upholds-ruling-against-chinese-banks-in-north-korea-sanctions-probe-idUSKCN1UQ03U.

370 John Haltiwanger, "How Would Trump Attack North Korea? President Considering 'Bloody Nose' Strike, Reports Say," *Newsweek*, February 1, 2018, https://www.newsweek.com/how-would-trump-attack-north-korea-president-considering-bloody-nose-strike-797807; Alex Lockie, "Trump Promises an 'Event the Likes of Which Nobody's Ever Seen' If North Korea Attacks Guam," *Insider*, August 10, 2017, https://www.businessinsider.com/trump-north-koreas-guam-nuclear-event-posture-2017-8.

371 United Nations Security Council, "Resolution 2371," S/RES/2371, August 5, 2017, https://documents-dds-ny.un.org/doc/UNDOC/GEN/N17/246/68/PDF/N1724668.pdf; United Nations Security Council, "Resolution 2375," S/RES/2375, September 11, 2017, https://documents-dds-ny.un.org/doc/UNDOC/GEN/N17/283/67/PDF/N1728367.pdf; United Nations Security Council, "Resolution 2397," S/RES/2397,

December 22, 2017, https://documents-dds-ny.un.org/doc/UNDOC/ GEN/N17/463/60/PDF/N1746360.pdf.

372 "North Korean Nuclear Negotiations," Council on Foreign Relations.

373 Michael J. Green, "Six Reasons Why Trump Meeting with Kim Jong Un Is a Very Bad Idea," *Foreign Policy*, May 18, 2016, https://foreignpolicy.com/2016/05/18/ six-reasons-why-trump-meeting-with-kim-jong-un-is-a-very-bad-idea/.

374 Nick Gass, "Trump: I'll Meet with Kim Jong Un in the U.S." *Politico*, June 15, 2016, https://www.politico.com/story/2016/06/ donald-trump-north-korea-nukes-224385.

375 "North Korean Nuclear Negotiations," Council on Foreign Relations.

376 Daniel Williams, "U.S. Warns N. Korea on Nuclear Weapons," *The Washington Post*, July 11, 1993, https://www.washingtonpost.com/ archive/politics/1993/07/11/us-warns-n-korea-on-nuclear-weapons/ d7461b91-e0c1-439b-a309-dacac721ea0b/; Amy Goldstein, "Two Leaders Warn North Korea," *The Washington Post*, May 24, 2003, https://www.washingtonpost.com/archive/politics/2003/05/24/two-leaders-warn-north-korea/8401cf26-172a-44d9-821e-84c2bd8e5d7d/; Office of the Press Secretary, "Statement by the President on North Korea's Nuclear Test," White House: President Barack Obama, September 9, 2016, https://obamawhitehouse.archives.gov/the-press-office/2016/09/09/statement-president-north-koreas-nuclear-test; "The Day North Korea Talks Collapsed, Trump Passed Kim a Note Demanding He Turn Over His Nukes," CNBC, March 30, 2019, https:// www.cnbc.com/2019/03/30/with-a-piece-of-paper-trump-called-on-kim-to-hand-over-nuclear-weapons.html; "G7 Leaders' Hiroshima Vision on Nuclear Disarmament," White House, May 19, 2023, https:// www.whitehouse.gov/briefing-room/statements-releases/2023/05/19/ g7-leaders-hiroshima-vision-on-nuclear-disarmament/.

377 Bressler, "Nuclear Nonproliferation Treaty."

378 Andrew Yeo, "Why Further Sanctions against North Korea Could Be Tough to Add," Brookings, July 8, 2022, https:// www.brookings.edu/blog/order-from-chaos/2022/07/08/ why-further-sanctions-against-north-korea-could-be-tough-to-add/.

379 Polina Nikolskaya, "Exclusive: Despite Sanctions, Russian Tanker Supplied Fuel to North Korean Ship-Crew Members," Reuters, February 26, 2019, https://www.reuters.com/article/us-northkorea-sanctions-russia-exclusive/exclusive-despite-sanctions-russian-tanker-supplied-fuel-to-north-korean-ship-crew-members-idUSKCN1QF0XX.

380 Askia Collins, "Republic of Korea, U.S. Navies Conclude Carrier Strike Group Exercise," US Navy, June 4, 2022, https://www.navy.mil/Press-Office/News-Stories/Article/3053309/republic-of-korea-us-navies-conclude-carrier-strike-group-exercise/.

381 Peter Baker and David E. Sanger, "In Turn to Deterrence, Biden Vows 'End' of North Korean Regime If It Attacks," *The New York Times*, April 26, 2023, https://www.nytimes.com/2023/04/26/us/politics/biden-south-korea-state-visit.html.

382 Ash Jain and Matthew Kroenig, *Present at the Re-Creation: A Global Strategy for Revitalizing, Adapting, and Defending a Rules-Based International System*, Atlantic Council, October 30, 2019, https://www.atlantic-council.org/wp-content/uploads/2019/10/Present-at-the-Recreation.pdf.

383 Bill Schneider, "Republicans Are the New Isolationists; Will US Retreat from World Stage?," *The Hill*, October 2, 2022, https://thehill.com/opinion/campaign/3670801-republicans-are-the-new-isolationists-will-us-retreat-from-world-stage/; Ronald Brownstein, "In 2024, Republicans May Complete a Historic Foreign Policy Reversal," CNN, March 28, 2023, https://www.cnn.com/2023/03/28/politics/gop-foreign-policy-debate-2024/index.html.

384 Mitch McConnell, "ICYMI: McConnell Remarks at Munich Security Conference," Mitch McConnell: Senate Republican Leader, February 17, 2023, https://www.republicanleader.senate.gov/newsroom/press-releases/icymi-mcconnell-remarks-at-munich-security-conference-.

385 Dean Acheson, *Present at the Creation: My Years in the State Department* (New York: W. W. Norton, 1969).

386 John R. Bolton, "A World without Rules," *National Review*, January 20, 2022, https://www.nationalreview.com/magazine/2022/02/07/a-world-without-rules/; Douglas J. Feith, John Fonte, and Jon Kyl, "The War of Law: How New International Law Undermines Democratic Sovereignty," Hudson Institute, July 1, 2013, https://www.hudson.org/national-security-defense/the-war-of-law-how-new-international-law-undermines-democratic-sovereignty.

387 "Vladimir Putin Meets with Members of the Valdai International Discussion Club. Transcript of the Final Plenary Session," Valdai Club, October 25, 2014, https://web.archive.org/web/20141025230537/http:/valdaiclub.com/valdai_club/73300.html.

388 Donald J. Trump and Tony Schwartz, *Trump: The Art of the Deal* (New York: Random House, 1987).

389 Ash Jain and Matthew Kroenig, *Toward a Democratic Technology Alliance: An Innovation Edge that Favors Freedom*, Atlantic Council, June

2022, https://www.atlanticcouncil.org/wp-content/uploads/2022/06/To-ward-a-Democratic-Technology-Alliance-An-Innovation-Edge-that-Fa-vors-Freedom.pdf; Martijn Rasser et al., *Common Code: An Alliance Framework for Democratic Technology Policy*, Center for a New American Security, October 21, 2020, https://www.cnas.org/publications/reports/common-code.

390 Michael R. Pompeo, "Communist China and the Free World's Future," US Department of State, July 23, 2020, https://2017-2021.state.gov/com-munist-china-and-the-free-worlds-future-2/index.html.

391 Frederick Kempe, "The Fourth Inflection Point: Testimony of Frederick Kempe to the House Permanent Select Committee on Intelligence," Atlantic Council, February 28, 2023, https://www.atlanticcouncil.org/commentary/testimony/the-fourth-inflection-point-testimony-of-freder-ick-kempe-to-the-house-permanent-select-committee-on-intelligence/.

392 "World of Change: Global Temperatures," Earth Observatory, NASA, ac-cessed June 6, 2023, https://earthobservatory.nasa.gov/world-of-change/global-temperatures.

393 "Carbon Dioxide," Vital Signs of the Planet, NASA, accessed June 6, 2023, https://climate.nasa.gov/vital-signs/carbon-dioxide/.

394 "Climate Change Impacts," National Oceanic and Atmospheric Ad-ministration, last modified August 13, 2021, https://www.noaa.gov/education/resource-collections/climate/climate-change-impacts; Nathan Rott, "Extreme Weather, Fueled By Climate Change, Cost the U.S. $165 Billion in 2022," NPR, January 10, 2023, https://www.npr.org/2023/01/10/1147986096/extreme-weather-fueled-by-climate-change-cost-the-u-s-165-billion-in-2022; Somini Sengupta, "Climate Change Is Making Armed Conflict Worse. Here's How.," *The New York Times*, March 18, 2022, https://www.nytimes.com/2022/03/18/climate/climate-armed-conflict-water.html; Shirley Cardenas, "How Climate Change Could Make Some Areas of Earth Uninhabitable by 2500," World Economic Forum, October 21, 2021, https://www.weforum.org/agenda/2021/10/climate-change-could-make-some-areas-of-earth-unin-habitable-by-2500/.

395 Steven E. Koonin, *Unsettled: What Climate Science Tells Us, What it Doesn't, and Why It Matters* (New York: BenBella Books, 2021).

396 Council of Economic Advisers and Office of Management and Budget, *Climate-Related Macroeconomic Risks and Opportunities*, White Paper (Washington, DC: Executive Office of the President, 2022), https://www.whitehouse.gov/wp-content/uploads/2022/04/CEA_OMB_Climate_Macro_WP_2022.pdf.

397 Council of Economic Advisers and Office of Management and Budget, *Methodologies and Considerations for Integrating the Physical and Transition Risks of Climate Change into Macroeconomic Forecasting for the President's Budget*, White Paper (Washington, DC: Executive Office of the President, 2023), https://www.whitehouse.gov/wp-content/uploads/2023/03/CEA-OMB-White-Paper.pdf.

398 Oren M. Cass, "Testimony of Oren M. Cass before the House Committee on Science, Space, and Technology May 16, 2018," Manhattan Institute, May 16, 2018, https://media4.manhattan-institute.org/sites/default/files/Cass-Testimony-May2018.pdf.

399 Chris Lafakis et al., "The Economic Implications of Climate Change," Moody's Analytics, June 2019, https://www.moodysanalytics.com/-/media/article/2019/economic-implications-of-climate-change.pdf.

400 Pete Evans, "Canada's Economy Would Be Less Hurt by Climate Change Than Other Countries, Moody's Says," CBC, July 4, 2019, https://www.cbc.ca/news/business/climate-change-moody-s-1.5199652.

401 Geoff Dembicki, "DC's Trumpiest Congressman Says the GOP Needs to Get Real on Climate Change," Vice, March 25, 2019, https://www.vice.com/en/article/zma97w/matt-gaetz-congress-loves-donald-trump-climate-change.

402 "U.S. Energy Facts Explained," U.S. Energy Information Administration, June 10, 2022, https://www.eia.gov/energyexplained/us-energy-facts/.

403 "Table 1. Total Energy Supply, Disposition, and Price Summary," *Annual Energy Outlook 2022*, US Energy Information Administration, accessed June 13, 2023, https://www.eia.gov/outlooks/aeo/data/browser/.

404 "Each Country's Share of CO_2 Emissions," Union of Concerned Scientists, updated January 14, 2022, https://www.ucsusa.org/resources/each-countrys-share-co2-emissions.

405 Hannah Ritchie, Max Roser, and Pablo Rosado, "CO_2 and Greenhouse Gas Emissions," OurWorldInData.org, 2020, https://ourworldindata.org/co2-and-greenhouse-gas-emissions.

406 "Each Country's Share," Union of Concerned Scientists.

407 Ritchie, Roser, and Rosado, "CO_2 and Greenhouse Gas."

408 Joe Biden, "Remarks by President Biden in Address to a Joint Session of Congress" (speech, Washington, DC, April 29, 2021), White House, https://www.whitehouse.gov/briefing-room/speeches-remarks/2021/04/29/remarks-by-president-biden-in-address-to-a-joint-session-of-congress/.

409 Anmar Frangoul, "President Xi Tells UN that China Will Be 'Carbon Neutral' within Four Decades," CNBC, September 23, 2020, https://www.

cnbc.com/2020/09/23/china-claims-it-will-be-carbon-neutral-by-the-year-2060.html.

410   "The First Big Energy Shock of The Green Era," *The Economist*, October 16, 2021, https://www.economist.com/leaders/2021/10/16/the-first-big-energy-shock-of-the-green-era.

411   Clara Ferreira Marques, "China Is Redrawing the World's Energy Map," *Bloomberg*, August 10, 2021, https://www.bloomberg.com/news/articles/2021-08-10/china-is-redrawing-the-world-s-energy-map; Michael Schuman, "Where US-China Competition Leaves Climate Change," *The Atlantic*, November 21, 2022, https://www.theatlantic.com/international/archive/2022/11/us-china-relations-climate-change/672170/.

412   "China Uses Uyghur Forced Labour to Make Solar Panels, Says Report," BBC, May 14, 2021, https://www.bbc.com/news/world-asia-china-57124636.

413   Navin Singh Khadka, "COP26: Did India Betray Vulnerable Nations?" BBC, November 16, 2021, https://www.bbc.com/news/world-asia-india-59286790.

414   John Bowden, "Ocasio-Cortez: 'World Will End in 12 Years' If Climate Change Not Addressed," *The Hill*, January 22, 2019, https://thehill.com/policy/energy-environment/426353-ocasio-cortez-the-world-will-end-in-12-years-if-we-dont-address/.

415   "The Green New Deal," Bernie Saunders, accessed June 13, 2023, https://berniesanders.com/issues/green-new-deal/.

416   "Readout of President Joe Biden's Meeting with President Xi Jinping of the People's Republic of China," White House, November 14, 2022, https://www.whitehouse.gov/briefing-room/statements-releases/2022/11/14/readout-of-president-joe-bidens-meeting-with-president-xi-jinping-of-the-peoples-republic-of-china/; Megan Cassella, "Democrats Press Trump to Commit to Paris Climate Deal as Part of USMCA," *Politico*, September 17, 2019, https://www.politico.com/story/2019/09/17/democrats-trump-paris-climate-deal-usmca-1739745.

417   Oliver Milman, "Governments Falling Woefully Short of Paris Climate Pledges, Study Finds," *The Guardian*, September 15, 2021, https://www.theguardian.com/science/2021/sep/15/governments-falling-short-paris-climate-pledges-study; "Green New Deal," Bernie Saunders; "Executive Order on Tackling the Climate Crisis at Home and Abroad," White House, January 27, 2021, https://www.whitehouse.gov/briefing-room/presidential-actions/2021/01/27/executive-order-on-tackling-the-climate-crisis-at-home-and-abroad/.

418 Tucker Carlson, "Tucker Carlson: Climate Is Now Our State Religion," Fox News, February 10, 2023, https://www.foxnews.com/opinion/tucker-carlson-climate-now-state-religion.

419 Justin Gillis, "The Montreal Protocol, A Little Treaty That Could," *The New York Times*, December 9, 2013, https://www.nytimes.com/2013/12/10/science/the-montreal-protocol-a-little-treaty-that-could.html.

420 "1990 Clean Air Act Amendment Summary," United States Environmental Protection Agency, last modified November 28, 2022, https://www.epa.gov/clean-air-act-overview/1990-clean-air-act-amendment-summary.

421 Helen Dewar and Kevin Sullivan, "Senate Republicans Call Kyoto Pact Dead," *The Washington Post*, December 11, 1997, https://www.washingtonpost.com/wp-srv/inatl/longterm/climate/stories/clim121197b.htm.

422 "Text of a Letter from the President to Senators Hagel, Helms, Craig, and Roberts," White House, March 13, 2001, https://georgewbush-whitehouse.archives.gov/news/releases/2001/03/20010314.html.

423 Nicolas Loris, "Paris Climate Agreement: Instead of Regulations and Mandates, Embrace Markets," Heritage Foundation, February 25, 2021, https://www.heritage.org/energy-economics/report/paris-climate-agreement-instead-regulations-and-mandates-embrace-markets.

424 Meghan L. O'Sullivan, *Windfall: How the New Energy Abundance Upends Global Politics and Strengthens America's Power* (New York: Simon & Schuster, 2018).

425 Jim Banks, "A Promise Kept: Biden's War on American Energy," Congressman Jim Banks, March 25, 2022, https://banks.house.gov/uploaded-files/a_promise_kept.pdf.

426 "Wrap-Up: President Biden's Unprecedented Assault on American Energy Increased Costs on American Consumers And Businesses," United States House Committee on Oversight and Accountability, March 30, 2023, https://oversight.house.gov/release/wrap-up-president-bidens-unprecedented-assault-on-american-energy-increased-costs-on-american-consumers-and-businesses.

427 Myah Ward, "White House Is Pressed on Potential Oil Deals with Saudi Arabia, Venezuela and Iran," *Politico*, March 7, 2022, https://www.politico.com/news/2022/03/07/white-house-oil-deals-saudi-arabia-venezuela-iran-00014803; Thomas Catenacci, "GOP Lawmakers Blast Biden for Turning to Venezuelan Dictator for Oil While Curbing Domestic Production," Fox Business, November 29, 2022, https://www.foxbusiness.

com/politics/gop-lawmakers-blast-biden-turning-venezuelan-dicta-
tor-oil-while-curbing-domestic-production.

428 David W. Kreutzer and Paige Lambermont, *The Environmental Quality Index: Environmental Quality Weighed Against Oil and Gas Production*, Institute for Energy Research, February 2023, https://www.instituteforen-ergyresearch.org/wp-content/uploads/2023/02/IER-EQI-2023.pdf.

429 Callie Patteson, "John Kerry Prioritizes Climate Change, Not Uyghur Abuses, with China," *New York Post*, September 23, 2021, https://nypost.com/2021/09/23/john-kerry-says-climate-change-is-priority-with-china/.

430 "Public's Top Priority for 2022: Strengthening the Nation's Economy," Pew Research Center, February 16, 2022, https://www.pewresearch.org/politics/2022/02/16/publics-top-priority-for-2022-strengthening-the-nations-economy/.

431 Council on Environmental Quality, "Environmental Impact Statement Timelines (2010-2018)," Executive Office of the President, June 12, 2020, https://ceq.doe.gov/docs/nepa-practice/CEQ_EIS_Timeline_Report_2020-6-12.pdf.

432 Casey Crownhart, "We Were Promised Smaller Nuclear Reactors. Where Are They?" *MIT Technology Review*, February 8, 2023, https://www.technologyreview.com/2023/02/08/1067992/smaller-nuclear-reactors/.

433 Nicholas L. Miller and Tristan A. Volpe, "The Rise of the Autocratic Nuclear Marketplace," *Journal of Strategic Studies* (April 2022): 1-39, https://doi.org/10.1080/01402390.2022.2052725.

434 Council of Economic Advisors, *The Value of U.S. Energy Innovation and Policies Supporting the Shale Revolution*, Executive Office of the President of the United States, 2019, https://trumpwhitehouse.archives.gov/wp-content/uploads/2019/10/The-Value-of-US-Energy-Innovation-and-Policies-Supporting-the-Shale-Revolution.pdf.

435 Hannah Ritchie and Max Roser, "Forests and Deforestation," OurWorldInData.org, 2021, https://ourworldindata.org/forests-and-deforestation.

436 "Governor Ron DeSantis Signs Historic Executive Order Continuing Commitment to Stewardship of Florida's Natural Resources," Florida Governor, January 10, 2023, https://www.flgov.com/2023/01/10/governor-ron-desantis-signs-historic-executive-order-continuing-commitment-to-stewardship-of-floridas-natural-resources/.

437 Kenneth N. Waltz, *Theory of International Politics* (New York: McGraw-Hill, 1979).

438 Matthew Kroenig, *The Return of the Great Power Rivalry*.

439 Jeanne Batalova and Michael Fix, *New Brain Gain: Rising Human Capital among Recent Immigrants to the United States*, Migration Policy Institute,

May 2017, https://www.immigrationresearch.org/system/files/RisingHumanCapital_FS-FINAL.pdf.

440 Max Roser and Lucas Rodés-Guirao et al., "Future Population Growth," OurWorldInData.org, last modified November 2019, https://ourworldindata.org/future-population-growth.

441 *The Demographic Outlook: 2023–2053*, Congressional Budget Office, January 2023, https://www.cbo.gov/system/files/2023-01/58612-Demographic-Outlook.pdf.

442 Adam Shaw, "Number of Illegal Migrants Who Entered US since Biden Took Office Approaching Two Million," Fox News, September 9, 2022, https://www.foxnews.com/politics/number-illegal-migrants-entered-us-since-biden-took-office-approaching-two-million.

443 Each year, tens of millions of people apply for the US's Diversity Visa Program. See "Diversity Visa Program, DV 2019–2021: Number of Entries During Each Online Registration Period by Region and Country of Chargeability," US Department of State, accessed June 16, 2023, https://travel.state.gov/content/dam/visas/Diversity-Visa/DVStatistics/DV-applicant-entrants-by-country-2019-2021.pdf.

444 Thebault, "Iranian Agents Once Plotted."

445 Ellen M. Gilmer, "Terrorists Crossing the US Border? Rising Encounters Explained," *Bloomberg Law*, April 12, 2023, https://news.bloomberglaw.com/immigration/terrorists-crossing-the-us-border-rising-encounters-explained.

446 Adam Shaw and Bill Melugin, "Border Patrol Apprehensions of Chinese Nationals at Southern Border Up 800%: Source," Fox News, February 9, 2023, https://www.foxnews.com/politics/border-patrol-apprehensions-chinese-nationals-southern-border-800-source.

447 "Fentanyl Trafficking Tests America's Foreign Policy," *The Economist*, May 11, 2023, https://www.economist.com/united-states/2023/05/11/fentanyl-trafficking-tests-americas-foreign-policy.

448 "Depression, War, and Civil Rights: Hispanics in the Southwest," Office of the House Historian, accessed June 16, 2023, https://history.house.gov/Exhibitions-and-Publications/HAIC/Historical-Essays/Separate-Interests/Depression-War-Civil-Rights/.

449 Andrew Becker, "Immigration Timeline," *Frontline*, accessed June 16, 2023, https://www.pbs.org/frontlineworld/stories/mexico704/history/timeline.html.

450 Philip L. Martin, "Select Commission Suggests Changes in Immigration Policy—A Review Essay." *Monthly Labor Review* 105 no. 2 (February 1982): 31–37, https://www.jstor.org/stable/41841751.

451   "1986: Immigration Reform and Control Act of 1986," Library of Congress, accessed June 5, 2023, https://guides.loc.gov/latinx-civil-rights/irca.

452   Alicia A. Caldwell, "Today's Immigration Debate Rooted in 'Reagan Amnesty,' Experts Say," PBS, August 23, 2016, https://www.pbs.org/newshour/nation/todays-immigration-debate-rooted-reagan-amnesty-experts-say.

453   Lucy Rodgers and Dominic Bailey, "Trump Wall: How Much Has He Actually Built?," BBC, October 31, 2020, https://www.bbc.com/news/world-us-canada-46824649.

454   "Migrant Protection Protocols," Department of Homeland Security, January 24, 2019, https://www.dhs.gov/news/2019/01/24/migrant-protection-protocols.

455   Ibid.

456   Kate Morrissey, "'Remain in Mexico' One Year Later: How a Single Policy Transformed the U.S. Asylum System," *The San Diego Union-Tribune*, January 29, 2020, https://www.sandiegouniontribune.com/news/immigration/story/2020-01-29/remain-in-mexico-one-year-later-how-a-single-policy-transformed-the-u-s-asylum-system.

457   Deepa Shivaram, "What to Know about Title 42, the Trump-Era Policy Now Central to the Border Debate," NPR, April 24, 2022, https://www.npr.org/2022/04/24/1094070784/title-42-policy-meaning.

458   Stuart Anderson, "A Review of Trump Immigration Policy," *Forbes*, August 26, 2020, https://www.forbes.com/sites/stuartanderson/2020/08/26/fact-check-and-review-of-trump-immigration-policy/?sh=35d779d756c0.

459   "Biden Has Taken Nearly 300 Executive Actions on Immigration in His First Year, Outpacing Trump," Migration Policy Institute, January 19, 2022, https://www.migrationpolicy.org/news/biden-executive-actions-immigration-first-year.

460   US President, Proclamation, "Termination of Emergency with Respect to the Southern Border of the United States and Redirection of Funds Diverted to Border Wall Construction, Proclamation 10142 of January 20, 2021," *Federal Register* 86, no. 16 (January 27, 2021): 7225–7227, https://www.govinfo.gov/content/pkg/FR-2021-01-27/pdf/2021-01922.pdf.

461   Elizabeth Lee, "Biden Immigration Changes Raise Hopes, Concerns on US-Mexico Border," Voice of America, March 5, 2021, https://www.voanews.com/a/usa_immigration_biden-immigration-changes-raise-hopes-concerns-us-mexico-border/6202931.html.

462 Kerry Sanders, "Honduran Migrants on Caravan Hope Biden Will Be Different from Trump Administration," NBC News, February 2, 2021, YouTube video, https://youtu.be/F-YFi0fd3rA.

463 Paul Bedard, "Illegal Border Crossings Set to Be 'Worst in US History,'" Yahoo! News, August 18, 2021, https://www.yahoo.com/now/illegal-border-crossings-set-worst-171900391.html.

464 Adam Gordon, "Fentanyl Seizures at Border Continue to Spike, Making San Diego a National Epicenter for Fentanyl Trafficking; U.S. Attorney's Office Prioritizes Prosecutions and Prevention Programs," United States Attorney's Office for the Southern District of California, August 11, 2022, https://www.justice.gov/usao-sdca/pr/fentanyl-seizures-border-continue-spike-making-san-diego-national-epicenter-fentanyl.

465 Tommy Hicks Jr., "Biden's Border Crisis Worsens in February: Magnitude of This Calamity Cannot Be Understated," *The Washington Times*, March 21, 2022, https://www.washingtontimes.com/news/2022/mar/21/bidens-border-crisis-worsens-in-february/.

466 Hannah Davis, "Fighting Human Trafficking and Battling Biden's Open Border," The Heritage Foundation, March 14, 2023, https://www.heritage.org/immigration/commentary/fighting-human-trafficking-and-battling-bidens-open-border.

467 Ibid.

468 "Fact Sheet: President Biden Sends Immigration Bill to Congress as Part of His Commitment to Modernize Our Immigration System," White House, January 20, 2021, https://www.whitehouse.gov/briefing-room/statements-releases/2021/01/20/fact-sheet-president-biden-sends-immigration-bill-to-congress-as-part-of-his-commitment-to-modernize-our-immigration-system/.

469 US Congress, House, *U.S. Citizenship Act*, HR 1177, 117th Cong., 1st sess., introduced in House February 18, 2021, https://www.congress.gov/117/bills/hr1177/BILLS-117hr1177ih.pdf; US Congress, House, *U.S. Citizenship Act*, HR 3194, 118th Cong., 1st sess., introduced in House, March 10, 2023, https://www.congress.gov/118/bills/hr3194/BILLS-118hr3194ih.pdf.

470 Julia Ainsley, "Migrant Border Crossings in Fiscal Year 2022 Topped 2.76 Million, Breaking Previous Record," NBC News, October 22, 2022, https://www.nbcnews.com/politics/immigration/migrant-border-crossings-fiscal-year-2022-topped-276-million-breaking-rcna53517.

471 Abby Budiman, "Key Findings about U.S. Immigrants," Pew Research Center, August 20, 2020, https://www.pewresearch.org/short-reads/2020/08/20/key-findings-about-u-s-immigrants/.

472 Daniel Griswold, *Reforming the US Immigration System to Promote Growth*, October 31, 2017, George Mason University Mercatus Center, October 31, 2017, https://www.mercatus.org/research/research-papers/reforming-us-immigration-system-promote-growth.

473 D'Vera Cohn and Neil G. Ruiz, "More than Half of New Green Cards Go to People Already Living in the US," Pew Research Center, July 6, 2017, https://www.pewresearch.org/short-reads/2017/07/06/more-than-half-of-new-green-cards-go-to-people-already-living-in-the-u-s/.

474 Ibid.

475 Jennifer Hunt, "Should Immigrants Be Admitted to the United States Based on Merit?," EconoFact, June 28, 2017, https://econofact.org/should-immigrants-be-admitted-to-the-united-states-based-on-merit.

476 Ibid.

477 "Immigration Bill Summary," *Politico*, June 28, 2013, https://www.politico.com/story/2013/06/immigration-bill-summary-093557.

478 Alison Snyder, "China Talent Program Increased Young Scientists' Productivity, Study Says," *Axios*, January 10, 2023, https://www.axios.com/2023/01/10/china-funding-young-scientists-productivity.

479 "Trump: I Want a 'Big, Fat, Beautiful, Open Door' for Legal Immigrants," NBC News, September 3, 2015, https://www.nbcnews.com/video/trump-i-want-a-big-fat-beautiful-open-door-for-legal-immigrants-518858307936.

480 Donald Trump, "Remarks by President Trump on Modernizing Our Immigration System for a Stronger America" (speech, Washington, DC, May 16, 2019), White House, https://trumpwhitehouse.archives.gov/briefings-statements/remarks-president-trump-modernizing-immigration-system-stronger-america/.

481 Ibid.

482 "Tear Down This Wall: Ronald Reagan, the Cold War, and Responsibility," Bill of Rights Institute, accessed June 14, 2023, https://billofrightsinstitute.org/activities/tear-down-this-wall-ronald-reagan-the-cold-war-and-responsibility-handout-a-narrative.